POCKET

Factfile

of

20TH CENTURY

EVENTS

**Lowe & B. Hould
Publishers**

Project Editor: Fiona Gold
Editor: Ann Furtado
Designer: Frankie Wood
Proof Reader: Lin Thomas
Researcher: Marian Dreier
Production Manager: Clive Sparling
Picture Manager: Claire Turner

Planned and produced by
Andromeda Oxford Ltd
11–15 The Vineyard
Abingdon
Oxfordshire OX14 3PX

Published by Borders Press,
a division of Borders, Inc.
311 Maynard, Ann Arbor,
Michigan, 48104.

Lowe & B. Hould, Publishers is a
trademark of Borders Properties, Inc.

ISBN 0-681-21997-1

Origination by Perdana Grafik, Malaysia

Printed by Tien Wah Press, Singapore

CONTENTS

INTRODUCTION

How do we define an "event" in the 20th century? The vast majority of the events presented here have featured in the international newspaper headlines of their day. They tend to be the political highpoints and disasters – treaties, wars, formal declarations and changes of government; or the social landmarks – scientific breakthroughs or cultural firsts. There are relatively few references to slow-moving trends. They may be powerful forces for change, but are less easy to regard as events because of the difficulties in associating them with a date, time and place.

In reality, choosing which events should feature in a book such as this is much like putting together the front page of a morning newspaper. Some events are world-changing, for instance, the assassination of Franz Ferdinand in Sarajevo on 28 June 1914, or the dropping of the atomic bomb on Hiroshima on 6 August 1945. Others are quieter parts of a longer story evolving over time, important fragments of a much larger pattern. Sometimes the pattern only becomes clear with the benefit of decades of hindsight. In the light of more recent events, the ferment of nationalism in the Baltic states during the early part of the century holds renewed interest for the reader in the 1990s. A mere ten years ago, many would have considered the declaration of Yugoslavian independence on 29 October, 1918 to be of academic interest to historians of World War I. Yet the continuing legacy of the decisions made at that time has filled our newspapers and television screens for most of this decade. The outbreak of civil war has sent us back to our history books to understand just how Serbia, Croatia and Bosnia could ever have been joined together as a single nation in the first place, and why they might not want to remain united following the collapse of communism throughout eastern Europe.

To gain some perspective on how history has shaped the world we live in today, we need to know what happened, and when it happened; the events of the past give us a framework to which we turn, again and again, as we try to make sense of new events as they occur.

About This Book

Selected events of the 20th century are arranged in chronological order, with one spread (two pages) devoted to each year. Within each year, events are divided into two broad sections; politics and culture. Most events are given a precise date, but some (particularly changes in the political climate or new social trends) can only be attributed to a month or are generally associated with the year in question. A heading and subheading highlight significant news items, and each spread is illustrated by a picture of one of the year's events described in the text.

Inevitably, space has restricted what can be included. Within these limits, this book offers a picture of the century as a series of happenings and as a network of interconnected events through which the browser or serious student can surf for information on landmark events of the 20th century.

WORLD EYES TURN TO PARIS

European powers extend territory under "new imperialism"

POLITICS

• **27 FEB:** Trade unions and socialist societies meet in London to establish the Labor Representation Committee. Led by Ramsay MacDonald. It became the Labor Party in 1906.

• **28 FEB:** In the Boer War, the British stronghold of Ladysmith is relieved after a siege of 118 days.

• **16 MAR:** The Social Democratic Party is founded in the United States. It became the Socialist party in 1901.

• **30 MAR:** Russia and Korea sign two agreements: a pact to prevent any other powers from gaining advantage in Korea; and a treaty by which Korea grants Russia sites for a coal depot and a naval hospital.

• **19 MAY:** A British protectorate is established over Tonga (formerly the Friendly Islands) to obstruct German interests.

• **28 MAY:** The Boxer Rebellion begins in China. During the next few months

The purpose-built exhibition center, Paris.

over 230 foreigners, missionaries and Christian converts are killed in the northern province of Shansi.

• **12 JUN:** A new German naval law allows for a 20-year program of shipbuilding which will make the German navy one of the largest and most powerful in the world.

• **16 JUN:** The German emperor formally opens the Kiel Canal, connecting the North Sea and the Baltic.

• **29 JUL:** The Italian king Umberto I is assassinated by an anarchist. He is succeeded by the more liberal Victor Emmanuel III.

• **21 SEPT:** Russia annexes Manchuria.

• **22 Sept:** The fifth congress of the Socialist International meets in Paris and creates an international socialist bureau to organize against war and militarism.

• **8 Oct:** Lord Ranfurly, governor of New Zealand, formally annexes the Cook Islands, at the unanimous request of the chiefs and people.

• **16 Oct:** An Anglo-German agreement regarding the Yangtze Basin provides for the continuance of the "open door" policy toward China and eschews territorial ambitions on the part of the Great Powers.

• **6 Nov:** Republican William McKinley is re-elected for a second term as United States president.

• **14 Dec:** France and Italy negotiate an agreement on North Africa which gives France a free hand in Morocco and Italy a free hand in Libya.

CULTURE

• The Cake Walk becomes the most fashionable dance in the United States and Europe. The dance arose among American blacks as a satire of elegant white ballroom dances.

• The first offshore oil wells, fixed to piers, are drilled along the shore of the Caspian Sea and along the west coast of the United States.

• The hamburger goes on sale for the first time in New Haven, Connecticut, in the United States.

• William Muldoon is declared the first ever professional wrestling champion of the United States.

• **19 Mar:** The Minoan civilization is discovered by Sir Arthur Evans while excavating at Knossos, Crete.

• **14 Apr:** The World Exhibition opens in Paris, France, demonstrating new inventions such as the escalator. By the time it closes in November, it has had over 50 million visitors.

• **26 Apr:** In Canada, a 36-hour fire destroys the city of Hull on the north shore of Ottawa River, and a large proportion of Ottawa City. Fifteen thousand people are left homeless and damage runs into hundreds of thousands of dollars.

• **14 May–22 Jul:** The second modern Olympic Games are held in Paris, France, and women athletes take part for the first time.

• **2 Jul:** First flight of the German airship Graf Zeppelin.

• **19 Jul:** The Paris Metro is opened. Begun in 1898, it features Art Nouveau station entrances designed by Hector Guimard.

END OF THE VICTORIAN ERA

Consumers welcome instant coffee and mass-produced cars

POLITICS

• The Socialist Revolutionary Party is created in Russia. It aims to nationalize land through terrorism.

• **1 Jan:** The Commonwealth of Australia is created. Lord Hopetoun becomes Governor-general and Edmund Barton is declared first prime minister.

• **22 Jan:** Queen Victoria, monarch of the British Empire dies. Her son Edward VII succeeds her.

• **8 Feb:** Russian expansionism in China is opposed by China, Japan and Britain.

• **4 Mar:** President William McKinley and Vice-President Theodore Roosevelt are inaugurated in the United States.

• **17 Mar:** In Russia, anti-czarist riots occur in St. Petersburg, Moscow, Odessa, Kiev and Karkov, following the excommunication of Leo Tolstoy.

• **23 Mar:** Rebel leader Emilio Aguinaldo is captured after a revolt in the Philippines.

Victoria, the most powerful woman of her day.

• **25 May:** In Norway, limited franchise is granted to women in local elections.

• **29 May:** British Prime Minister Lord Salisbury defends Britain's policy of isolation, ending negotiations for an Anglo-German alliance.

• **12 Jun:** Cuba becomes a United States protectorate.

• **4 Jul:** William H. Taft of the United States is installed as first governor of the Philippines

• **14 Jul:** An 8-week strike by US steelworkers begins.

• **22 Jul:** The decision of the British House of Lords in the Taff Vale case confirms the status of trade unions as legal bodies.

• **9 Aug:** Venezuela is invaded by Colombian troops.

• **7 Sept:** Boxer Rebellion ends with a peace protocol drawn up by 12 powers.

• **8 Sept:** Colombia is invaded by troops from Venezuela, Ecuador and Nicaragua.

• **9 Sept:** Austrian emperor Franz Josef restores diplomatic relations with Mexico after 34-year gap.

• **14 Sept:** US president William McKinley is assassinated by a Polish anarchist, and is succeeded by Theodore Roosevelt on the same day.

• **25 Sept:** Britain annexes the Ashanti kingdom in West Africa to form part of the Gold Coast.

• **18 Nov:** The Hay-Pauncefote Treaty recognizes the right of the United States to build the Panama Canal.

• **26 Nov:** Britain and Italy sign an agreement fixing the frontier between Sudan and Eritrea in North Africa.

CULTURE

• William K. D'Arcy of New Zealand secures a 60-year concession to exploit oil in Persia.

• J. P. Morgan forms the US Steel Corporation, the first billion-dollar corporation in the United States.

• Ragtime music sweeps the US.

• Instant coffee is invented by S. Kato in Japan.

• Acetylene gas lamps replace candles and oil lamps on cars.

• Hubert Booth invents the vacuum cleaner in Britain.

• **10 Feb:** Violent demonstrations against the Jesuits in Spain.

• **31 Mar:** Wilhelm Maybach constructs the first Mercedes car at the Daimler Works in Germany.

• **29 Jun:** In France, religious establishments are required to apply for parliamentary authorization.

• **16 Oct:** US president Roosevelt invites black educationalist and reformer Booker T. Washington to the White House.

• **18 Oct:** In Britain, William Henry-Wills creates the Imperial Tobacco Company.

• **24 Oct:** Following the success of the Box Brownie camera, the Eastman Kodak Company is incorporated.

• **10 Dec:** The first Nobel Prizes are awarded in Sweden.

• **21 Dec:** Guglielmo Marconi sends first transatlantic telegraph message.

THE BIRTH OF SCIENCE FICTION

The motor car achieves 74.5 m.p.h. and the telephone system is born

POLITICS

• **JAN:** The first Labor Office is established in the United States.

• **16 JAN:** Turkey grants Germany a license to build a railroad from Konia to Baghdad in Mesopotamia.

• **30 JAN:** The Anglo-Japanese Treaty recognizes the independence of China and Korea.

• **4 FEB:** Political opposition to the czarist government in Russia grows as 30,000 students go on strike.

• **14 FEB:** In Italy, martial law is declared in Trieste when violent strikers demand reduced working hours.

• **20 FEB:** In Barcelona, Spain, 500 strikers die in clashes with government troops. A state of siege is declared.

• **8 APR:** Russia agrees to evacuate her troops from Manchuria in 18 months.

• **10 MAY:** Alsace-Lorraine is granted a measure of self-government by the German kaiser.

A still from the Méliès film A Trip to the Moon.

• **12 MAY:** In the United States anthracite miners strike (until Oct.) for increased pay and reduced hours.

• **30 MAY:** King Alfonso XIII of Spain responds to increased labor unrest by suspending the *Cortes*. Martial law is declared next day.

• **31 MAY:** The Boer War is ended by the Treaty of Vereeniging. The Boers accept British sovereignty

• **7 JUN:** Mass strikes in favor of electoral reform begin in Belgium.

• **13 JUN:** In Finland, Russian is imposed as the official language.

• **28 JUN:** The Triple Alliance (between Germany, Austro-Hungary and Italy) is renewed for 12 years.

- **Jul:** In Australia the Immigration Restriction Act allows exclusion by a language test. Female suffrage is established for all federal elections.

- **12 Jul:** A . J. Balfour becomes British prime minister after the resignation of Lord Salisbury the previous day.

- **9 Aug:** In Britain, King Edward VII is crowned at the age of 60.

- **3 Sept:** Violent disturbances at Agram, Croatia, between Croats and Serbs. Martial law is declared.

- **14 Sept:** 20,000 Irish nationalists demonstrate in Phoenix Park, Dublin, against the British government.

- **22 Sept:** The Russian czar abolishes Finnish autonomy and appoints a Russian governor-general.

- **7 Oct:** France and Siam sign a treaty to settle the Siamese frontier.

- **9 Oct:** Two thirds of French miners go on strike.

- **20 Nov:** Lord Tennyson becomes governor-general of Australia.

- **26 Nov:** In New Zealand, the Progressive Party win their fifth consecutive general election victory.

- **30 Dec:** The Spanish government sends battleships to Tangiers and prepares to invade Morocco.

CULTURE

- Pepsi-Cola is founded in the US.

- Sew-on press studs for clothing are invented in France.

- Italian tenor Enrico Caruso makes his first recording, singing into a wax disc recorder in a hotel room in Milan.

- **Jan:** In the US, American football college teams play in the inaugural Rose Bowl game. Michigan beats Stanford.

- **1 Feb:** China officially abolishes the binding of women's feet.

- **15 Feb:** A subway system opens in Berlin, Germany.

- **24 Feb:** The British Post Office opens its telephone system to subscribers.

- **22 Mar:** Britain and Persia agree to build a telegraph link between Europe and India.

- **1 May:** In France, *A Trip to the Moon,* the first science fiction film, is released by Georges Méliès.

- **21 Aug:** *Cedric,* the largest vessel in the world (21,000 tons) is launched from Belfast shipyards in Britain.

- **10 Dec:** In Egypt, the Aswan Dam is completed after four years' construction.

- **17 Dec:** The first Cadillac is made in Detroit, Michigan.

POWERED AIRCRAFT FLIGHT

Pioneering work begins on radiation therapy for cancer

POLITICS

• **1 Jan:** In Delhi, Edward VII is proclaimed emperor of India.

• **22 Jan:** The US and Colombia agree to build the Panama Canal.

• **14 Feb:** The US Department of Commerce and Labor is set up.

• **3 Mar:** The US imposes new anti-immigration laws to bar "undesirables".

• **12 Mar:** The czar of Russia promises reforms, including freedom of religion.

• **15 Mar:** The British army takes Sokoto, the last major town in its conquest of northern Nigeria.

• **Apr:** A diplomatic crisis develops over the German–Baghdad Railroad from Konia to Basra, which was due to be financed by France and Britain.

• **13 Apr:** A week-long general strike in the Netherlands is abandoned.

• **15 May:** Striking railway workers in Victoria, Australia, abandon their demands after five days.

Marie Curie working in her laboratory.

• **21 May:** The Tariff League is set up to promote preferential trading within the British Empire.

• **11 Jun:** Alexander I and Queen Draga of Serbia are murdered in a military conspiracy.

• **14 Jun:** Peter I is elected to the throne of Serbia.

• **12–13 Aug:** Tension rises between Russia and Japan over the presence of Russian troops in Manchuria.

• **19 Aug:** At the Sixth Zionist Conference in Basel, Britain offers to set up a Jewish nation in Uganda.

• **8 Sept:** Turkish troops are reported to have massacred thousands of civilians in Bulgaria.

• **15 Sept:** Britain agrees to back a Russian–Austrian plan to settle the Bulgarian crisis.

• **16 Sept:** Emperor Franz Josef plans to maintain a joint Austrian–Hungarian army despite Hungarian opposition.

• **10 Oct:** Emmeline Pankhurst sets up the British Women's Social and Political Union, committed to achieving social reform and votes for women.

• **14 Oct:** Britain and France agree to refer judicial or treaty questions to the Hague Tribunal.

• **16 Oct:** A border dispute between Canada and the United States is resolved in favor of the United States.

• **3 Nov:** Panama undergoes a revolution and, supported by the United States, declares its independence from Colombia.

• **12 Nov:** China moves 10,000 troops into Manchuria.

• **17 Nov:** The Russian Social democratic party splits at its London conference into the moderate Mensheviks ("minority party") and radical Bolsheviks ("majority party").

• **20 Dec:** Some 50,000 Chinese coolies arrive in South Africa to work in the mines. A mass meeting condemns the decision to import Chinese labor.

CULTURE

• Milton Hershey's chocolate factory is established in Pennsylvania

• German surgeon Georges Perthes initiates radiation therapy for cancer, using X-rays on malignant tumors.

• Marie and Pierre Curie share the Nobel Prize for Physics with A. Becquerel; the Curies for work on radioactivity and Becquerel for natural radiation.

• In the United States, Richard Steiff designs the first "teddy bear" (named after Theodore Roosevelt).

• **29 Mar:** A radio news service between London and New York is established.

• **15 Jun:** *The Great Train Robbery*, the first film to employ cinematic effects, such as intercutting, opens in the US.

• **16 Jun:** Henry Ford establishes the Ford Motor Company in the US.

• **19 Jul:** The first Tour de France cycle race is won by Maurice Garin.

• **13 Oct:** In the United States, the first World Series in baseball is won by the Boston Red Sox.

• **21 Sept:** *Kit Carson*, the first Western movie, opens in the United States.

• **17 Dec:** Orville and Wilbur Wright undertake the first powered flights, at Kitty Hawk, North Carolina.

RUSSO-JAPANESE WAR CRISIS

Pavlov discovers how conditioned reflexes work

POLITICS

• **10 JAN:** Herrero tribesmen in German Southwest Africa massacre over 100 Germans in a tribal lands dispute.

• **31 JAN:** Russian warships sail to intercept a Japanese squadron off the Russian naval base of Port Arthur.

• **4 FEB:** The Russian czar offers Japan a free hand in Korea in return for Japanese neutrality in Manchuria.

• **5 FEB:** US troops leave the new republic of Cuba having assisted in the 1898 rebellion against Spain.

• **6 FEB:** The US state of Maryland joins other southern states in disenfranchising black voters.

• **8 FEB:** Japan launches a surprise attack on the Russian naval base at Port Arthur. The Russian fleet are trapped.

• **10 FEB:** Japan declares war on Russia and sends troops to occupy Seoul, Korea.

• **18 FEB:** Turks kill 800 Albanians in the siege of Shemsi Pasha, Macedonia.

The Japanese attack the Russian fleet at Port Arthur, 8th February.

• **31 MAR:** British troops kill 300 Tibetans attempting to halt a British mission to Tibet.

• **8 APR:** Britain relinquishes all claims to Madagascar.

• **8 APR:** An *Entente Cordiale* is signed between Britain and France settling outstanding territorial disputes.

• **27 APR:** John C. Watson becomes the first Labor prime minister of Australia.

• **15 JUN:** Brazil and Britain sign an arbitration convention resolving border disputes in British Guyana.

• **24 Jun:** The Russian army suffers large losses in a failed attempt to relieve the siege of Port Arthur.

• **12 Jul:** Britain and Germany sign a 5-year treaty to resolve disputes by arbitration.

• **19 Jul:** Britain dispatches warships to protect neutral shipping from attack by the Russian navy.

• **3 Aug:** British forces take Lhasa, the capital of Tibet.

• **16 Aug:** Britain protests to Russia over the sinking of merchant shipping.

• **7 Sept:** Tibet signs a treaty with Britain to forbid foreign intervention and to give Britain trading posts.

• **20 Oct:** Bolivia and Chile sign a formal treaty marking the end the war of the Pacific (1879–1884).

• **21 Oct:** The Dogger Bank incident: the Russian fleet fires on British trawlers, sinking two, while on its way through the North Sea to the Far East.

• **8 Nov:** Theodore Roosevelt wins a second US presidential election.

• **Dec:** Roosevelt threatens to invoke the Monroe Doctrine to restrict European expansion in the western hemisphere.

• **26 Dec:** The Russian czar pledges to improve conditions for the masses.

CULTURE

• The caterpillar tractor is developed in California.

• The hamburger and ice cream cone become the rage at the St. Louis exposition, Missouri.

• The ultraviolet lamp is invented.

• Thomas Sullivan pioneers the teabag in the US.

• **17 Jan:** Anton Chekhov's play *The Cherry Orchard* premières in Moscow.

• **1 Jul–29 Aug:** The third modern Olympic Games take place in St. Louis, Missouri; the US team dominate.

• **29 Jul:** France severs diplomatic links with the Vatican.

• **7 Sept:** In the US, an Alabama mob burn a black man accused of murder.

• **27 Oct:** The New York subway opens and is used by 150,000 people on the first day.

• **10 Dec:** Russian scientist Ivan Pavlov discovers conditioned reflexes and receives the Nobel Prize for Physiology or Medicine.

• **27 Dec:** *Peter Pan*, the classic children's play by J. M. Barrie, premières in London, popularizing a new girl's name, Wendy.

REBELLION PARALYZES RUSSIA

Albert Einstein redefines human understanding of the universe

"Bloody Sunday" in St. Petersburg.

POLITICS

• **JAN:** General Louis Botha founds *Het Volk*, to promote responsible government in the Transvaal, South Africa.

• **2 JAN:** Russian forces surrender Port Arthur to the Japanese after a seven-month siege.

• **22 JAN:** Bloody Sunday: protesting workers led by the priest Father Gapon march on the Winter Palace in St. Petersburg, Russia. Troops open fire without warning killing and wounding large numbers of unarmed people.

• **25 JAN:** In Poland, strikers fire at troops and bomb buildings.

• **17 FEB:** Grand Duke Sergei, the uncle of Czar Nicholas II, is assassinated in Moscow.

• **3 MAR:** The Russian czar announces his intention to create a consultative assembly.

• **10 MAR:** After a 12-day battle, the Japanese inflict a massive defeat on the Russian army at Mukden.

• **27–29 MAY:** The Russian Baltic fleet is destroyed by the Japanese in the Battle of Tsushima Straits.

• **7 JUN:** Norway declares independence from Sweden. Prince Karl of Denmark becomes Haakon VII of Norway.

• **27 JUN:** A general strike is called in Odessa, Russia. Sailors mutiny on the Russian battleship *Potemkin* which is moored offshore.

• **3 JUL:** Russian troops kill 6,000 before restoring order in Odessa. A general strike is called in St. Petersburg.

• **24 JUL:** The Treaty of Bjorko establishes a Russo-German alliance.

• **19 AUG:** The Russian czar sets up a consultative body to be called the Duma.

• **1 Sept:** The provinces of Alberta and Saskatchewan are formed in Canada.

• **5 Sept:** Russia and Japan sign the Treaty of Portsmouth, mediated by President Roosevelt in the United States. Russia agrees to accede to Japan in Korea and withdraw from Manchuria.

• **16 Oct:** In India, the partition of East Bengal and Assam from the remainder of the province provokes nationalist opposition.

• **26 Oct:** The first workers' soviet is formed in St. Petersburg under Leon Trotsky to coordinate the general strike which is paralyzing Russia.

• **30 Oct:** Nicholas II announces the creation of a semi-constitutional monarchy and guaranteed civil liberties.

• **31 Oct:** A general strike begins in Finland.

• **12 Nov:** Martial law is declared in Poland by the Russians.

• **28 Nov:** Universal suffrage is granted in Austria.

• **28 Nov:** The nationalist party Sinn Féin is founded in Dublin to work for Irish independence.

• **22 Dec:** A revolt in Moscow by students and workers is brutally crushed by Russian troops.

CULTURE

• Albert Einstein publishes his seminal papers on the special theory of relativity, the photoelectric effect and Brownian motion.

• The opening of the first nickelodeon in Pittsburgh, Pennsylvania.

• Elastic rubber replaces traditional whalebone and lacing in women's undergarments.

• The Pathé Company in France automates the coloring of movie films.

• **26 Jun–8 Jul:** May Sutton of the United States becomes the first non-Briton to win a Wimbledon tennis title.

• **1 Jul:** Salvation Army General Booth buys 20,000 acres of land in Australia for the settlement of poor immigrants.

• **14 Oct:** Christabel Pankhurst and Annie Kenney become the first British suffragettes to be sent to prison.

• **30 Oct:** The drug Aspirin goes on sale in Britain.

• **8 Nov:** During a pogrom in Odessa, Russia, over 1,000 Jews are massacred by police, troops and officials.

• **9 Dec:** The French pass a law removing state funding from religious establishments, effectively separating Church and state.

SAN FRANCISCO EARTHQUAKE

Rivalry between western powers is reflected in a naval building race

POLITICS

• **1 JAN:** In Britain, the Aliens Act comes into force, with strict controls on poor immigrants from eastern Europe.

• **16 JAN:** The Algeciras conference opens in Morocco, affirming autonomy but recognizing France's special role.

• **22 JAN:** In Germany, the "Red Monday" socialist rally attracts crowds of 250,000.

• **3 FEB:** The Japanese government increases its navy dramatically.

• **7 FEB:** The Liberals under Sir Henry Campbell-Bannerman win the British General Election.

• **10 FEB:** HMS *Dreadnought*, the most powerful warship in the world to date, is launched in Britain.

• **7 MAR:** In Finland, all taxpayers over 24 are given the vote.

• **27 APR:** Britain gains control of Tibet in a treaty with China.

• **MAY:** The German Navy Bill increases

Devastated San Franciscans in the rubble.

the tonnage of battleships being built in Germany and accelerates the naval building race with Britain.

• **3 MAY:** Britain issues an ultimatum to Turkey to relinquish control of the Sinai peninsula.

• **10 MAY:** The first Russian Duma, elected by universal suffrage, meets.

• **22 MAY:** The last British troops to be stationed in Canada depart.

• **10 JUN:** Dick Seddon, prime minister of New Zealand since 1893, dies.

• **12 JUL:** In France, Jewish army officer Alfred Dreyfus is rehabilitated after charges of treason brought against him in 1894 are proved false.

• **21 JUL:** The Russian Duma is dismissed; many of the deputies urge civil disobedience and go into exile.

• **1 SEPT:** British New Guinea is placed under Australian control and is renamed Papua (the former Portuguese name).

• **29 SEPT:** Following uprisings in Cuba, the United States sets up a provisional government, under William Taft, the US war secretary.

• **2 NOV:** The Russian revolutionary, Leon Trotsky, is exiled to Siberia for his activities.

• **26 NOV:** President Roosevelt returns to the US after a visit to Panama, the first visit abroad by a serving president.

• **12 DEC:** The Transvaal is granted autonomy with white male suffrage.

• **30 DEC:** The shah of Persia signs a liberal constitution drawn up by the national assembly. He dies the next day.

• **30 DEC:** The All-India Muslim League is founded.

CULTURE

• The Coca-Cola Company replaces cocaine in their drink with caffeine.

• Foundation of the Mercedes automobile company in Berlin.

• The New Zealand Rugby Union "All Blacks" tour Britain for the first time.

• The first Victorian Football League final is held in Melbourne.

• In the United States, William Kellogg founds the Battle Creek Toasted Cornflake Company.

• American Lee de Forest invents the triode valve, an essential component of electronic equipment until the 1950s.

• The first full-length feature film, *The Story of the Kelly Gang*, is released in the United States.

• **4 JAN:** British dancer Isadora Duncan is banned from dancing in Berlin after allegations of obscenity.

• **22 MAR:** The first rugby international is played in Paris: England beat France.

• **7 APR:** The Italian volcano Vesuvius erupts, destroying the town of Ottaiano and killing more than 100 people.

• **19 APR:** San Francisco, California, suffers a major earthquake which leaves over 1,000 dead and 200,000 homeless.

• **19 MAY:** The Simplon tunnel is opened linking France and Italy.

• **30 JUN:** The Pure Food and Drug Act, outlawing food adulteration, is passed in the United States.

• **17 OCT:** German professor Alfred Korn sends a photograph by telegraph for more than 1,000 miles.

PEACE CONFERENCE AT THE HAGUE

Pablo Picasso introduces a new experimental age in art

POLITICS

• **26 Jan:** Austria introduces universal suffrage for parliamentary elections.

• **11 Feb:** The shah of Persia, Muhammad Ali Mirza, recognizes constitutional government.

• **26 Feb:** In the first elections in Transvaal, South Africa, Gen. Botha of the *Het Volk* party, becomes premier.

• **11 Mar:** Bulgarian Prime Minister Petkov is assassinated by an anarchist.

• **15 Mar:** Finland elects the first women to parliament.

• **22 Mar:** In South Africa, Mohandas Gandhi and the Indian population of the Transvaal exercise passive resistance in response to government restrictions on the immigration of Indians.

• **8 Apr:** The Anglo-French convention confirms the independence of Siam.

• **12 Apr:** Switzerland creates a standing defense militia.

Lord Baden-Powell, founder of the Boy Scouts.

• **16 May:** Britain, France and Spain sign the Pact of Cartagena to thwart German interests in the Mediterranean.

• **10 Jun:** Franco-Japanese agreement to preserve the independence of China.

• **14 Jun:** Norway grants limited women's suffrage.

• **15 Jun–18 Oct:** The Second Peace Conference at the Hague fails to stop the arms race but agrees conventions on the rules of war and neutrality.

• **16 Jun:** The Russian czar is forced to dissolve the Duma and increase political representation of the propertied classes.

• **1 Jul:** Orange Free State in S. Africa is granted self-government by Britain.

• **25 Jul:** Japan places Korea under its control, provoking an uprising.

• **30 Jul:** Russo-Japanese treaty agrees spheres of influence in Manchuria.

• **4 Aug:** The French fleet bombards Casablanca after violent uprisings.

• **31 Aug:** Anglo-Russian agreement on Persia, Afghanistan and Tibet allows the alignment of Russia with Britain and France against the Central Powers.

• **8 Sept:** Guomindang nationalist party is established by Sun Yat-sen in China.

• **26 Sept:** New Zealand becomes a dominion of the British Empire.

• **21 Oct:** In a financial crisis in the United States, 31 national banks and 212 state banks collapse.

• **8 Nov:** The concept of a basic wage is established by the Australian Arbitration Court in the Harvester decision.

• **14 Nov:** In Russia, the Third Duma meets with a conservative majority.

• **15 Dec:** The Persian shah attempts a *coup d'etat* and imprisons the prime minister. Popular protest forces the shah to yield.

CULTURE

• The first electric washing machine, designed by Budd Fisher in 1906, is marketed in the United States.

• In New York, Florenz Ziegfeld stages the first *Ziegfeld Follies*.

• Persil washing powder is introduced in Germany.

• Lord Baden-Powell founds the Boy Scout movement in Britain.

• William Harley and Arthur Davidson set up their motorcycle company.

• Frenchman Pierre Cornu builds a prototype vertical-takeoff helicopter.

• Pablo Picasso shows his first Cubist painting *Les Demoiselles d'Avignon*.

• In the US, William Randolph Hearst founds the International News Service.

• J. M. Synge's drama *The Playboy of the Western World* opens at the Abbey theater, Dublin, and provokes riots on the grounds of its "indecency"

• **14 Feb:** In Britain, 57 suffragettes appear in court following their arrest after violent clashes with police.

• **Apr:** Twenty million people are reported to be starving in Russia's worst ever famine.

• **13 Sept:** The British ocean liner SS *Lusitania* completes the crossing of the Atlantic in a record five days.

• **11 Dec:** Fire destroys the parliament buildings at Wellington, New Zealand.

TROUBLE BREWS IN THE BALKANS

The Buick and Oldsmobile companies merge to form General Motors

POLITICS

• In the United States, the Federal Bureau of Investigation (FBI) is set up.

• Australia begins a 22-year program of construction of its first naval force.

• Australia introduces old age and invalid pensions.

• **27 JAN:** In the US, Oklahoma becomes the 47th state of the Union.

• **1 FEB:** King Carlos I and the crown prince of Portugal are murdered; the king is succeeded by Manuel II.

• **12 APR:** Herbert Henry Asquith becomes British prime minister, succeeding Henry Campbell-Bannerman who resigns on grounds of ill health.

• **30 APR:** Violent nationalist demonstrations continue in India; two Englishwomen are killed by a terrorist bomb in Muzaffarpur.

• **MAY:** The government of Australia is defeated in a confidence vote and Labor takes office under Andrew Fisher.

The Model-T Ford, launched in 1908.

• **7 MAY:** British prime minister H. H. Asquith introduces old age pensions for people over 70.

• **21 JUN:** In London, 200,000 suffragettes attend a rally in Hyde Park.

• **23 JUN:** Shah Muhammad Ali overthrows the liberal government in Persia.

• **5 JUL:** The "Young Turks" stage an insurrection and force the sultan to restore the 1876 constitution.

• **20 AUG:** King Leopold of Belgium hands over the Congo, formerly his private possession, to the Belgian state.

• **16 SEPT:** At the Buchlau conference, Russia agrees to acquiesce in Austria's annexation of Bosnia-Herzegovina.

• **25 Sept:** The Casablanca incident creates rising tension between France and Germany.

• **Oct:** The Australian parliament agrees to establish a new federal capital at Canberra.

• **5 Oct:** Ferdinand I of Bulgaria declares independence from Turkey.

• **6 Oct:** Austria annexes Bosnia-Herzegovina, angering Serbia and Montenegro; Russia backs the Serbs.

• **7 Oct:** Crete proclaims its union with Greece.

• **10–14 Oct:** Intensive diplomatic activity takes place between the great powers to avoid a crisis in the Balkans.

• **12 Oct:** A constitutional convention opens in South Africa, at which the Union of South Africa is proposed.

• **27 Oct:** The British *Daily Telegraph* publishes a controversial interview with Kaiser Wilhelm II of Germany in which he states that the German people are hostile to Britain.

• **3 Nov:** In the United States' elections, the republican William Howard Taft is elected president.

• **14–15 Nov:** In China, Emperor Guangxu and Dowager Empress Cixi die, and the boy-Emperor Pu Yi succeeds.

CULTURE

• The General Motors Corporation is founded in Detroit, Michigan.

• In the US, Florence Lawrence is the "Biograph Girl", the first star promoted by the Hollywood publicity machine.

• Completion of the Hejaz Railroad from Turkey to the holy places of Islam.

• French scientists A. Calmette and C. Guérin develop the first tuberculosis vaccine, not marketed until the 1920s.

• Paper cups are introduced in the US.

• The Hoover electric vacuum cleaner company is founded in Britain.

• **11 Feb:** Thomas Alva Edison wins patent rights for the movie projector.

• **Aug–Oct:** Wilbur Wright makes record-breaking flights in Europe.

• **Sept:** The International Conference for the Protection of Labor demands prohibition of night work by children.

• **1 Oct:** The Ford Motor Company puts the Model-T Ford, the first mass market automobile, into production.

• **14 Nov:** Albert Einstein proposes the quantum theory of light.

• **26 Dec:** Jack Johnson (USA) is the first black man to become world heavyweight boxing champion.

FRANCE RULES THE SKIES

British and US explorers attempt to reach the North and South Poles

POLITICS

• Compulsory military service is introduced in Australia.

• **JAN:** Serious riots break out between Hindus and Muslims in India.

• **9 JAN:** Colombia signs a convention with the US recognizing Panama.

• **27 JAN:** José Gomez is sworn in as the president of Cuba.

• **8 FEB:** France and Germany sign an agreement acknowledging Morocco's independence, and recognizing France's interests in that country.

• **2 MAR:** War between Austria and Serbia over Bosnia-Herzegovina is avoided when Serbia backs down.

• **26 MAR:** Russian troops invade northern Persia in support of the shah.

• **19 APR:** Turkey recognizes Bulgarian independence.

• **26 APR:** Sultan Abdul Hamid of Turkey is deposed and replaced by Muhammad V.

Louis Blériot flies the English Channel, 25 July.

• **29 APR:** British prime minister David Lloyd George introduces a radical budget of social reform and higher taxation.

• **APR–MAY:** French postal workers strike over demands to unionize; civil servants are denied the right to strike.

• **25 MAY:** The Indian Councils Act increases the power of the legislative councils, granting separate electorates for Muslims and other minorities.

• **14 JUL:** Count von Bülow resigns as German imperial chancellor, and is replaced by Theobald von Bethmann Hollweg.

• **16 JUL:** The shah of Persia is deposed by Ali Kuli Khan, and is replaced by the 12-year-old Sultan Ahmad

• **21 Jul:** Georges Clemenceau resigns as head of the French government and Aristide Briand takes over as premier.

• **26 Oct:** Prince Ito of Japan is assassinated by a Korean nationalist. Japan imposes a dictatorship in Korea.

• **28 Oct:** Belgium announces major liberalizing reforms in the Congo.

• **14 Nov:** US president William Taft approves a naval base at Pearl Harbor.

• **30 Nov:** British prime minister Lloyd George's "People's Budget" is rejected by the House of Lords.

• **7 Dec:** A royal proclamation creates the Union of South Africa, bringing together the colonies of the Cape, Natal, Transvaal and the Orange River.

• **12 Dec:** The British House of Lords rules it illegal to use trade union funds to sponsor Labor Members of Parliament.

C U L T U R E

• The General Electric Company produces the first electric toaster.

• Australian longterm residents are awarded the right to old age pensions.

• Belgian Leo Baekeland patents the process for making Bakelite.

• The Girl Guides are established in London, as a parallel organization to the Boy Scouts.

• First performance of Gustav Mahler's song-cycle *Das Lied von der Erde*.

• **1 Jan:** The Motion Picture Patents Company is set up in the United States.

• **9 Jan:** British explorer Ernest Shackleton passes within 112 mi (180 km) of the South Pole.

• **11 Jan:** Public executions are resumed in France as four gangsters are guillotined.

• **18 Jan:** New Zealand women are severely restricted from buying alcohol in bars.

• **24 Feb:** The first color moving pictures are demonstrated in Brighton, England.

• **15 Mar:** US businessman H.G. Selfridge opens his department store in Oxford Street, London.

• **6 Apr:** Robert Peary (USA) claims to be the first person to reach the North Pole.

• **18 Apr:** Joan of Arc is beatified by the Vatican.

• **18 May:** Serge Diaghilev's *Ballets Russes* has its première in Paris.

• **25 Jul:** Frenchman Louis Blériot flies from Calais to Dover in the *Bleriot XI*, becoming the first person to fly across the English Channel in a monoplane.

MUSIC TAKES THE AIR

Radio spawns a wider audience for all kinds of music

POLITICS

• In Mexico, a revolutionary movement emerges led by Francisco Madero and Emiliano Zapata.

• **13 Jan:** Unrest in India leads to the banning of "seditious" meetings in five provinces.

• **15 Jan:** The British general election ends with a dead heat between the Liberals and Conservatives; Asquith remains prime minister.

• **20 Feb:** Boutros-Ghali, first native prime minister of Egypt, is assassinated.

• **23 Feb:** A Chinese army invades Tibet; the Dalai Lama flees to India.

• **27 Apr:** Louis Botha and James Hertzog found the South Africa Party, calling for independence for the Boers.

• **6 May:** Death of Edward VII and succession of George V.

• **1 Jul:** The Union of South Africa is formed and becomes a dominion of the British Empire.

The tango becomes all the rage.

• **4 Jul:** Russia and Japan agree spheres of influence in the world and on mutual defense of interests.

• **22 Aug:** Hostility toward Japan continues in Korea; Japan formally annexes the territory on 29 Aug.

• **28 Aug:** Montenegro declares full independence from the Ottoman Empire under the newly-proclaimed king, Nicholas I.

• **31 Aug:** Ex-president Theodore Roosevelt, expounds his concept of "The New Nationalism".

• **2 Sept:** In Britain, employers lock out striking dockers (longshoremen). 10,000 miners strike in support.

• **12 Sept:** British statistics show that 300,000 workers were on strike in 1909, a fourfold increase on 1908.

• **15 Sept:** The first Union of South Africa elections result in victory for the South African party. Louis Botha becomes prime minister.

• **3–5 Oct:** The Portuguese monarchy is overthrown by revolution. As King Manuel II flees to Britain, a republic is declared under Theophilo Braga.

• **7 Oct:** The Portuguese government expels all nuns and monks.

• **18 Oct:** Eleutherios Venizelos becomes prime minister of Greece and begins a program of reform.

• **4–5 Nov:** Russia gains a free hand in north Persia by agreeing to cease opposition to German construction of the Baghdad Railway.

• **18 Nov:** British prime minister, Asquith calls his second general election of the year as talks concerning reform of the House of Lords fail.

• **14 Dec:** In Palestine, Turkish troops are sent to suppress an uprising of 20,000 Bedouin Arabs.

• **20 Dec:** The British general election results in a tie between Liberals and Tories. Asquith continues as prime minister of a minority government.

CULTURE

• Britain opens the first Labor Exchanges, to help the unemployed get work.

• Boy Scouts of America and Camp Fire Girls are founded in the United States.

• Father's Day first celebrated in the US.

• The tango becomes the latest dance craze in the United States and Europe.

• Pathe Gazette's first film newsreel.

• US band leader, John Philip Sousa tours the world with his band.

• The first radio receivers go on sale in kit form in the United States.

• Opening of the 5,000-seat Gaumont Palace cinema in Paris.

• French scientist Marie Curie isolates pure radium with André Debierne and publishes her *Treatise on Radiography*.

• **1 Jan:** New York's Metropolitan Opera broadcasts tenor Enrico Caruso on radio.

• **May:** Halley's Comet passes within 13 million miles of Earth. Comet parties are held in the US but fears abound concerning its effects on health.

• **25 Jun:** Igor Stravinsky's ballet *The Firebird* for the *Ballets Russes* is an outstanding success.

• **Aug:** In the US, Thomas Edison demonstrates "talking pictures".

CONQUEST AND CHALLENGE

Territorial ambitions and social revolution stalk the world

POLITICS

• **1 JAN:** In Australia, the Northern Territory transfers to direct Commonwealth administration.

• **25 JAN:** Civil war in Mexico prompts the US to send troops to guard against Mexican insurgents.

• **24 FEB:** The German Reichstag votes to increase the German standing army by 515,000.

• **28 FEB:** In Australia, prime minister Andrew Fisher plans to nationalize monopolies.

• **1 APR:** Mexican president Porfirio Diaz promises extensive reforms in the face of growing rebellion.

• **15 APR:** US troops begin fighting Mexican rebels led by Francisco Madero.

• **23 APR:** French government sends troops to Morocco to suppress revolt.

• **15 MAY:** US Supreme Court dissolves J. D. Rockefeller's Standard Oil Trust on the basis of antitrust legislation.

Amundsen reaches the South Pole.

• **21 MAY:** French troops enter Fez, Morocco; Germany accuses France of violating the Algeciras agreement concerning Moroccan independence.

• **25 MAY:** Mexican dictator Porfirio Diaz flees ending a 45-year rule. Francisco Madero becomes president.

• **26 MAY:** Germany grants Alsace-Lorraine its own legislature and a substantial degree of autonomy.

• **1 JUL:** Germany sends the gunboat *Panther* to Morocco as talks with France make little progress. The French request for British assistance is rejected.

• **10 JUL:** Russia indicates its alliance with France over Morocco.

- **16 JUL:** Lord Kitchener of Britain becomes consul-general in Egypt.

- **26 JUL:** US president Taft signs a reciprocity bill with Canada.

- **8 AUG:** In Britain, a nationwide strike by stevedores, railwaymen, carters and transport workers brings chaos.

- **10 AUG:** British House of Lords passes the Parliament Bill exchanging their power of veto over House of Commons bills for powers of suspension.

- **20 AUG:** Portugal adopts a liberal constitution under Manoel de Arriaga.

- **14 SEPT:** Russian prime minister Pyotr Stolypin is assassinated and replaced by Vladimir Kokovtsoff.

- **21 SEPT:** The Canadian Liberal Party is defeated in general election. Robert K. Borden forms a Conservative ministry.

- **29 SEPT:** Italy declares war on Turkey after being refused peaceful entry into Tripoli. The Italian fleet bombs the Tripoli coast.

- **26 OCT:** An almost bloodless Chinese revolution begins the overthrow of the Manchu dynasty after nearly 300 years.

- **4 NOV:** France and Germany agree that Morocco should become a French protectorate while Germany gains territory in the French Congo.

- **5 NOV:** Italy annexes Libya, Tripoli and Cyrenaica.

- **12 DEC:** King George V of Britain is crowned Emperor of India. New Delhi replaces Calcutta as capital.

- **30 DEC:** Sun Yat-sen is elected president of the Chinese republic by a revolutionary assembly at Nanjing.

CULTURE

- Military training for men aged from 14 to 40 is established in New Zealand.

- The *Der Blaue Reiter* (The Blue Rider) group of painters by Franz Marc and Wassily Kandinsky hold first exhibition.

- "Alexander's Ragtime Band" by Irving Berlin becomes popular in the US.

- Official Secrets Act is passed in Britain.

- In Britain, authors and musicians win lifetime copyright on their work and for 50 years thereafter.

- C. F. Kettering (USA) develops the first effective electric starter-motor for cars.

- **DEC:** French scientist Marie Curie wins an unprecedented second Nobel Prize for Chemistry but the Academie des Sciences in Paris refuses to admit her because she is a woman.

- **14 DEC:** Norwegian explorer Roald Amundsen reaches the South Pole.

SINKING OF THE TITANIC

Crisis looms in the Balkans despite international intervention

POLITICS

• **JAN:** After elections, the socialists become the strongest party in the German Reichstag.

• **6 JAN:** In the US, New Mexico becomes the 47th state of the Union.

• **10 JAN:** The French cabinet resigns. Raymond Poincaré becomes prime minister of a coalition government.

• **26 JAN:** In Britain, 30,000 people demonstrate in Ulster against proposals for Irish home rule.

• **3 FEB:** Japan plans to build eight Dreadnoughts and eight cruisers.

• **12 FEB:** Boy emperor Pu Yi of China is forced to abdicate. Yuan Shikai is installed as president of the provisional republic of China on 15 Feb.

• **14 FEB:** Arizona becomes the 48th state of the Union.

• **1 MAR:** British suffragettes begin a window-smashing campaign in the West End of London.

S.S. Titanic *is destroyed by an iceberg.*

• **8 MAR:** A German naval bill further enlarges the navy. Britain vows to retain naval superiority in the North Sea and recalls battleships from Mediterranean.

• **29 MAR:** A Minimum Wage Bill is passed in Britain to bring an end to a 6-week strike by 1,500,000 coal miners.

• **18 APR:** The Turks close the Dardanelles straits to shipping after bombardment by Italy. They are reopened on 4 May after protests from other powers.

• **5 MAY:** The Bolshevik newspaper *Pravda* ("Truth") begins publication in Russia.

• **31 MAY:** US Marines land in Cuba to protect American interests there.

• **25 JUN:** In Britain, Parliament hears protests against the forcible feeding of imprisoned suffragettes.

• **JUL:** Beginning of the civil war in Nicaragua, with intervention by the US in support of president Adolfo Diaz.

• **9 JUL:** Elections in New Zealand won by the new Reform Party over the Liberals. W. F. Massey becomes premier.

• **30 JUL:** In Japan, the Meiji emperor Mutsuhito dies and is succeeded by his son Yoshihito.

• **30 SEPT:** Bulgaria and Serbia mobilize to attack Turkey over reforms in Macedonia.

• **8 OCT:** Montenegro declares war on Turkey. (Bulgaria, Serbia and Greece do the same on 18 Oct).

• **18 OCT:** Treaty of Lausanne brings peace between Italy and Turkey. Italy is to withdraw from the Aegean and Turkey will withdraw from Tripoli.

• **3−5 NOV:** The Bulgarians advance toward Constantinople; Russia warns that their fleet will resist occupation.

• **5 NOV:** Democrat Woodrow Wilson is elected president of the United States.

• **12 NOV:** Assassination of Jose Canalejos y Méndez, liberal and anticlerical premier of Spain.

• **28 NOV:** Declaration of Albanian independence.

• **3 DEC:** Armistice between Turkey, Bulgaria and Serbia; Greece and Montenegro maintain offensives in Janina and Scutari respectively.

• **16 DEC:** London peace conference opens on the Balkan question.

CULTURE

• In Paris, Cinzano display the first neon advertising sign.

• The fossil remains of the "Piltdown Man" are found in south-east England.

• Richard Hellmann, proprietor of a New York delicatessen, begins to sell ready-made mayonnaise.

• Fashion designer Coco Chanel opens her first salon in Deauville, France.

• In US, Fox and Universal film companies are established.

• Britain appoints first film censor.

• Dixieland Jazz Band opens in cabaret in New Orleans, Louisianna.

• The US states of Arizona, Kansas and Wisconsin adopt women's suffrage.

• **14−15 APR:** The British ship, *S.S. Titanic,* sinks on her maiden voyage from Southampton to New York with the loss of 1,513 lives.

SUFFRAGETTES FIGHT ON

Balkan conflict continues and China tries out democracy

POLITICS

• The United Federation of Labor and the Social Democratic Party are founded in New Zealand.

• In the US, the Department of Labor is created after pressure from the American Federation of Labor.

• **6 JAN:** The London peace conference on the Balkan question collapses.

• **17 JAN:** Raymond Poincaré is elected president of France.

• **23 JAN:** *Coup d'état* by Young Turks. Turkey refuses to cede Adrianople to Bulgaria.

• **3 FEB:** Balkan War is resumed by the Bulgarians. Adrianople is captured from the Turks on 26 Mar.

• **18 FEB:** Overthrow and execution of Mexican president Madero by Victoriano Huerta. Civil war breaks out against his repressive regime.

• **19 FEB:** British suffragettes bomb the chancellor Lloyd George's new house.

Emmeline Pankhurst under arrest.

• **18 MAR:** Aristide Briand, prime minister of France, resigns following rejection by the senate of his proposals for electoral reform.

• **18 MAR:** King Giorgios I of Greece is assassinated; Constantine I succeeds.

• **3 APR:** British suffragette Emmeline Pankhurst is imprisoned for three years for inciting persons to plant explosives.

• **8 APR:** Republic of China's first parliament meets with the Guomindang (National People's party) holding a majority of seats.

• **8 APR:** US president, Woodrow Wilson, becomes the first leader for 112 years to deliver the "State of the Union" address in person to Congress.

• **30 May:** The London treaty brings peace to the Balkans. Bulgaria retains Adrianople.

• **6 Jun:** The Reichstag funds a large increase in the German army.

• **30 Jun:** Second Balkan War breaks out. Bulgaria attacks Serbia and Greece.

• **10 Jul:** Rebellion breaks out in the southern provinces of China.

• **12 Jul:** In Britain, 150,000 Ulstermen pledge to resist Irish home rule and threaten civil war.

• **10 Aug:** Treaty of Bucharest leads to Bulgarian loss of territory to Romania, Serbia and Greece

• **23 Sept:** Serbs invade Albania.

• **29 Sept:** Treaty of Constantinople ends Second Balkan War. Adrianople remains under Turkish rule.

• **6 Oct:** Yuan Shik'ai is elected president of the Chinese Republic.

• **11 Oct:** Mexican president Huerta dissolves Congress and declares himself dictator.

• **Nov:** Mohandas Gandhi, leader of the Indian Passive Resistance Movement, is jailed in South Africa, provoking riots.

• **3 Nov:** US demands resignation of General Huerta of Mexico.

• **4 Nov:** In China, president Yuan Shik'ai purges parliament of its Guomindang members.

• **5 Nov:** Recognition of the autonomy of Outer Mongolia by China and Russia.

• **13 Nov:** Greek-Turkish peace treaty allows division of southern Albania and grants Crete and Aegean islands to Greece.

CULTURE

• The foxtrot becomes fashionable

• Igor Stravinsky's ballet *The Rite of Spring* causes controversy.

• The Ford Motor Company (USA) introduces a moving assembly line.

• The Armory Show in New York brings modern European art, including a Picasso exhibition, to the US.

• Canada's Transcontinental Railway opens.

• The first electric refrigerator for home use is marketed in the US and Germany.

• 'Camel' cigarettes are launched in the United States.

• **17 Oct:** In Germany, the world's biggest airship, Zeppelin L2 explodes with the loss of all 28 crew on board.

• **21 Dec:** *The New York World* prints the first modern crossword puzzle.

HOME BY CHRISTMAS?

*The diplomatic tightrope in Europe
gives way; general war ensues*

POLITICS

• **11 Jan:** In China, Yuan Shihk'ai dissolves parliament.

• **20 Mar:** British troops stationed at the Curragh near Dublin "mutiny" at the prospect of being ordered to enforce Home Rule in northern Ireland.

• **21 Apr:** US marines occupy Vera Cruz in Mexico; a peace agreement is signed on July 3.

• **26 May:** British parliament passes a Home Rule Bill for Ireland.

• **28 Jun:** Archduke Franz Ferdinand of Austria-Hungary is assassinated in Sarajevo.

• **23 Jul:** Austria demands an apology from Serbia for the assassination and a cessation of anti-Austrian activities.

• **24 Jul:** Russia, supported by France, announces it will protect Serbia against invasion.

• **28 Jul:** Austria–Hungary declares war on Serbia.

Students in Berlin at the outbreak of war.

• **30 Jul:** Russia mobilizes for war.

• **31 Jul:** Germany declares war on Russia; Austria–Hungary and France mobilize their forces.

• **31 Jul:** French socialist leader Jean Jaurès is assassinated.

• **2 Aug:** Germany begins to invade Luxembourg, and demands free passage for its armies through Belgium.

• **3 Aug:** Germany declares war on France, which has already been pledged support by Britain.

• **4 Aug:** Germany invades Belgium; Britain declares war on Germany.

• **6 Aug:** Austria–Hungary declares war on Russia.

• **13 Aug:** Austria–Hungary invades Serbia, and is repulsed.

• **15 Aug:** The Panama Canal is opened to shipping.

• **16 Aug:** The British Expeditionary Force lands in France.

• **20 Aug:** The Germans take Brussels, capital of Belgium, and invade France.

• **20 Aug:** Pope Pius XI dies; he is succeeded by Benedict XV on 3 Sept.

• **23 Aug:** Japan declares war on Germany and begins its takeover of German colonies in East Asia.

• **26–30 Aug:** A German army defeats the Russians at Tannenberg.

• **30 Aug:** German air-raid on Paris.

• **3 Sept:** The French government evacuates to Bordeaux.

• **5 Sept:** French and British troops stop the German advance at the Battle of the Marne (to 12 Sept).

• **6 Sept:** The Germans defeat the Russian army at the Masurian Lakes, East Prussia (to 15 Sept).

• **30 Oct:** German troops in Belgium are halted at First Battle of Ypres; trench warfare begins.

• **2 Nov:** Russia declares war on Turkey.

• **6 Nov:** Britain and France declare war on Turkey.

• **29 Nov:** Former president Theodore Roosevelt criticizes US neutrality.

• **8 Dec:** British Royal Navy defeats German Navy off the Falkland Islands.

• **25 Dec:** German and Allied soldiers in trenches declare an informal Christmas Day truce.

CULTURE

• *St. Louis Blues* by W.C. Handy.

• First brassière patented, by Mary Phelps Jacob (Caresse Crosby) (USA).

• Movie star Charlie Chaplin first appears in the "tramp" costume in *Kid Auto Races at Venice*.

• **8 Jan:** First successful use of radiotherapy to treat cancer, in the Middlesex Hospital, London.

• **18 Feb:** British explorer Campbell Beazley announces the discovery of three ruined Inca cities in Peru.

• **13 Apr:** Premiere of George Bernard Shaw's play *Pygmalion*.

• **18 Apr:** Premiere of the movie *Cabiria* (directed by Giovanni Pastrone) in Turin.

• **15 Jul:** Paramount Pictures, a major Hollywood movie studio, is established.

A YEAR OF STALEMATE

The military fail to make headway while war impinges on civilians

POLITICS

• **19 Jan:** The Germans first use Zeppelin airships to bomb Britain.

• **24 Jan:** The Battle of Dogger Bank takes place as the Royal Navy sink the German cruiser *Blucher*.

• **2 Feb:** The Germans announce a U-boat submarine blockade of British shipping; Britain announces that all goods bound for Germany will be seized.

• **8–22 Feb:** In the winter battle of Masuria on the Eastern Front, the Germans advance against the Russians.

• **19 Feb:** A naval action by Britain against the Dardanelles begins to divert the Turks from their military objectives in the Caucasus.

• **10–13 Mar:** The Battle of Neuve Chapelle is fought on the Western Front; the Allies make limited gains.

• **22 Apr–18 May:** At the Second Battle of Ypres, on the Western Front, the Germans make the first effective use of chlorine gas as a weapon.

Charlie Chaplin becomes a popular hero.

• **25 Apr:** ANZAC (Australian and New Zealand Army Corps) and British forces land at Anzac cove, Gallipoli, in the Dardanelles campaign.

• **26 Apr:** Italy, previously neutral in the European war, concludes a secret treaty with the Allies.

• **7 May:** The British passenger liner S.S. *Lusitania* is sunk by a German U-boat, 128 US citizens are among the 1,195 people who lose their lives.

• **23 May:** Italy declares war on Austria–Hungary.

• **26 May:** The British government becomes a coalition, led by H. H. Asquith.

• **1 Jul:** Austria–Hungary and Germany jointly invade Poland.

• **6 Aug:** The Allies land fresh troops at Suvla Bay, in the Gallipoli campaign.

• **31 Aug:** Germany and Austria–Hungary partition Poland.

• **6 Sept:** Bulgaria concludes an alliance with Germany and mobilizes against Serbia on 24 Sept.

• **16 Sept:** Following the murder of president Vibrun Sam (27 Jul), Haiti becomes a US protectorate.

• **25 Sept:** The Allies launch a "great offensive" at the Second Battle of Champagne and Third Battle of Artois.

• **5 Oct:** Allied troops begin to disembark at Salonika in an attempt to block the Bulgarian advance on Serbia.

• **29 Oct:** Socialist Aristide Briand becomes prime minister of France.

• **2 Dec:** General Joseph Joffre is appointed Commander-in-Chief of the French army.

• **7 Dec:** Turks besiege British forces at Kut-el-Amara (Mesopotamia). British capitulate 29 Apr 1916.

• **8 Dec:** Allied and ANZAC troops begin to withdraw from Sulva Bay and Anzac Cove in Gallipoli.

• **17 Dec:** Douglas Haig replaces John French as commander of the British forces on the Western Front.

CULTURE

• The sale of absinthe is banned in France, because of blindness and premature death among heavy drinkers.

• *The Rainbow*, a novel by D. H. Lawrence, is published in Britain and banned on charges of obscenity

• *Metamorphosis*, by Czech writer Franz Kafka, is published.

• German-born physicist Albert Einstein publishes his general theory of relativity.

• English poet Rupert Brooke dies on active service.

• German Fokker aircraft are equipped with an interrupter gear to allow machine guns to shoot through the propeller blades.

• **8 Feb:** *The Birth of a Nation*, an epic film by D. W. Griffiths about the history of the United States, is released.

• **18 Mar:** The British government appeals for women to take jobs in trade, industry and agriculture.

• **19 Nov:** The US labor leader Joe Hill is executed in Utah for murder; he later became a folk hero.

• **25 Nov:** The racist, anti-Semitic, anti-Catholic Ku Klux Klan reemerges in the US in the state of Georgia. It is led by William Joseph Simmons.

THE WAR OF SLAUGHTER

Casualties on the Western Front exceed two million men.

POLITICS

• **6 JAN:** The compulsory military service bill is passed by the British Parliament.

• **10 JAN–16 APR:** The Russians lead an offensive against Turkey in Armenia.

• **14 JAN:** Montenegro capitulates to Austrian troops; however a week later it resolves to continue fighting.

• **21 FEB:** Germany begins a policy of wearing down her opponents with an offensive against French positions in Verdun. The battle ends on 18 Dec with massive losses on both sides.

• **22 FEB:** US president Woodrow Wilson lays out terms for his proposed mediation between the Allies and the Central Powers.

• **9 MAR:** Germany declares war on Portugal.

• **24 APR:** The Irish Republican Brotherhood takes advantage of Britain's preoccupation with war in Europe to start a nationalist rising in Dublin.

Dublin smolders after the Easter rising.

• **1 MAY:** British forces violently suppress the Irish rising.

• **9 MAY:** France and Britain agree on a postwar plan for partitioning Turkey.

• **31 MAY:** At the Battle of Jutland, the British and German navies meet but neither wins a decisive advantage.

• **4 JUN–10 AUG:** Russia launches the Brusilov offensive against the Austrians, aiding Italy, but suffering heavy losses.

• **5 JUN:** The British minister of war Lord Kitchener dies when the *H.M.S. Hampshire* is sunk by a German U-boat off the Orkneys in Scotland; he is succeeded by David Lloyd George.

• **6 JUN:** An Arab revolt against the Turks is launched in the Hejaz.

• **1 JUL:** The British army launches a major offensive on the Somme in northern France, but suffers enormous losses, including 60,000 casualties (20,000 dead) on the first day alone.

• **27 AUG:** Romania joins the Allies and declares war on Austria–Hungary.

• **30 AUG:** The German chief of general staff Erich von Falkenhayn is replaced by Paul von Hindenburg.

• **1 SEPT:** Bulgaria declares war on Romania and launches a successful joint invasion with Germany and Austria-Hungary.

• **15 SEPT:** Tanks are used by the British army for the first time on the Somme.

• **28 OCT:** An Australian referendum rejects conscription.

• **7 NOV:** Woodrow Wilson is reelected president of the United States.

• **19 NOV:** The Battle of the Somme on the Western Front comes to an inconclusive end.

• **21 NOV:** The Austrian emperor Franz Josef dies, and is succeeded by his grandnephew as Charles I.

• **7–10 DEC:** David Lloyd George becomes British prime minister, and forms a war cabinet .

• **12 DEC:** Germany announces that it is ready to negotiate peace, but the Allies reject this advance on 30 Dec.

• **18 DEC:** US president Wilson makes peace proposals for the war in Europe, but the Allies reject his terms on 10 Jan 1917.

CULTURE

• Irish novelist James Joyce's autobiographical novel *Portrait of the Artist as a Young Man* is published.

• French designer Coco Chanel makes jersey a fashionable material; previously it was only used for underwear.

• The first artificial silk (Rayon) knitwear is marketed in the USA.

• Plastic surgery techniques are developed to treat war wounds.

• **FEB:** Romanian poet, Tristan Tzara, becomes one of the founder members of the Dada movement of avant-garde art founded in Zurich, Switzerland.

• **18 MAY:** Britain introduces a daylight saving scheme (British Summer Time).

• **16 OCT:** Margaret Sanger founds the first birth control clinic in the United States in Brooklyn, New York.

• **30 DEC:** Gregory Rasputin, the confidant of the czarina of Russia, is murdered.

REVOLUTION IN RUSSIA

The US enters the war and turns the tide for the Allies

POLITICS

• **29 Jan:** The US Congress passes a new immigration act banning all Asians other than Japanese.

• **31 Jan:** A radical constitution is adopted by the Mexican Congress, providing for universal suffrage, an eight-hour day and a minimum wage.

• **1 Feb:** The Germans recommence unrestricted U-boat warfare in the Atlantic, causing the Americans to sever relations with Germany.

• **17 Feb:** A coalition Commonwealth war government is set up in Australia by prime minister William Hughes.

• **2 Mar:** Puerto Rico becomes a United States territory.

• **8–14 Mar:** Strikes and unrest break out in Petrograd, Russia.

• **11 Mar:** British troops take Baghdad.

• **11 Mar:** The Russian Duma forms a provisional government headed by Prince Gyorgy Lvov.

Russian soldiers join striking workers to topple the Russian monarchy.

• **15 Mar:** Czar Nicholas II of Russia abdicates, in favor of his brother, who himself abdicates the next day.

• **24 Mar:** The provisional government of Russia recognizes the independence of Finland, Poland and Estonia (12 Apr).

• **6 Apr:** The United States declares war on Germany.

• **9 Apr:** In the first Allied push of the year on the Western front, Vimy Ridge is taken, with major Canadian losses.

• **16 Apr:** V. I. Lenin and other Bolshevik leaders return to Petrograd from exile.

• **28 Apr:** Philippe Pétain becomes commander of the French forces.

- **7 Jun:** British troops launch an attack on Messines Ridge.

- **12 Jun:** King Constantine of Greece abdicates; Greece declares war on the Central Powers on 29 Jun.

- **14 Jun:** The American Expeditionary Force arrives in France, led by General John J. Pershing.

- **26 Jun:** The British royal family drop their German titles, and adopt the family name of Windsor.

- **16–18 Jul:** The Bolsheviks stage a failed coup in Petrograd.

- **20 Jul:** Alexander Kerensky heads the Russian provisional government.

- **20 Jul:** Serbia, Montenegro, Slovenia and Croatia agree to form a single state.

- **31 Jul–10 Nov:** The Third Battle of Ypres (Passchendaele) in which 325,000 British soldiers died.

- **3 Sept:** On the Eastern Front, the Germans take Riga and most of Latvia.

- **15 Oct:** Convicted Dutch spy and dancer Mata Hari is executed in Paris.

- **31 Oct:** The Italian army is defeated by the Germans at Caporetto.

- **2 Nov:** Balfour Declaration of the British government in favor of Palestine as a national home for the Jews.

- **6 Nov:** In Russia, Bolshevik forces storm the Winter Palace in Petrograd and overthrow the government. Lenin forms a Bolshevik government the next day, Trotsky is appointed prime minister.

- **20 Nov–8 Dec:** The use of tanks makes a decisive contribution to victory in the Battle of Cambrai.

- **7 Dec:** The United States declares war on Austria–Hungary.

- **15 Dec:** An armistice is concluded on the Eastern Front.

- **17 Dec:** Unionist Robert Borden wins the Canadian general election.

CULTURE

- Canada grants women suffrage, with the exception of Quebec, where it was delayed until 1940.

- Pablo Picasso's designs for the *Ballets Russes* ballet *Parade* are described as "surrealist" by Guillaume Apollinaire.

- Marcel Duchamp's *Fountain,* made out of a urinal, is displayed in New York.

- The first jazz record, *Dixieland Jazz Band One-Step*, is released by Victor.

- Clarence Birdseye develops a method of freezing to preserve food.

- **17 Oct:** The first section of the transaustralian railroad between Port Augusta and Kalgoorlie is completed.

END OF THE WAR TO END WARS

Central and eastern Europe collapse into chaos and revolution

POLITICS

• **8 Jan:** US president Wilson sets out his 14 points for peace in Europe.

• **12 Jan:** Latvia declares its independence from Russia.

• **15 Jan:** General strikes take place in Vienna, Prague and Budapest as part of a workers' peace movement.

• **21 Feb:** Australian forces take Jericho from the Turks.

• **3 Mar:** The treaty of Brest-Litovsk brings the war on the Eastern Front to an end, with Russia ceding a large amount of territory, and recognizing the independence of the Baltic states.

• **21 Mar:** The Germans begin a "spring offensive" on the Western Front.

• **1 Apr:** The Royal Air Force is established by the British, replacing the Royal Flying Corps.

• **21 Apr:** German flying ace Manfred von Richthofen (the "Red Baron") is shot down.

Czar Nicholas II, murdered with his family.

• **15 May:** An Allied counterattack pushes the Germans back.

• **16 Jul:** Czar Nicholas II of Russia and his family are murdered by Bolsheviks at Ekaterinburg.

• **2 Aug:** British troops intervene in the Russian civil war against the Bolsheviks, landing at Archangel, and at Vladivostok on 3 Aug.

• **8 Aug:** Allied troops make a decisive break in the German line near Amiens.

• **15–24 Sept:** The Allies begin a major advance into Bulgaria. The Bulgarians ask for an armistice.

• **18 Sept:** The British, aided by the Arabs, begin an attack on Turkish positions in Palestine.

• **1 Oct:** A British force led by Major T. E. Lawrence captures the Middle Eastern city of Damascus.

• **16 Oct:** Austrian emperor Charles I proclaims a reorganization of the monarchy as a federal state, with complete self-government for each subject nationality.

• **17 Oct:** Hungary declares independence from Austria.

• **24 Oct:** The Italians launch an offensive against the Austrians, and take Fiume and Trieste.

• **28 Oct:** Czechoslovakia proclaims independence. Tomas Masaryk becomes first Czech president.

• **28 Oct:** German sailors mutiny at Kiel after orders to attack the British.

• **29 Oct:** Yugoslavia's independence is proclaimed in Zagreb.

• **1 Nov:** British and French forces occupy Constantinople.

• **3 Nov:** The Allies and Austria–Hungary sign an armistice.

• **6 Nov:** German and Allied delegations meet at Compiègne and negotiate armistice terms.

• **9 Nov:** German kaiser Wilhelm II abdicates and flees to Holland; a German republic is proclaimed.

• **11 Nov:** At 11 a.m. an armistice comes into force on the Western Front.

• **12 Nov:** Abdication of Austrian emperor Charles I.

• **1 Dec:** British and American troops begin the occupation of Germany.

• **4 Dec:** Alexander I becomes prince-regent of the Serbs, Croats, and Slovenes.

• **13 Dec:** US president Wilson arrives in France to attend the peace conference.

• **14 Dec:** At the "Khaki Election" in Britain, Lloyd George wins a large majority, pledging punishment for Germany and demanding full reparations.

CULTURE

• The first three-color traffic lights are installed in New York.

• An influenza epidemic in Europe and Asia kills 20 million people by 1919.

• The first Tarzan film, *Tarzan of the Apes*, is released in the United States.

• **6 Feb:** Women over the age of 30 are given the vote in Britain.

• **19 Jun:** General rationing is introduced in Britain.

• **25 Aug:** The US War Industries Board declares motion pictures to be an essential industry.

REMAKING EUROPE

Break up of the Austro-Hungarian empire; civil war in Russia

POLITICS

• **3 JAN:** Bolshevik army invades Latvia.

• **5–15 JAN:** A Communist (Spartacist) uprising takes place in Berlin, led by Rosa Luxembourg and Karl Liebknecht who are shot after the revolt is squashed.

• **10 JAN:** The British occupy Baghdad.

• **17 JAN:** Ignace Paderewski forms a coalition cabinet in Poland, with Gen. Pilsudski as provisional president.

• **18 JAN:** Opening of the Paris Peace Conference chaired by French prime minister Georges Clemenceau.

• **19 JAN:** Elections in Germany for national assembly leave Social Democrats as the largest party.

• **21 JAN:** Sinn Fein MPs elected to the British parliament at Westminster organize their own assembly in Ireland and declare an Irish Republic with Éamon de Valera as president.

• **22 JAN:** Czechs occupy the disputed Teschen area on the Polish border.

President Woodrow Wilson (center) and Georges Clemenceau (right) lead the way to Versailles.

• **25 JAN:** The Paris Peace Conference resolves to create a League of Nations.

• **2 MAR:** Foundation of the third Communist International, to propagate communism and world revolution.

• **12 MAR:** Karl Renner becomes chancellor of Austria after the Socialists win 16 Feb elections.

• **18 MAR:** In India, the internment of political agitators without trial leads Gandhi to proclaim a day of fasting and work stoppage. Riots erupt in Amritsar.

• **21 MAR:** Formation of a socialist-communist government in Hungary.

• **23 MAR:** Benito Mussolini founds the Italian fascist movement.

• **10 APR:** Romanian troops begin an invasion of Hungary.

• **13 APR:** The Amritsar massacre occurs in India. British troops fire on unarmed demonstrators killing 379 people. Gandhi suspends his campaign of civil disobedience.

• **18 APR:** Beginning of Vilnius dispute (1919–1922) between Poland and Lithuania.

• **30 APR:** China walks out of the Paris peace conference in protest when Japan is granted territorial rights over the Shandong peninsula.

• **MAY:** In Russia, the Red Army begins a counteroffensive against White army.

• **7 MAY:** Paris peace conference mandate for the German colonies south of the equator is assigned to Australia. (Samoa goes to New Zealand, Nauru Island is jointly administered by Australia, New Zealand and Britain).

• **15 MAY:** Greeks land at Smyrna, and with the support of the Allies, begin an attempted conquest of Turkey.

• **6 JUN:** Beginning of Russo-Finnish war over Karelia.

• **19 JUN:** Turkish nationalist leader Mustafa Kemal, and other nationalists declare their hostility to Allied plans for the dismemberment of Turkey.

• **20 JUN:** In Germany, Scheidermann government resigns in protest at Allied demands. Social Democrat Gustav Bauer forms a new government.

• **21 JUN:** German fleet is scuttled at Scapa Flow by its own crew.

• **28 JUN:** Treaty of Versailles is signed. Germany is compelled to accept "war guilt," to make reparations and to concede territory to the Allies.

• **31 JUL:** Germany adopts the Weimar constitution.

• **4 AUG–14 NOV:** Romanian troops occupy Budapest.

• **10 SEPT:** The Treaty of St.-Germain between Austria and the Allies ratifies Austria's breakup into sovereign states and provides for reparations.

• **27 NOV:** Treaty of Neuilly between Bulgaria and the Allies deprives Bulgaria of its Aegean seaboard.

CULTURE

• The Bauhaus school of design is founded in Germany by Walter Gropius.

• Jazz music becomes popular in Europe.

• **11 APR:** In a referendum, New Zealand rejects prohibition of alcohol.

• **15 JUN:** British aviators, Alcock and Brown make the first transatlantic flight.

THE RISE OF THE NEW WOMAN

The League of Nations attempts to wipe out war for good

POLITICS

• **16 Jan:** The League of Nations is inaugurated, members being signatories to the Treaty of Versailles. Exceptions are USA, China, Ecuador and Nicaragua.

• **23 Jan:** The Dutch refuse to hand over ex-Kaiser Wilhelm II as demanded by Supreme Allied War Command.

• **2 Feb:** Russia recognizes Estonian independence.

• **10 Feb, 14 Mar:** Plebiscites in Schleswig divide the province between Denmark and Germany.

• **26 Feb:** As agreed at Versailles, France acquires the Saar's coal deposits.

• **1 Mar:** Admiral Miklós Horthy is made regent and head of state of Hungary. He proclaims himself dictator on 28 Mar.

• **13–17 Mar:** Kapp Putsch: an insurrection in Berlin led by Dr. Wolfgang Kapp. The government flees but the movement collapses after a general strike.

Tennis star Suzanne Lenglen in short skirts!

• **16 Mar:** Turkish nationalist agitation leads to the occupation of Constantinople by allied forces.

• **9 Apr:** Mexico suffers a *coup d'état*. During May, Mexico City is captured and President Carranza is murdered.

• **23 Apr:** A provisional government is set up in Ankara, Turkey by the Nationalists led by Mustafa Kemal.

• **25 Apr:** Mandates are granted over former Turkish territory: Syria and the Lebanon go to France; Britain is assigned Palestine and Transjordania

• **25 Apr–12 Oct:** Poland launches an offensive against the Russian Bolsheviks in an attempt to capture the Ukraine. Kiev is taken on 7 May.

• **4 Jun:** Treaty of Trianon provides for Hungarian reparations, military limitations and loss of territory.

• **6 Jun:** German electors vote in a coalition government of the Center party, Social Democrats, and the People's Party.

• **22 Jun:** Greeks advance into Turkey capturing Bursa (9 Jul) and Adrianople (25 Jul).

• **1 Jul:** The "Black and Tans", a special military police, are sent to Ireland to suppress dissent.

• **1 Jul:** Robert Borden, premier of Canada, resigns because of ill health. Arthur Meighen takes over on 10 Jul.

• **5–16 Jul:** At a conference on German reparations in Spa in Belgium, it is established that France will receive 52 percent of the total, and Britain 22 percent.

• **12 Jul:** Russia recognizes Lithuanian independence.

• **10 Aug:** Treaty of Sevres between Turkey and the Allies leads to territorial gains for Greece.

• **11 Aug:** By the Treaty of Riga, Russia recognizes Latvian independence.

• **2 Nov:** Republican Warren Harding wins the US presidential election.

• **9 Nov:** Danzig (Gdansk) is confirmed to be a free city under the mandate of the League of Nations.

• **12 Nov:** Treaty of Rapello between Italy and Kingdom of the Serbs, Croats and Slovenes.

• **16 Nov:** Bolsheviks win the Russian civil war.

• **3 Dec:** Treaty of Alexandropol ends hostilities between Armenia and Turkey.

• **23 Dec:** The British parliament passes the Government of Ireland Act setting up Southern and Northern Ireland as discrete political entities.

CULTURE

• Trial of Italian-born anarchists, Sacco and Vanzetti in Massachusetts, USA.

• Soviet Russia becomes first country to legalize abortion.

• **16 Jan:** Prohibition comes into force in the US.

• **Feb:** The first commercial radio station, KDKA, begins broadcasting in Pittsburgh, Pennsylvania.

• **Jun–Jul:** French tennis star Suzanne Lenglen wears daring short skirts on court at the Wimbledon tournament and wins all three titles, the ladies' singles, ladies' doubles and mixed doubles.

• **Aug:** In the US, ratification of 19th Amendment enfranchises women.

THE RISE OF THE MOVIE STAR

Southern Ireland achieves full independence from Britain

POLITICS

• **JAN:** Greek-Turkish war begins.

• **13–22 JAN:** The Italian Socialist party splits into moderates and radicals.

• **21 FEB:** Reza Khan seizes power in Persia through a *coup d'état*.

• **26 FEB:** Treaty between Persia and Soviet Russia secures Persian integrity.

• **27 FEB:** Fascist and Communist riots in Florence, Italy heralds a period of civil war between the two groups.

• **8 MAR:** Allied troops occupy Ruhrort, Dusseldorf and Duisburg when Germany fails to meet demands for reparations.

• **17 MAR:** Polish constitution adopted.

• **17 MAR:** Collapse of Russian economy leads Lenin to introduce the New Economic Policy (NEP) allowing a measure of economic freedom.

• **23 MAR:** Germany announces that it cannot pay reparations due. British Reparations Act of 24 Mar imposes 50 percent duty on German goods.

Rudolph Valentino stars in The Sheik.

• **31 MAR–1 JUL:** In Britain, a national coal strike follows attempts to negotiate pay locally, not nationally.

• **27 APR:** The Allied Reparations Commission sets Germany's debt at 132 billion gold marks.

• **29 APR–5 MAY:** An ultimatum is sent to Germany demanding a payment of one billion gold marks by 12 May or the Allies will occupy the Ruhr. Germany borrows the money in London.

• **24 MAY:** Elections in Southern Ireland result in 124 Sinn Féin delegates being returned to power unopposed.

• **7 JUN:** New parliament of Northern Ireland opens with the Unionists as the majority party led by Sir James Craig.

• **16 Aug:** In Southern Ireland, the Sinn Féin members of parliament declare themselves to be a separate parliament and begin to negotiate total independence from Britain.

• **23 Aug:** After a plebiscite in his favor, Faisal is crowned king of Iraq.

• **15 Sept:** Guatemala, Honduras and El Salvador form a Republic of Central America.

• **12 Oct:** Upper Silesia is partitioned between Poland and Germany after a plebiscite. Poland gains most of the coal mines and steelworks.

• **21 Oct:** King Karoly marches on Budapest, Hungary, to regain the throne. He is defeated and exiled to Madeira.

• **5 Nov:** Crown Prince Hirohito takes over as regent of Japan.

• **12 Nov:** The Washington Conference on disarmament and Far East questions opens, attended by the major world powers. It lasts until 6 Feb 1922.

• **6 Dec:** Southern Ireland is granted full independence with dominion status within the British Commonwealth. Britain becomes the United Kingdom of Great Britain and Northern Ireland (UK).

• **13 Dec:** USA, UK, France, and Japan sign a treaty to respect each others' rights in the Pacific.

• **15 Dec:** Australia adopts higher tariffs to protect new industries.

• **29 Dec:** Conservatives lose Canadian general election to Liberals. W. L. Mackenzie King becomes premier.

CULTURE

• *The Sheik,* with Rudolph Valentino and Agnes Ayres, is a smash hit.

• Kotex begins to market sanitary towel products.

• Band Aid sticking plasters are available for the first time.

• Wassily Kandinsky founds the Academy of Arts and Sciences of All the Russias in Moscow.

• Australian cricketer, Jack Gregory scores the fastest century in Test cricket history while batting against South Africa.

• In the United States, W. G. Cady pioneers the use of the quartz crystal in radio reception leading to the popular crystal "cat's whisker" radio.

• Canadian scientists, F. G. Banting, C. Best, J. McLeod and J. Collip extract insulin from the human pancreas.

• **Mar:** Britain's first birth control clinic is opened in London by Marie Stopes.

• **Aug:** Russia suffers a great famine in which up to 18 million people starve.

TREASURES OF THE PHARAOH

Hollywood cashes in with a series of "mummy" films

POLITICS

• **6 JAN:** Conference of Cannes postpones German reparations payments.

• **21 JAN:** Éamon De Valera resigns as president of Ireland after *Dáil Eireann* (the Irish parliament) ratifies the treaty setting up dominion status for Ireland.

• **2 FEB:** In India, an attack on a police station by nationalists results in the death of 22 policemen. Gandhi suspends civil disobedience campaign on 13 Feb.

• **4 FEB:** Japan agrees to restore the Shandong peninsula to China.

• **15 FEB:** Permanent Court of International Justice opens at The Hague in The Netherlands.

• **20 FEB:** After a plebiscite, Vilnius is incorporated into Poland.

• **28 FEB:** Egypt declares independence and Fuad I becomes king on 15 Mar.

• **15 MAR:** In Ireland, Éamon De Valera organizes a new Republican party to fight the pro-treaty *Dáil Eireann*.

The jeweled death mask of Tutankhamun.

• **18 MAR:** In India, Gandhi is sentenced to six years' imprisonment on charges of sedition.

• **16 APR:** The Treaty of Rapallo establishes close economic and political ties between Russia and Germany.

• **31 MAY:** Reparations Commission grants Germany a moratorium on reparations payments until year end.

• **24 JUN:** Walter Rathenau, cabinet minister and Jewish industrialist, is assassinated by German nationalists.

• **JUL:** In Southern Ireland, there is heavy fighting between Government troops and anti-Treaty Republicans.

• **29 JUL:** Allies forbid the Greeks to occupy Constantinople.

• **31 Jul:** In Italy, fascists led by Benito Mussolini seize Milan and Genoa.

• **Aug:** The German mark suffers hyper-inflation due to wartime reparations.

• **22 Aug:** Michael Collins, first premier of Southern Ireland, is killed in an IRA ambush after 10 days in office.

• **9 Sept:** A successful Turkish counteroffensive against the Greeks includes recapture of the city of Smyrna.

• **9 Sept:** Adoption of a constitution by *Dáil Eireann,* to take effect from 6 Dec.

• **16 Sept:** A British force is sent to defend the Dardanelles against Turkey.

• **13 Oct:** Armistice of Mudanya ends the Greek-Turkish War.

• **19 Oct:** In Britain, prime minister Lloyd George resigns. Andrew Bonar Law forms a conservative ministry on 23 Oct.

• **28 Oct:** Italian fascists, led by Mussolini, march on Rome. King Victor Emmanuel refuses prime minister Facta's proposal for martial law.

• **31 Oct:** King Victor Emmanuel III requests that Mussolini form a cabinet of fascists and nationalists. On 25 Nov he is granted dictatorial powers.

• **1 Nov:** Mustafa Kemal abolishes the sultanate in Turkey and proclaims a Turkish republic.

• **26 Dec:** Reparations Commission declares "deliberate default" of Germany.

• **30 Dec:** Proclamation of the Union of Soviet Socialist Republics (USSR).

CULTURE

• Dance marathons sweep the US.

• The American cocktail becomes popular in Europe.

• Chanel No. 5 perfume is launched.

• Completion of the largest hydro-electric power station in the world at Niagara Falls, Canada.

• Empire Settlement Act: Britain pledges to promote emigration to, and aid settlement in, Australia.

• The British Broadcasting Company (BBC) is founded.

• Jazz music becomes the rage in northern cities of the United States.

• **Jan:** James Joyce's novel, *Ulysses,* is published in Paris, and subsequently banned in the US and UK.

• **Feb:** First issue of *Reader's Digest.*

• **Aug:** The unofficial women's Olympic Games are held in Paris.

• **Nov:** British archeologists Howard Carter and Lord Carnarvon discover the tomb of the pharaoh Tutankhamun in the Valley of the Kings at Luxor, Egypt.

HYPERINFLATION RACKS GERMANY

The city of Tokyo is almost demolished by an earthquake

POLITICS

• **11 Jan:** Allied forces occupy the Ruhr district of Germany. A period of hyper-inflation results as the government prints large amounts of paper money.

• **21 Jan:** Ruhr miners strike in protest against the Allied occupation.

• **27 Jan:** The National Socialist (Nazi) Party holds its first rally in Germany.

• **2 Feb:** Australian prime minister William Hughes resigns; and is replaced by Stanley Bruce, leading a coalition.

• **9 Mar:** Lenin retires from Soviet Union politics, due to ill-health.

• **21 May:** Stanley Baldwin becomes British prime minister following the resignation of Andrew Bonar Law due to ill-health.

• **26 May:** The kingdom of Transjordania (later Jordan) is recognized as an autonomous state.

• **8 Jun:** British women win the right to divorce their husbands for adultery.

German Marks become children's playthings.

• **24 Jul:** At the treaty of Lausanne, Turkey gives up all claims to territory lost during World War I but recovers eastern Thrace.

• **3 Aug:** Calvin Coolidge is sworn in as US president following the death of Warren Harding the previous day.

• **6 Aug:** Gustav Stresemann is appointed German chancellor.

• **31 Aug:** The Italians occupy the town of Corfu (until 27 Sept).

• **1 Sept:** Tokyo is completely devastated by an earthquake, which kills more than 200,000 people. Tidal waves and aftershocks continue for some time.

• **10 Sept:** The Irish Free State is admitted to the League of Nations.

- **13 Sept:** A *coup d'état* in Spain is led by Miguel Primo de Rivera.

- **28 Sept:** Ethiopia is admitted to the League of Nations.

- **27 Oct:** French troops occupy the German Rhineland.

- **28 Oct:** Reza Khan becomes premier of the state of Persia.

- **29 Oct:** Mustafa Kemal becomes president of the new Turkish republic.

- **8–11 Nov:** Nazi leader Adolf Hitler and General von Ludendorff stage the abortive Beer Hall putsch in Munich.

- **15 Nov:** The Rentenmark is introduced in Germany in an attempt to replace the inflated currency.

- **20 Nov:** The value of the old German Mark drops to an incredible low of 4,200 billion to the US dollar.

- **6 Dec:** At a British general election, no party wins an overall majority.

CULTURE

- The Charleston becomes popular following its debut in *Ziegfeld Follies*.

- The Cotton Club, home of much important jazz over the following 20 years, opens in Harlem, New York.

- The Yankee Baseball Stadium opens in New York City.

- Public exhibitions are held of work completed in the Bauhaus, a German center of modern design.

- The Ku Klux Klan claims 1 million members in the United States.

- **12 Feb:** Première of *Rhapsody in Blue*, by George Gershwin.

- **16 Feb:** Singer Bessie Smith makes her first record, *Down-hearted Blues*.

- **3 Mar:** *Time* magazine is founded in the United States by Henry Luce and Briton Hadden.

- **29 Mar:** The French actress Sarah Bernhardt is commemorated in a funeral service in Paris.

- **26 Apr:** In London, Lady Elizabeth Bowes-Lyon marries the duke of York, the future monarch George VI.

- **28 Apr:** Wembley soccer stadium opens in London, with the FA Cup Final, between Bolton Wanderers and West Ham United.

- **25–26 May:** The first 24-hour motor race is held at Le Mans, France.

- **6 Jul:** French tennis player Suzanne Lenglen wins the Wimbledon Ladies' Singles title for a record fifth time.

- **21 Dec:** Cecil B. de Mille's landmark movie *The Ten Commandments* premières in New York.

FASCISM TAKES ROOT IN EUROPE

First wave of Russian Communism ends with the death of Lenin

The Hollywood studio MGM is founded in April, promoting the motto Art for Art's Sake.

POLITICS

• **20–30 JAN:** The first Guomindang (Chinese nationalist party) congress in Canton admits Communist delegates.

• **21 JAN:** The death of the Soviet leader, Lenin, triggers a power struggle between Stalin and Trotsky.

• **22 JAN:** Ramsey MacDonald becomes the first British Labor prime minister.

• **25 JAN:** France and Czechoslovakia sign a treaty of alliance.

• **1 FEB:** Britain recognizes the USSR.

• **4 FEB:** In India, Gandhi is released from prison due to ill-health.

• **3 MAR:** The Turkish national assembly abolishes the monarchy and caliphate (successor of Muhammad).

• **25 MAR:** Greece is proclaimed a republic, confirmed by plebiscite 13 Apr.

• **1 APR:** Adolf Hitler writes *Mein Kampf* while imprisoned for the "Munich Putsch".

• **6 APR:** In the Italian general election, Fascists poll 64 percent of the votes.

• **31 MAY:** China recognizes the USSR, which in turn relinquishes its territorial claims in China.

• **10 JUN:** In Italy, Giacomo Matteotti, a socialist deputy and antifascist, is assassinated by Fascist agents.

• **16 AUG:** The German *Reichstag* approves the Dawes Plan (originally proposed in April) which reorganizes war reparations.

• **2 OCT:** The League of Nations adopts the Geneva Protocol for compulsory arbitration of international disputes.

• **3 OCT:** King Hussein of Arabia is forced to abdicate in favor of his son, Ali.

• **5 Oct:** British parliament is dissolved after Labor is defeated over the withdrawn prosecution of a newspaper editor.

• **24 Oct:** The British Foreign Office publishes the "Zinoviev Letter" inciting revolutionary activity in Britain. The Soviets claim that the letter is a hoax.

• **28 Oct:** France recognizes the USSR.

• **29 Oct:** The British general election results in landslide victory for the Conservatives.

• **4 Nov:** Republican Calvin Coolidge decisively wins the presidential election.

• **19 Nov:** The British governor-general of Sudan is murdered in Cairo. Britain demands withdrawal of Egyptian troops.

• **21 Nov:** In Britain, the Conservative government cancels treaties with the USSR set up by the Labor government.

• **24 Dec:** Albania becomes a republic.

C U L T U R E

• British hairdresser Antoine creates the fashionable "blue rinse".

• Australia introduces compulsory voting in elections.

• Denmark appoints the first woman cabinet minister, Nina Bang.

• William Randolph Hearst founds the *Daily Mirror* tabloid in New York.

• Native Americans are granted full United States citizenship.

• Clarence Birdseye (USA) founds the General Sea Foods Co. to sell frozen fish.

• The first execution using a gas chamber takes place in the US.

• The Surrealist movement is founded in France with the publication of André Breton's *Surrealist Manifesto*.

• US movie star Charlie Chaplin marries 16-year old Lita Grey.

• **Jan:** The first Winter Olympic Games are held in Chamonix, France.

• **Feb:** Radio broadcasts are first used for educational purposes by Columbia University in the United States.

• **Apr:** Metro-Goldwyn-Meyer (MGM) is founded when Metro Pictures, Goldwyn Pictures and the Louis B. Meyer Company amalgamate.

• **Apr:** The British Empire Exhibition opens in London.

• **Jun:** Over 10,000 American Indians gather at Sand Springs, Oklahoma, to discuss their problems in modern USA.

• **Jul:** US swimmer Johnny Weissmuller wins two golds at the Paris Olympics.

• **4 Nov:** Texas elects the first woman state governor, "Ma" Miriam Ferguson.

APARTHEID IS OFFICIAL

"Art Deco" goes on display for the first time

POLITICS

• The Vietnamese Nationalist party is founded by Ho Chi Minh.

• **5 JAN:** In Italy, Mussolini begins a purge against the opponents of Fascism.

• **16 JAN:** In the USSR, Leon Trotsky is dismissed as commissar for war, leaving power to Stalin, Zinoviev and Kamenev.

• **20 JAN:** The Russo-Japanese convention establishes a relationship of mutual benefit and cooperation.

• **FEB – APR:** A Kurdish uprising is suppressed by the Turkish government.

• **9 FEB:** Germany suggests a Rhineland mutual guarantee pact to replace the Geneva Protocol.

• **12 MAR:** In China, Sun Yat-sen dies and is succeeded as leader of the Guomindang party by Jiang Jieshi.

• **28 APR:** The UK returns to the Gold Standard.

• **1 MAY:** Cyprus is declared a British crown colony.

"Flappers" from a vaudeville show.

• **12 MAY:** Uzbekistan, Kazakhstan and Turkmenistan join the USSR.

• **30 MAY:** Student demonstrations in China are dispersed by armed British troops provoking boycott of British goods and shipping.

• **30 MAY:** Following the death of W. F. Massey, Joseph Coates of the Reform Party becomes prime minister of New Zealand.

• **25 JUN:** Gen. Theodoros Pangalos seizes power by *coup d'état* in Greece.

• **29 JUN:** In South Africa, the color bar (apartheid) becomes legal.

• **13 JUL:** French and Belgian troops begin evacuation of the Ruhr.

• **18 Jul:** Uprising of the Druses in Syria (to Jun 1927).

• **8 Aug:** In Washington D.C., the Ku Klux Klan hold their first national congress.

• **28 Aug:** Britain resumes diplomatic relations with Mexico.

• **23 Sept:** New immigration restriction Act in Australia allows the governor-general to refuse entry arbitrarily.

• **16 Oct:** The European powers sign the Locarno Pact to stabilize borders.

• **22 Oct:** The Greeks invade Bulgaria over a border dispute. League of Nations imposes fines against Greece (14 Dec).

• **31 Oct:** Reza Khan deposes the shah of Persia and declares himself shah.

• **9 Nov:** In Germany, the Nazi Party founds the SS *(Schutzstaffel)*.

• **3 Dec:** The border is confirmed between Northern and Southern Ireland.

• **17 Dec:** USSR and Turkey sign economic and political alliance.

• **28 Dec:** Polish land law provides for redistribution of land to the peasantry.

CULTURE

• Lux soap goes on sale in the US.

• French Fashion designer Madeleine Vionnet begins to use the bias cut.

• Russian-born George Balanchine becomes principal choreographer of the *Ballets Russes*.

• The Exposition des Arts Décoratifs in Paris, an international show case of design and architecture, introduces the new style "Art Deco".

• The world's first motel opens in San Luis Obispo, California.

• Dancer Josephine Baker wins great acclaim for her daring performance in *La Revue Nègre* in Paris.

• Foundation of American automobile manufacturer Chrysler Corporation.

• Sergey Eisenstein's film *Battleship Potemkin* is notable for its use of dramatic intercutting techniques.

• In the US, financial difficulties result in 500,000 farmers leaving the land per year despite government assistance.

• Emily Dickenson's *Complete Poems* is published posthumously in the US.

• **23 Mar:** Amidst anti-evolutionary theory fervor in the southern states of the US, Tennessee bans the teaching of evolution in its schools.

• **Sept:** The British government discusses using white lines on the roads and at traffic lights to reduce traffic congestion and accidents.

JOSEPH STALIN DOMINATES USSR

The British Commonwealth of Nations is established

POLITICS

• **3 Jan:** Theodoros Pangalos assumes the dictatorship of Greece.

• **8 Jan:** Abd al-Aziz ibn Saud is proclaimed king of the Hejaz (later Saudi Arabia).

• **10 Feb:** Germany applies for admission to the League of Nations. (Admitted 8 Sept.)

• **1 May:** British miners go on strike over withdrawal of government subsidy.

• **3–12 May:** The British Trades Union Congress calls a general strike in sympathy with the miners.

• **12–15 May:** In Poland, Józef Pilsudski leads a military revolt against the government. Ignace Moscicki becomes president.

• **16 May:** In Ireland, Éamon de Valera resigns from Sinn Féin and forms Fianna Fáil (Warriors of Ireland).

• **28 May:** A military coup in Portugal deposes the democratic regime.

The new Japanese emperor, Hirohito.

• **5 Jun:** A large part of the oil-rich Mosul area (formerly Turkish territory) is ceded to Iraq.

• **Jul:** A financial crisis in France causes the fall of Aristide Briand's ministry. Raymond Poincaré becomes the new prime minister.

• **Jul–Aug:** In the USSR, Stalin triumphs over Trotsky's leftist faction. Trotsky and others are expelled from the Politburo and Central Committee.

• **9 Jul:** In Portugal, the new military regime is deposed by Gen. António de Fragoso Carmona.

• **28 Jul:** Panama and the United States sign a treaty to protect the Panama Canal during wartime.

• **28 JUL:** King Albert I of Belgium is given dictatorial powers to deal with a financial crisis.

• **7 AUG:** Spain and Italy sign a treaty of mutual friendship.

• **22 AUG:** In Greece, dictator Pangalos is overthrown by Gen. Georgios Kondylis.

• **6 SEPT:** In China, Jiang Jieshi's Guomindang forces capture Hankou.

• **2 OCT:** Józef Pilsudski becomes prime minister of Poland.

• **19 OCT–18 NOV:** The Imperial Conference in London declares a British Commonwealth of autonomous and equal nations united by allegiance to the British crown.

• **31 OCT:** In Italy, Mussolini narrowly avoids being assassinated.

• **NOV:** There is a Communist revolt in the Dutch East Indies (until Jun 1927).

• **27 NOV:** Italy and Albania sign a treaty promising mutual assistance and recognition of the status quo.

• **17 DEC:** In Lithuania, Antanas Smetona deposes the government and appoints himself dictator.

• **25 DEC:** Death of the Japanese emperor Yoshihito ends the Taishō period. Hirohito's succession begins the Shōwa period (lasting until 1989).

CULTURE

• Charles Atlas (Angelo Siciliano) opens a gym in New York to promote body-building techniques.

• The death of the artist Antoni Gaudi, brings to a halt work on the cathedral of the Sagrada Familia, Barcelona, Spain.

• The Women's Cricket Association is formed in Britain.

• In Britain, the Central Electricity Generating Board is formed to create a national grid.

• **24 MAR:** M. B. Skaggs establishes the Safeway chainstores in the western US.

• **30 APR:** Pictures are transmitted by radio between London and New York.

• **9 MAY:** Richard Byrd and Floyd Bennett reach the North Pole in 15 hours in a Fokker monoplane.

• **6 AUG:** American Gertrude Ederle becomes the first woman to swim the English Channel.

• **18 AUG:** England regains the Ashes after 14 years.

• **23 AUG:** The death of film star Rudolph Valentino (31) from a ruptured ulcer causes hysteria among fans.

• **1 OCT:** British pilot Alan Cobham completes the first round trip to Australia in 58 days.

THE GOLDEN TWENTIES

The Jazz Singer heralds the new age of the "talkie"

POLITICS

• **31 Jan:** Allied military control ends in Germany.

• **3 Feb:** Revolt in Portugal is suppressed after heavy fighting.

• **24 Mar:** In the Chinese civil war, the Guomindang takes Nanjing.

• **18 Apr:** In China, a split appears in the Guomindang nationalist party leading Jiang Jieshi to conduct a purge against communists in the party.

• **1 May:** After the Bavarian government lifts its ban on Adolf Hitler speaking in public, the Nazi party holds a meeting in Berlin.

• **4 May:** The USA intervenes in the civil war in Nicaragua and is asked to supervise elections.

• **9 May:** In Australia, Parliament House in Canberra is opened.

• **20 May:** Britain signs a treaty with Abd al Aziz ibn Saud recognizing the independence of the kingdom of Hejaz.

Charles Lindbergh with the Spirit of St. Louis.

• **26 May:** Britain severs diplomatic links with the USSR on the grounds of espionage and subversion.

• **27 May:** Japanese troops block the advance of the Chinese toward Beijing.

• **Jun:** The Indonesian Nationalist party (PNI) is founded.

• **23 Jun:** The UK Trades Disputes Act outlaws general strikes and compulsory political levying by trade unions.

• **Jul–Oct:** Complaints by native chiefs in Samoa against the New Zealand-run administration lead to the deportation of a number of German citizens.

• **15 Jul:** There is a general strike and riots in Vienna, Austria, after three nationalists are acquitted of the murder of two Socialists.

• **7 Aug:** The International Peace Bridge is opened between the US and Canada.

• **12 Aug:** In the Irish Free State, Éamon de Valera and other Republicans agree to take their seats in the Dáil.

• **Oct:** There is an insurrection in Mexico after president Calles stops the nationalization of church property.

• **17 Oct:** Norway elects its first Labor government.

• **14 Nov:** Trotsky and Zinoviev are expelled from the Soviet Communist Party.

• **15 Nov:** Canada is elected to a seat on the Council of the League of Nations.

• **22 Nov:** Persia claims the Bahrain Islands in the Persian Gulf.

• **14 Dec:** Britain recognizes Iraq's independence and wins military concessions.

• **27 Dec:** The fifteenth All-Union Congress of the Communist party of the USSR condemns all deviation from the party line as laid down by Stalin.

CULTURE

• *The Jazz Singer,* starring Al Jolson, is released and becomes the first talkie to be seen widely in the United States.

• Shingled (short) hair becomes all the rage for women and girls.

• US film star Mae West is imprisoned for indecency in her Broadway show *Sex*.

• A transatlantic telephone service begins between London and New York.

• Greyhound racing becomes a popular sport in Britain.

• Martha Graham opens her school of Contemporary Dance in New York.

• US blues singers Ma Rainey and Bessie Smith begin to make recordings.

• German architect Ludwig Mies van der Rohe, launches the "International Style".

• **6 Feb:** 10-year-old American violinist Yehudi Menuhin causes a sensation in Paris with his performance of Lalo's *Symphonie Espagnole.*

• **29 Mar:** Major Henry Segrave (UK) sets a new world land-speed record of 203.841 mph (328.05 kph) in his "mystery" car in Florida, beating the previous record set by Malcolm Campbell (UK) in *Bluebird* on 4 Feb.

• **21 May:** Capt. Charles Lindbergh (USA) makes the first solo transatlantic flight in the *Spirit of St. Louis.*

• **14 Sept:** US dancer Isadora Duncan dies, aged 49, when her scarf becomes entangled in the wheels of her car.

THE "WONDER ANTIBIOTIC"

Television becomes available to householders in the US

POLITICS

• Italian Communist party leader, Antonio Gramsci is sentenced to 20 years' imprisonment.

• Guerrilla resistance to US intervention in Nicaragua escalates.

• **JAN:** In the USSR, Stalin sends 30 of his rivals, including Trotsky, into exile.

• **31 JAN:** Britain sends 12,000 troops to China to defend British nationals caught up in the Chinese civil war.

• **MAR:** The British colony of Malta becomes a dominion.

• **25 MAR:** Gen. António Carmona is elected president of Portugal.

• **30 MAR:** In Rome, non-fascist youth movements are given 30 days to disband.

• **3–11 MAY:** A Chinese nationalist offensive clashes with Japanese forces. Japan reoccupies Shandong peninsula.

• **12 MAY:** In Italy, the electorate is slashed from 10 million to three million as the government restricts suffrage.

Alexander Fleming, the father of penicillin.

• **8 JUN:** Chinese nationalists occupy Beijing, the capital is moved to Nanjing.

• **2 JUL:** In Britain, women are enfranchised on the same terms as men, universal suffrage over the age of 21.

• **17 JUL:** Alvaro Obregón, president of Mexico, is assassinated.

• **19 JUL:** King Fuad dissolves the Egyptian parliament and rules instead by decree.

• **1 AUG:** In the kingdom of the Serbs, Croats and Slovenes (later Yugoslavia), the Croats set up a separatist parliament in Zagreb.

• **13 AUG:** Indian nationalists issue a draft constitution calling for dominion status for India.

- **25 Aug:** President Ahmed Zog of Albania declares Albania a kingdom and himself the king.

- **27 Aug:** The Kellogg-Briand Pact, a multilateral agreement condemning war, is signed in Paris by 15 nations.

- **30 Aug:** The Independence of India League is organized by Nehru, Bose and Iyengar to oppose dominion status.

- **1 Oct:** Joseph Stalin begins his first five-year plan in the USSR to develop industry and collectivize farms.

- **6 Oct:** Jiang Jieshi becomes president of the Republic of China.

- **7 Oct:** Ras Tafari becomes king *(regis)* of Ethiopia and initiates a policy of modernization.

- **3 Nov:** The Roman alphabet is introduced in Turkey.

- **6 Nov:** Republican Herbert Hoover wins the US presidential election.

- **14 Nov:** The New Zealand general election is a tie between the United (Liberal) party and the Reform party.

- **Dec:** Fighting breaks out between Paraguay and Bolivia over Chaco Boreal.

- **20 Dec:** Britain signs a treaty officially recognizing the Guomindang government in China.

CULTURE

- The first black and white television sets go on sale in the United States.

- In Britain, Morris Motors launch the Morris Minor, a cheap family car.

- Walt Disney creates first Mickey Mouse cartoon, *Steamboat Willie*.

- British scientist, Alexander Fleming discovers penicillin.

- H. Geiger and W. Muller construct the "Geiger counter," an instrument for measuring radioactive radiation.

- A. Szent-Györgyi (Hungarian US citizen) discovers vitamin C.

- Peanut butter goes on sale in the US.

- **Feb:** John Logie Baird demonstrates color television in Britain and makes the first transatlantic transmission.

- **May:** In the United States, the first scheduled television service begins, for 90 minutes three times a week.

- **Jun:** Captain Charles Kingford-Smith arrives at Brisbane, Australia, after a trans-Pacific flight from California, USA.

- **Jun:** Amelia Earhart (USA) becomes the first woman to fly the Atlantic.

- **Jul:** The eighth modern Olympic Games, held in Amsterdam, include women's athletics for the first time.

THE GREAT DEPRESSION

The Nazis grow more powerful in Germany

Stock market crash creates instant bankrupts.

POLITICS

• **JAN:** Leon Trotsky is expelled from the USSR and flees to Constantinople and then to Mexico.

• **6 JAN:** The kingdom of the Serbs, Croats and Slovenes is renamed Yugoslavia, under a dictatorship established by King Alexander.

• **14 JAN:** Civil war breaks out in Afghanistan and king Amanullah is forced to abdicate.

• **11 FEB:** The Lateran Treaties between the Papacy and Italy guarantee the sovereignty of the Vatican.

• **24 MAR:** In Italy, Fascists announce victory in a heavily-engineered, single party election.

• **20 MAY:** Japan evacuates the Shandong Peninsula in China.

• **5 JUN:** Ramsay MacDonald forms a second Labor government in Britain.

• **1 JUL:** The 1924 Immigration Act comes into force in the United States.

• **AUG:** Germany accepts the Young Plan and the Allied forces begin evacuation of the Rhineland.

• **4 AUG:** Jewish demands for exclusive use of the Wailing Wall in Jerusalem draw a violent Arab response.

• **11 AUG:** Zionist leader Chaim Weizmann forms the Jewish Agency in Zurich, Switzerland to encourage Jews from around the world to settle in Israel.

• **SEPT:** The United States joins the International Court of Justice.

• **16 SEPT:** The Bolivia-Paraguay peace treaty ends a 10-month border dispute between the two nations.

• **22 SEPT:** Fighting erupts between armed groups of Communists and Nazis in Berlin, Germany.

• **8 Oct:** Gen. Muhammad Nadir Khan conducts a coup in Afghanistan and is proclaimed shah on 16 Oct.

• **13 Oct:** In Australia, Labor, led by James Scullin, wins the general election.

• **24 Oct:** "Black Thursday", the great stock market crash on New York's Wall Street precipitates the Great Depression.

• **17 Nov:** Nikolai Bukharin and other rightists in the Politburo are expelled from the USSR by Stalin.

• **Dec:** In Germany, the Nazis win the Bavarian municipal elections.

• **Dec:** The All-India National Congress, meeting in Lahore, demands independence from Britain under threat of civil disobedience.

• **22 Dec:** The Khabarovsk Protocol between the USSR and China defuses conflict which verged on war.

• **22 Dec:** In Egypt, the extreme nationalist Wafd Party wins the general election.

CULTURE

• *Popeye the sailor* is created by US cartoonist, Elzie Segar.

• Hergé's cartoon *Tintin* first appears in a Belgian newspaper.

• The Museum of Modern Art is founded in New York.

• Ludwig Mies van der Rohe's German Pavilion in Barcelona creates a stir.

• "Happy Days are Here Again" becomes a popular song in the United States.

• *St. Louis Blues* starring singer Bessie Smith is suppressed for its "bad taste".

• Clarence Birdseye markets his quick-freezing method for food in the US.

• **14 Feb:** The St. Valentine's Day massacre occurs in Chicago, Illinois. Gangster Al Capone's mob kill six members of a rival gang.

• **14 Feb:** Dancer Josephine Baker is banned from performing in Munich, Germany on the grounds of "indecency".

• **Mar:** Airmail begins from London to India, Egypt, Palestine and Iraq.

• **11 Mar:** Henry Segrave sets new world land-speed record of 359 k.p.h. (223 m.p.h.) at Daytona Beach, Florida.

• **16 May:** The first Academy Awards are made in the United States.

• **Aug:** The German airship Graf Zeppelin completes a trip around the world in 21 days, 7 hours, 26 minutes.

• **14 Oct:** The world's biggest airship (R101) makes its maiden voyage.

• **Dec:** Public telephone boxes appear in Britain for the first time.

UNEMPLOYMENT SOARS

Western economies plummet despite protectionist tariffs

Australia's Don Bradman, cricketer of the decade.

POLITICS

• **5 Jan:** Stalin orders the collectivization of farms throughout the USSR.

• **21 Jan:** Britain, USA, France, Italy and Japan meet in London to discuss naval disarmament.

• **28 Jan:** In Spain, the dictator Primo de Rivera resigns. Gen. Damaso Berenguer is asked to form a ministry.

• **23 Feb:** Rafael Leonidas Trujillo begins a 31-year dictatorship in the Dominican Republic.

• **12 Mar:** In India, Gandhi's salt march begins the campaign of civil disobedience threatened in 1929.

• **16 Mar:** Stalin orders the kulaks (rich farmers) to be "liquidated as a class" in the USSR.

• **28 Mar:** The city of Constantinople in Turkey is renamed Istanbul.

• **31 Mar:** Revolt in Ethiopia. Ras Tafari becomes Emperor Haile Selassie.

• **21 Apr:** The London disarmament Conference treaty limits numbers of warships and aircraft carriers.

• **5 May:** In India, Gandhi is arrested and imprisoned.

• **22 May:** Syria, formerly under French control, is granted a constitution.

• **28 May:** George W. Forbes becomes prime minister of New Zealand.

• **8 Jun:** Crown Prince Carol is elected king of Romania.

• **13 Jun:** Australia allocates £1 million to unemployment relief.

• **17 Jun:** The US passes the Hawley-Smoot Tariff Bill raising tariffs on imported goods.

• **21 Jun:** In Germany, the Berlin chief of police bans the wearing of swastikas.

• **24 Jun:** The Simon Report is published in Britain recommending provincial self-government for India.

• **30 Jun:** Britain agrees to recognize the independence of Iraq.

• **28 Jul:** In Canada, the conservatives win the general election; Richard B. Bennett becomes prime minister.

• **7 Aug:** Unemployment in the UK reaches 2 million.

• **25 Aug:** A *Coup d'état* in Peru results in a military leader, Col. Luis Sánchez Cerro, taking on the presidency.

• **5 Sept:** Revolt in Argentina brings down the government.

• **14 Sept:** In Germany, unemployment reaches three million. The Socialists win general election but the Nazi Party increases its representation in the *Reichstag* from 12 to 107 seats.

• **Oct:** Unemployment reaches 4.5 million in the USA. President Hoover appoints a Committee on Unemployment and (4 Nov) requests $150 million from Congress for public works.

• **1–14 Oct:** As wheat prices fall worldwide, Britain rejects a Canadian proposal to impose preferential tariffs.

• **16 Oct:** France announces its intention to build a line of defenses along the Franco-German border (The Maginot line).

• **20 Oct:** Revised British policy on Palestine allows limited self-government and aims to deal impartially with the problems of land shortage.

• **26 Oct:** Military coup in Brazil; Getúlio Vargas is provisional president.

• **12 Dec:** Military rising in Spain is suppressed.

CULTURE

• Cricketer Don Bradman scores 974 runs (av. 139.14) for Australia in a Test against England, the highest number of runs ever scored in a Test by one player.

• Ready-sliced bread appears for the first time in Britain.

• The Chrysler Building, typifying the Art Deco style, is completed in New York.

• Perspex, a plastic glass, is created by W. Chalmers (USA).

• **13 Mar:** American astronomer, Clyde Tombaugh, discovers the planet Pluto.

• **24 Apr:** Amy Johnson, 27, flies solo from Britain to Australia.

• **5 Oct:** British airship R101 explodes in France; 44 people die.

BANK FAILURES SWEEP EUROPE

The horror movie provides a new form of escapism

POLITICS

• **JAN:** Bolivia defaults on foreign debt; other Latin American countries follow.

• **2 JAN:** A military government takes over in Panama.

• **26 JAN:** In India, Gandhi is released from prison for talks with the British.

• **3 FEB:** A devastating earthquake in New Zealand kills 256 people.

• **28 FEB:** In Britain, Sir Oswald Mosley leaves the Labor party and organizes the fascist New party.

• **4 MAR:** The viceroy of India and Gandhi sign the Delhi Pact which suspends Gandhi's campaign of civil disobedience in return for concessions.

• **12 APR:** The Republicans win an overwhelming victory in the Spanish elections. Calls for abdication result in King Alfonso fleeing on 14 Apr.

• **11 MAY:** The failure of Credit-Anstalt in Austria begins the financial collapse of Central Europe.

Dracula, the face that launched 1,000 sequels.

• **16 JUN:** The Bank of England advances money to Austria.

• **20 JUN:** US president Herbert Hoover proposes a one-year moratorium for reparations and war debts.

• **13 JUL:** Bankruptcy of the German Danatbank leads to the closure of all German banks until 5 Aug.

• **25 JUL:** In Britain, the May Committee reports a massive budget deficit and recommends drastic cuts including unemployment benefit.

• **2 AUG:** The Bank of France and New York Federal Reserve each lend the Bank of England £25,000,000.

• **24 AUG:** Following a split in the Labor cabinet, British prime minister

Ramsey MacDonald resigns. A National Coalition government is formed.

• **SEPT–DEC:** The second Round Table conference on India fails to reach agreement. Campaign of civil disobedience resumes.

• **3 SEPT:** The royal dictatorship of King Alexander ends and Yugoslavia adopts a new constitution.

• **10 SEPT:** Economy measures provoke riots and a naval mutiny in Britain.

• **20–21 SEPT:** Britain abandons the gold standard.

• **18 SEPT:** Japanese invasion of Manchuria begins with siege of Mukden.

• **27 OCT:** British National Coalition government wins 558 seats in election.

• **NOV:** Mao Zedong establishes the first Chinese Soviet Republic in the remote Jiangxi province of China.

• **11 DEC:** The Statute of Westminister defines the status of the dominions, (Can, Aus, NZ, S. Afr, Irish Free State, Newfoundland), as autonomous and equal with their own legal systems and foreign policies.

CULTURE

• One of the last silent films, *City Lights* starring Charlie Chaplin is a success in the United States.

• Alka Seltzer is introduced in the US by Miles Laboratories of Indiana.

• The 2,500 mi (4,000 km) uncharted Antarctic coast is explored by a British, Australian and New Zealand team who demonstrate that the coast is continuous.

• The first teleprinter exchange, prelude to the telex, begins operating in the UK.

• CFCs are first produced for use in aerosols in the United States.

• Bela Lugosi stars in the first *Dracula* movie.

• **JAN:** Pope Pius XI denounces trial marriages, divorce and birth control.

• **3 MAR:** *The Star Spangled Banner* becomes the US national anthem.

• **4 APR:** The first airmail leaves Australia for England.

• **1 MAY:** The Empire State Building opens; it is the world's tallest structure.

• **JUN:** US aviators, Wiley Post and Harold Gatty, circumnavigate the globe in 8 days, 15 hours and 51 minutes.

• **1 JUL:** The Benguella–Katanga railroad, the first to cross the African continent, is completed.

• **24 AUG:** Gangster Al Capone is sentenced to 11 years in prison for tax evasion in Chicago, Illinois.

FARMERS IN CRISIS

An agricultural depression hits the United States and Europe

POLITICS

• **4 JAN:** In India, the government is granted emergency powers; the National Congress is declared illegal and Gandhi is arrested.

• **7 JAN:** US secretary of state, Henry Stimson, declares opposition to Japanese aggression in Manchuria and refuses to recognize gains through armed force.

• **28 JAN:** Japan occupies Shanghai.

• **2 FEB:** 60 nations including USA and USSR attend a Geneva disarmament conference at which a French proposal for an international police force is opposed by Germany.

• **16 FEB:** Fianna Fáil, the Republican party, win the Irish general election.

• **18 FEB:** The Japanese set up a puppet republic of Manzhouguo in Manchuria.

• **9 MAR:** Pu-Yi, the last emperor of China, is installed as head of state.

• **9 MAR:** Éamon de Valera is elected president of the Irish Free State.

Sydney harbor bridge opens 18 March.

• **13 MAR:** In Germany, Field Marshal Paul von Hindenburg wins the presidency, but not an overall majority.

• **24 APR:** The Nazis win elections in Prussia, Bavaria, Würtemberg and Hamburg.

• **10 MAY:** Albert Lebrun succeeds to the presidency in France, following the murder of President Paul Doumer.

• **15 MAY:** Tsuyoshi Inukai, prime minister of Japan, is murdered by the military. Makoto Saito succeeds.

• **30 MAY:** The German chancellor, Heinrich Brüning, resigns.

• **15 JUN:** The Chaco War between Bolivia and Paraguay begins.

• **16 JUN:** A final payment of 3,000

million marks in German reparations is agreed at Lausanne.

• **16 Jun:** The ban on Nazi para-military groups is lifted in Germany.

• **5 Jul:** Antonio de Olivera Salazar becomes prime minister of Portugal with virtual dictatorial powers.

• **18 Jul:** Turkey is admitted to the League of Nations.

• **21 Jul:** The Imperial conference at Ottawa, Canada, negotiates new protectionist tariffs giving preference to dominion and British products.

• **31 Jul:** The *Reichstag* elections result in stalemate; the Nazis win 230 seats but have no overall majority.

• **13 Aug:** In Germany, Adolf Hitler refuses Hindenburg's offer of vice-chancellorship under von Papen.

• **22 Sept:** The Kingdom of the Hajas and Najd becomes Saudi Arabia.

• **25 Sept:** In Spain, the province of Catalonia is granted autonomy.

• **2 Oct:** The Lytton Report to the League of Nations recommends the establishment of an independent government in Manzhouguo under Chinese sovereignty

• **3 Oct:** Iraq achieves independence and joins the League of Nations.

• **8 Nov:** Democrat Franklin D. Roosevelt wins the US presidency.

• **17 Nov:** Fresh German elections produce deadlock; von Papen resigns.

• **11 Dec:** The Geneva Protocol is signed giving Germany equal rights with other nations.

CULTURE

• The dishwasher goes on sale in the US.

• Redundant agricultural workers in the US and Europe flock to towns for work.

• **Mar:** The suicide of Swedish "match king", Ivan Kreuger, precedes the collapse of his business empire.

• **2 Mar:** US aviator Charles Lindbergh's infant son is kidnapped; he is found murdered on 12 May.

• **18 Mar:** In Australia, Sydney harbor bridge is opened linking north Sydney to the city of Sydney.

• **9 May:** Neon lights are used to illuminate the first flashing advertisements in the world at London's Piccadilly Circus.

• **21 May:** American aviator Amelia Earhart becomes the first woman to make a solo flight across the Atlantic.

• **Dec:** Radio City Music Hall, with seating for 6,000 people, opens in New York city.

FASCISM SWEEPS EUROPE

Unemployment and discontent promote extreme politics

POLITICS

• **13 Jan:** The US Congress votes for independence for the Philippines; the Philippino government rejects the plan.

• **24 Jan:** Fianna Fáil wins the general election in the Irish Free State.

• **28 Jan:** In Germany, Adolf Hitler is appointed chancellor.

• **16 Feb:** The Little Entente countries (Czech., Rom., Yugo.) establish a permanent governing body in response to the rise of the Nazis in Germany.

• **28 Feb:** In Germany, the *Reichstag* building is destroyed by fire. The Nazis use this as a pretext for suspending civil liberties and freedom of the press.

• **5 Mar:** The German elections result in the Nazis winning 44% of the vote.

• **6 Mar:** In the US, financial crisis leads to the closure of the banks for four days and an embargo on gold export.

• **12 Mar:** In the US, President Roosevelt begins radio "fireside chats".

Hitler rises to absolute power in Germany.

• **16 Mar:** At the Geneva Disarmament Conference, Britain proposes a reduction in European army sizes; Germany walks out and leaves the League of Nations.

• **20 Mar:** The first concentration camp is opened at Dachau, Germany.

• **23 Mar:** The *Reichstag* passes the Enabling Act giving Hitler dictatorial powers for four years.

• **27 Mar:** The League of Nations condemns Japanese military action in Manchuria; Japan leaves the League.

• **1 Apr:** A national boycott of Jewish shops and businesses begins in Germany. Other forms of persecution escalate.

• **8 Apr:** Western Australia votes 2:1 to secede from the Commonwealth of Australia, but Britain rejects the move.

• **19 APR:** The US abandons the gold standard, Canada follows suit on 25th.

• **MAY:** In the US, Roosevelt's "New Deal" initiates economic recovery and provides unemployment relief.

• **2 MAY:** In Germany, trade unions are suppressed.

• **3 MAY:** The oath of allegiance to the British Crown is removed from the Irish constitution.

• **17 MAY:** In Spain, the Associations Law nationalizes Church property.

• **26 MAY:** Australia claims possession of one third of Antarctica.

• **28 MAY:** The Nazis win the elections in the free city of Danzig.

• **31 MAY:** China and Japan sign an armistice, the T'ang-Ku Truce.

• **19 JUN:** Chancellor Engelbert Dollfuss dissolves the Nazi party throughout Austria.

• **14 JUL:** In Germany, the Nazis become the only legal political party.

• **12 AUG:** A military coup in Cuba, supported by the United States, ousts President Machedo.

• **25 AUG:** Canada, USA, USSR, Australia and Argentina sign a wheat agreement to stabilize prices.

• **12 NOV:** In the German elections, 92% of voters vote for the Nazi party.

• **16 NOV:** The United States resumes trade relations with the USSR.

• **19 NOV:** In Spain, elections result in victory for right-wing parties.

• **5 DEC:** Prohibition ends in the US.

• **29 DEC:** Ion Duca, Liberal premier of Romania is murdered by the fascist Iron Guard. George Tartarescu succeeds.

CULTURE

• French fashion designer Elsa Schiaparelli reintroduces broad shoulders to the female silhouette.

• The Nazi policy banning modern art causes an exodus of German artists.

• German Jews are banned from taking part in the 1936 Olympics.

• UK Imperial Chemicals Ind. (ICI) markets the first synthetic detergent.

• England regains the Ashes after the "Bodyline" tour of Australia but aggressive English bowling techniques threaten diplomatic relations.

• The speaking clock of the Paris Observatory is put into operation.

• **JUN:** The American aviator Wiley Post makes the first solo flight around the world in 7 days, 18 hours and 49 mins.

COMMUNISM BOOMS IN CHINA

Hitler and Mussolini join forces to plan Europe's future

Agricultural depression worsens in the US.

POLITICS

• **JAN:** Libya is formed by the union of Cyrenaica and Tripolitania with Fezia.

• **14 JAN:** In Spain, the Catalonian elections are won by the moderate left.

• **26 JAN:** Germany signs a 10-year non-aggression pact with Poland.

• **1 FEB:** In Austria, all political parties are banned except the Fatherland Front.

• **9 FEB:** The Balkan Pact is established between Greece, Romania, Yugoslavia and Turkey.

• **12 FEB:** In France, an anti-fascist one-day general strike is called by the trade unions and left-wing parties.

• **16 FEB:** In Austria, a socialist uprising is brutally suppressed.

• **1 MAR:** Japan consolidates her position in Manchuria by supporting Pu-Yi, who assumes the title Emperor of Manzhouguo.

• **17 MAR:** The Rome Protocols are signed by Austria, Hungary and Italy.

• **24 MAR:** The US Congress passes the Tydings-McDuffie Act which guarantees Philippine independence within 10 years.

• **7 APR:** In Spain, Socialists lead a strike in Barcelona.

• **30 APR:** Chancellor Dollfuss establishes a dictatorship in Austria.

• **19 MAY:** In Bulgaria, fascists aided by King Boris seize power in a coup.

• **5 JUN:** The South African party led by Jan Smuts and the Nationalist party led by prime minister Hertzog join to form the United Party.

• **14–15 JUN:** Hitler and the Italian dictator, Mussolini, meet in Venice to discuss an alliance between Germany and Italy.

• **29–30 JUN:** Germany experiences the "Night of the Long Knives": a purge of the Nazi party by Hitler and the SS.

• **2 JUL:** Revolutionary leader Lázaro Cárdenas is elected president of Mexico.

• **12 JUL:** The Belgian government prohibits uniformed political parties.

• **25 JUL:** Chancellor Dollfuss is murdered in an attempted Nazi coup.

• **30 JUL:** Dr Kurt von Schuschnigg is appointed Austrian chancellor.

• **2 AUG:** President Hindenburg of Germany dies; Hitler succeeds.

• **19 AUG:** A German plebiscite shows that 89.9% of voters approve of Adolf Hitler as leader (*Führer*).

• **12 SEPT:** Latvia, Lithuania and Estonia sign the Baltic Pact.

• **15 SEPT:** The United Australia Party wins the Australian general election. Joseph Lyons becomes prime minister.

• **18 SEPT:** The USSR joins the League of Nations.

• **5 OCT:** The Spanish government declares martial law.

• **9 OCT:** King Alexander of Yugoslavia is assassinated by a Croat.

• **21 OCT:** In China, Mao Zedong sets off on the "Long March".

• **7 NOV:** The United Australia party, led by Joseph Lyons, forms a coalition government with the Country party.

• **30 NOV:** In Egypt, King Fuad suspends the constitution after riots.

• **1 DEC:** In the USSR, Communist leader Sergei Kirov is assassinated, provoking a Communist party purge.

• **16 DEC:** The National Union party provides the only candidates in the Portuguese general election.

• **21 DEC:** Daniel Salamanca, president of Bolivia, is overthrown in a military coup.

CULTURE

• The first viable quintuplets are born in Canada.

• In the US, the first utility car allows space for livestock or goods in the rear.

• Donald Duck makes his movie debut in Walt Disney's *The Orphan's Benefit*.

• **MAR:** Driving tests are introduced for the first time in Britain.

• **MAY:** Severe dust storms in the southern states of the US remove an estimated 300 million tons of topsoil. The rural slump gets worse.

• **23 MAY:** US criminals Bonnie Parker and Clyde Barrow (Bonnie and Clyde) are shot dead by Texas Rangers.

EUROPE REALIGNS ITS LOYALTIES

Italy makes the first aggressive move, by invading Ethiopia

POLITICS

• **7 Jan:** France and Italy sign the Marseille Pact over African territory.

• **13 Jan:** In a plebiscite in the Saar, 90% vote for reunion with Germany.

• **15 Jan:** In the USSR, Zinoviev and Kamenev and 17 other leading Communists are tried and imprisoned.

• **1 Feb:** German rearmament is discussed at a conference in London.

• **1 Mar:** The Saarland is restored to Germany by the Allies.

• **1–11 Mar:** An uprising in Greece is led by Venizelos who flees to France after the revolt is suppressed.

• **9 Mar:** In the USSR, Nikita Khrushchev is elected as secretary of the Soviet Communist party.

• **16 Mar:** Germany introduces military conscription thereby repudiating the Treaty of Versailles.

• **22 Mar:** Persia formally changes its name to Iran.

Fred and Ginger star in the movie Top Hat.

• **25 Mar:** Paul van Zeeland forms a ministry of National Unity in Belgium.

• **11 Apr:** Italy, France and Britain agree to act together against Germany.

• **23 Apr:** Poland adopts a new constitution.

• **2 May:** France and the USSR sign a five-year treaty of mutual assistance.

• **19 May:** In the Czech elections, the Sudeten German (Nazi) party becomes the second largest party in parliament.

• **7 Jun:** Stanley Baldwin takes over as prime minister of Britain.

• **18 Jun:** The Anglo-German naval accord limits the German navy.

• **25 JUL:** A meeting of the Communist Third International agrees to support democratic nations against fascist states.

• **2 AUG:** The Government of India Act separates Burma and Aden from India and grants a central legislature at Delhi.

• **20 AUG:** Federico Paez sets up a military dictatorship in Ecuador.

• **31 AUG:** The US Neutrality Act forbids shipments of arms to belligerents.

• **15 SEPT:** In Germany, the Nuremberg Laws legitimize persecution of the Jews and confirm the swastika as the official flag of Germany.

• **2 OCT:** Italy invades Ethiopia; the League of Nations imposes sanctions.

• **7 OCT:** In Austria, Kurt Schuschnigg carries out a bloodless coup against Emil Fey, the minister of the interior, and his Nazi allies.

• **14 OCT:** The Liberals, led by Mackenzie King, win an overwhelming victory in the Canadian general election.

• **20 OCT:** Mao Zedong's Long March ends as the Communists reach Yanan in Shaanxi province of north-west China.

• **3 NOV:** A plebiscite in Greece supports the restoration of the monarchy.

• **14 NOV:** Manuel Quezon is inaugurated first president of the Philippines.

• **27 NOV:** Following a general election, Michael J. Savage forms the first Labor government in New Zealand.

• **13 DEC:** Eduard Benes succeeds Tomàš Masaryk as Czech president.

CULTURE

• Musician Benny Goodman becomes known as the "king of swing".

• British scientist, Robert Watson Watt develops the first practical aerial radar.

• Alcoholics Anonymous is established in New York city.

• In Britain, Allen Lane launches Penguin paperbacks.

• The black American athlete, Jesse Owens, breaks five athletic world records in one day.

• Kodak launches Kodachrome in the US, the first multilayer color film.

• Fred Astaire and Ginger Rogers star in *Top Hat,* lyrics by Irving Berlin.

• **APR:** Increasingly severe dust storms hit the southern states of the US.

• **APR:** "Cat's Eyes" (glass reflectors) patented by P. Shaw are first used on British roads.

• **MAY:** Leicester Square underground (subway) station opens in London, featuring the world's longest escalator.

CIVIL WAR IN SPAIN

Racism flourishes in the Western world

POLITICS

• **20 Jan:** King George V of Britain dies, Edward VIII succeeds.

• **16 Feb:** In Spain, Manuel Azana (Popular Front) becomes prime minister and restores the 1931 constitution.

• **7 Mar:** German troops occupy the Rhineland, violating the Treaty of Versailles.

• **23 Mar:** Italy, Austria and Hungary sign the Rome Pact.

• **25 Mar:** Britain, USA and France sign the London Naval Treaty, limiting naval expansion.

• **1 Apr:** Military conscription is reinstated in Austria violating the 1919 Treaty of St. Germain.

• **19 Apr:** Rioting between Arabs and Jews in Tel Aviv, Palestine, leaves 11 dead and many injured.

• **28 Apr:** King Fuad of Egypt dies, his 16-year-old son, Prince Farouk, succeeds.

Jesse Owens challenges "white supremacy".

• **9 May:** Italy annexes Ethiopia.

• **24 May:** The Rexists (fascists) win 21 seats in the Belgian elections.

• **4 Jun:** In France, Léon Blum organizes the first Popular Front (Socialist) ministry. A program of social reform is instituted.

• **17 Jun:** Canada's "New Deal" of 1935 is ruled illegal by the Supreme Court.

• **15 Jul:** The League of Nations votes to repeal its sanctions against Italy.

• **17 Jul:** An anti-government revolt provokes the Spanish civil war.

• **20 Jul:** The Montreux Convention recognizes Turkish sovereignty of the Dardanelles.

• **4 Aug:** Greek premier Gen. John Metaxes appoints himself as dictator.

• **6 Aug:** In Spain, Franco's nationalist army captures Badajoz in the south west.

• **19–23 Aug:** After a five-day show trial in Moscow, 16 of Stalin's opponents are executed including Zinoviev and Kamenev.

• **9–17 Sept:** At a London conference, 27 countries vote for a policy of non-intervention in the Spanish Civil War.

• **1 Oct:** Spanish nationalists vote General Franco chief of state.

• **10 Oct:** In Austria, Chancellor Schuschnigg incorporates the Fascist militia in the Fatherland Front.

• **22 Oct:** Belgium declares martial law to curb the activities of Rexists.

• **1 Nov:** Mussolini proclaims the Rome–Berlin axis.

• **3 Nov:** Democrat F. D. Roosevelt wins a second term as US president.

• **6 Nov:** The siege of Madrid begins and the government flees to Valencia.

• **18 Nov:** Italy and Germany recognize Franco's government in Spain.

• **25 Nov:** Germany and Japan sign the Anti-Comintern Pact intended to combat international communism.

• **11 Dec:** In Britain, King Edward VIII abdicates. His brother, George VI succeeds.

CULTURE

• The black American athlete, Jesse Owens, wins four gold medals at the 11th Olympic Games held in Berlin.

• Roll-on Roll-off ferries operate between Britain and France for the first time.

• The International Surrealist Exhibition is opened in London by Salvador Dali, wearing a diving suit.

• The Fiat 500 is launched as Italy's "people's car".

• Adolf Hitler opens the first Volkswagen ("people's car") factory in Saxony.

• In the US, the Boulder (Hoover) Dam on the Colorado river is completed; it creates the world's largest reservoir.

• **Nov:** The British Broadcasting Corporation (BBC) starts regular television broadcasting from Alexandra Palace, London.

• **30 Nov:** In Britain, the Crystal Palace (originally designed for the 1851 Great Exhibition) is destroyed by fire.

THE HINDENBURG DISASTER

Heavier-than-air aircraft continue to develop with the new jet engine

POLITICS

• **1 Jan:** Political uniforms and private armies are banned in Britain.

• **9 Jan:** Bolshevik Leon Trotsky is given political asylum in Mexico.

• **25 Mar:** Italy and Yugoslavia agree a five-year nonaggression pact.

• **1 Apr:** The Government of India Act comes into force and seven provinces set up all-India governments.

• **27 Apr:** In Spain, the Basque town of Guernica is bombed by the Germans provoking international outrage.

• **6 May:** The German airship *Hindenburg* explodes at Lakehurst, New Jersey, killing 36 people.

• **28 May:** Neville Chamberlain becomes prime minister of Britain.

• **3 Jun:** The Duke of Windsor (the former King Edward VIII) marries Mrs. Wallis Simpson in Paris.

• **12 Jun:** In the Soviet Union, Stalin begins a purge of army generals.

The Hindenburg *bursts into flames, 6 May.*

• **18 Jun:** In the Spanish civil war, Franco's forces take Bilbao.

• **7 Jul:** Japanese troops on maneuver clash with the Chinese near Beijing, triggering the Sino-Japanese war.

• **28 Jul:** Japanese troops capture Peking, now Beijing.

• **8 Aug–8 Nov:** The Japanese wage a campaign to take Shanghai and arouse fierce international opposition for their bombing of civilians.

• **15 Aug:** Canadian prime minister Mackenzie King appoints a commission to revise the British North America Act.

• **13 Oct:** Germany guarantees the inviolability of Belgium.

• **23 Oct:** The United Australia and

Country Parties defeat Labor in the Australian general election.

• **3 Nov:** The Brussels conference meets to discuss the Sino-Japanese war.

• **6 Nov:** Italy joins the German–Japanese Anti-Comintern Pact.

• **10 Nov:** President Getúlio Vargas assumes dictatorial powers in Brazil.

• **17 Nov:** The British peer Lord Halifax visits Germany to attempt a settlement of the Sudetenland question.

• **20 Nov:** The Chinese capital moves from Nanjing to Chongqing.

• **13 Dec:** Nanjing falls to the Japanese, and widespread pillage ensues.

• **28 Dec:** Elections in Romania bring down the Titulescu regime; Octavian Goga is appointed prime minister despite winning only 10 % of the vote.

• **29 Dec:** The Irish Free State officially changes its name to Éire as a new constitution comes into force.

CULTURE

• The Golden Gate bridge opens to traffic across the San Francisco Bay.

• The first dry photocopier is devised by Chester Carlson, a New York law student.

• AEG/Telefunken (Germany) markets the first magnetic tape recorder.

• Aviator Amelia Earhart disappears during a flight over the Pacific Ocean.

• British engineer Frank Whittle builds and tests the first jet engine.

• Pope Pius XI brands Nazism as fundamentally anti-Christian, and criticizes atheistic communism.

• *La Grande Illusion*, a film by Jean Renoir about World War I, is released in Paris.

• Billy Butlin opens the first commercial holiday camp in Britain.

• **12 May:** King George VI is crowned in Westminster Abbey, Britain.

• **8 Jun:** Hollywood's first "sex goddess" Jean Harlow, dies aged 26.

• **Jul:** Adolf Hitler opens an exhibition of "degenerate art" in Munich, showing pieces by many important modern European artists.

• **11 Jul:** American composer George Gershwin dies aged 38.

• **Aug:** At the Paris world fair, the Spanish painter Picasso displays his painting *Guernica,* a reaction to the bombing of the Basque town in April.

• **Sept:** US jazz singer, Bessie Smith dies after she is refused treatment at a "whites only" hospital.

PEACE FOR OUR TIME?

Hitler continues to create a "Greater Germany" through bloodless coups

POLITICS

• **10 Jan:** The Japanese take Qingdao.

• **18 Jan:** King Carol of Romania suspends the constitution and dismisses the antisemitic premier Octavian Goga.

• **2–14 Mar:** The Soviet purges continue with the trial and execution of Nikolay Bukharin.

• **12 Mar:** German forces invade Austria; many Austrians welcome them.

• **13 Mar:** Austria is proclaimed a province of the German Reich. Hitler replaces Chancellor Schuschnigg with the Austrian Nazi, Artur Seyss-Inquart.

• **18 Mar:** The Mexican government nationalizes the oil companies.

• **16 Apr:** Britain recognizes Italian sovereignty in Ethiopia in return for non-interference in the Spanish civil war.

• **3–9 May:** Hitler visits Mussolini, consolidating the Rome–Berlin axis.

• **4 May:** Douglas Hyde, a Protestant, becomes the first Irish president.

Chamberlain returns from Munich, 30 Sept.

• **10 May:** The Japanese resume their advance into China.

• **19–20 May:** The Czechs mobilize in response to reports of German troops massing on the Czech border.

• **17 Jun:** In Ireland, de Valera's Fianna Fáil wins the general election.

• **7 Sept:** The Sudeten Germans break relations with the Czech government.

• **12 Sept:** Hitler demands self-determination for the Sudeten Germans; the Czechs proclaim martial law.

• **15 Sept:** British prime minister Neville Chamberlain meets Hitler to discuss the Czech crisis.

• **22 Sept:** The Japanese create a

United Council for China at Peking (Beijing), indicating their intention to turn China into a Japanese protectorate.

• **29 SEPT:** At the Munich conference, Hitler, Chamberlain, Mussolini and the French premier Deladier, agree to transfer the Sudetenland to Germany.

• **1–10 OCT:** Germany occupies the Sudetenland.

• **4 OCT:** The French Popular Front government collapses over the issue of the Munich agreement.

• **6 OCT:** Slovakia is granted full autonomy, and Ruthenia wins autonomy two days later under the name Carpatho–Ukraine.

• **24 OCT:** The US Wages and Hours Law stipulates minimum wages and maximum hours, outlawing child labor.

• **8 NOV:** In the US mid-term elections, the Republicans make their first gains for a decade.

• **9–10 NOV:** *Kristallnacht,* a night of anti-Jewish violence, takes place in Germany; 26,000 male Jews are arrested.

• **23 DEC:** In Spain, Franco begins his main offensive in Catalonia.

• **24 DEC:** In Peru, 24 American countries reaffirm mutual solidarity in the face of foreign intervention.

CULTURE

• Spanish painter Salvador Dalí is expelled from the Surrealist movement because of his support for Gen. Franco.

• German filmmaker Leni Riefenstahl releases *Olympiad,* a five-hour film of the Berlin Olympic Games.

• Ferdinand Porsche works on the design of the Volkswagen "beetle" car in Germany.

• Hungarian Ladislao Biró patents the ball-point pen.

• German physicist Otto Hahn becomes the first person to split the uranium atom.

• US chemical company du Pont begin the commercial manufacture of Nylon.

• **14 JAN:** Walt Disney's first full-length cartoon *Snow White and the Seven Dwarfs,* is released.

• **16 JAN:** Benny Goodman gives the first jazz concert at New York's Carnegie Hall.

• **3 JUL:** The British steam engine *Mallard* achieves 126 m.p.h. (203 k.p.h.) setting a new world speed record.

• **30 OCT:** Orson Welles's radio broadcast of *The War of the Worlds* causes widespread panic in New Jersey, when listeners believe it to be true.

CONFLICT ERUPTS

The Allies declare war on Germany following the invasion of Poland

POLITICS

• **17 Jan:** Norway, Sweden and Finland refuse a German bilateral nonaggression pact and insist on neutrality.

• **26 Jan:** In Spain, Franco's forces capture Barcelona with Italian help.

• **27 Feb:** Britain and France recognize Franco's regime in Spain.

• **10–14 Mar:** The Prague government deposes premier Joseph Tiso of Slovakia, who appeals to Hitler for assistance.

• **14 Mar:** Hungary invades and annexes Carpatho–Ukraine.

• **15 Mar:** German troops occupy Bohemia–Moravia in Czechoslovakia; Hitler enters Prague.

• **20 Mar:** Britain and France claim that the Munich agreement on Czechoslovakia no longer apply.

• **23 Mar:** Romania agrees to sell Germany oil at preferential rates.

• **29 Mar:** The civil war ends in Spain following the surrender of Madrid.

A father says goodbye to his evacuated son.

• **7 Apr:** Italy invades Albania; King Zog flees to Greece.

• **11 Apr:** Hungary withdraws from the League of Nations.

• **24 Apr:** Robert Menzies succeeds Joseph Lyons as Australian premier.

• **22 May:** Hitler and Mussolini agree a 10-year alliance (the Pact of Steel).

• **23 May:** Britain endorses a plan for an independent Palestinian state within 10 years.

• **22 Aug:** Britain guarantees the defense of Poland in the event of attack.

• **23 Aug:** Germany and the USSR sign a nonaggression treaty (the Hitler–Stalin Pact) and agree spheres of influence.

• **30 Aug:** The SS stages an attack on a German radio station in Gliewitz, Poland, to provide a pretext for invasion.

• **1 Sept:** German troops invade Poland and Germany annexes Danzig.

• **3 Sept:** Britain, France, Australia and New Zealand declare war on Germany; Mussolini announces Italian neutrality.

• **3 Sept:** In Britain, Chamberlain forms a war cabinet, with Winston Churchill as First Lord of the Admiralty.

• **5 Sept:** The United States announces its neutrality in the European war.

• **5 Sept:** South African premier Hertzog resigns; Jan Smuts succeeds.

• **10 Sept:** A British Expeditionary Force begins to land in France.

• **16 Sept:** The Germans surround Warsaw; Soviet troops invade Poland.

• **27 Sept:** Poland surrenders and is divided between Germany and the USSR.

• **4 Nov:** President Roosevelt signs an amendment to the Neutrality Act to allow the US to sell arms to the Allies.

• **30 Nov:** Soviet troops invade Finland and bomb Helsinki.

• **13 Dec:** British warships corner the German *Graf Spee* in Montevideo harbor; the crew scuttle the ship.

CULTURE

• Vivien Leigh and Clark Gable star in the romantic film *Gone with the Wind*.

• American actress Judy Garland stars in *The Wizard of Oz*.

• Nylon stockings first go on sale.

• John Wayne stars in John Ford's classic Western movie *Stagecoach*.

• The commercial production of polythene begins in Britain.

• **28 Jan:** German-Jewish nuclear physicists Otto Frisch and Lise Meitner alert the Allies to German research into nuclear fission.

• **9 Feb:** The British government begins to distribute air-raid shelters to Londoners.

• **2 Mar:** Pius XII is elected pope after the death of Pius XI.

• **30 Apr:** New York World's Fair opens, with a theme of "progress and peace".

• **20 May:** Pan-American Airways starts regular scheduled flights between Europe and the United States.

• **31 Aug:** The first British school-children are evacuated from urban areas.

• **2 Aug:** Albert Einstein writes to President Roosevelt about the possibility of making an atomic bomb.

GERMANY BATTERS EUROPE

*Germany, Italy and Japan
conclude a military pact*

POLITICS

• **1 Feb:** The USSR begins a new offensive against Finland, attacking the Karelian Isthmus and Lake Kuhmo.

• **11 Feb:** The Russians attack the Mannerheim Line on Finland's south-east border.

• **20 Feb:** German U-boat commanders are ordered to attack all shipping including supposedly neutral ships.

• **12 Mar:** Finland signs a peace treaty with the USSR ceding the Karelian Isthmus and other territory.

• **9 Apr–13 Jun:** Germany invades Norway and Denmark. The Norwegian government flees to Tromsö and the Germans set up a puppet administration under Quisling.

• **10 Apr:** The British navy attacks the German fleet in the First Battle of Narvik in Norway.

• **7 May:** British prime minister, Neville Chamberlain resigns and Winston Churchill forms an all-party coalition.

Mickey Mouse lights a gloomy Europe.

• **10 May–22 Jun:** Germany invades Belgium, Luxembourg and the Netherlands.

• **14 May:** The Dutch army surrenders.

• **21 May:** German troops march through Belgium and northern France capturing Amiens and Abbeville.

• **28 May:** Belgian army surrenders.

• **29 May–3 Jun:** German troops reach the French coast trapping British and French soldiers who are evacuated from Dunkirk.

• **10 Jun:** The Norwegian king flees to Britain ordering his army to cease fire. Italy declares war on Britain and France. The French government flees to Bordeaux as Germans enter Rouen.

- **14 Jun:** German troops enter Paris.

- **15 Jun:** The USSR occupies Lithuania, Estonia and Latvia.

- **16 Jun:** Winston Churchill offers France union with Britain as a means of continuing the war. France rejects the offer; prime minister Reynaud resigns and is replaced by Marshal Pétain.

- **20 Jun:** The first Australian and New Zealand troops arrive in Britain.

- **22 Jun:** France concludes an armistice with Germany. The country is divided between a German-occupied zone and a French-administered state centered on Vichy.

- **27 Jun:** Russia invades Romania.

- **30 Jun:** German troops invade the Channel Islands.

- **10 Jul:** Hitler launches the aerial Battle of Britain.

- **23 Aug:** An all-night bombing raid on London begins the "Blitz".

- **3 Sept:** The US sells 50 destroyers to Britain in exchange for leased bases in Newfoundland and the Caribbean.

- **4 Sept:** Ion Antonescu assumes dictatorial powers in Romania.

- **13 Sept:** Italy invades Egypt.

- **22 Sept:** Japan invades Indochina.

- **27 Sept:** Germany, Italy and Japan sign the Axis Pact of military and economic cooperation.

- **7 Oct:** German and Italian forces enter Romania.

- **28 Oct:** Italy invades Greece.

- **5 Nov:** In the US, Roosevelt wins a third presidential election.

- **11–12 Nov:** The British cripple the Italian fleet in the port of Taranto.

- **20 Nov:** Hungary joins the German-Italian-Japanese Pact; on 23 Nov Romania joins.

- **9 Dec:** Britain launches an offensive against the Italians in North Africa.

CULTURE

- Howard Florey and Ernst Chain develop penicillin as an antibiotic.

- Walt Disney's *Fantasia* is released in the US, featuring stereophonic sound.

- The Tacoma Narrows suspension bridge collapses in Washington state.

- Bing Crosby, Bob Hope and Dorothy Lamour star in the first "Road to" movie, *The Road to Singapore*.

- **Jan:** Food rationing begins in Britain.

- **Nov:** Prehistoric cave paintings are discovered in France at Lascaux.

GLOBAL WAR RAGES

The US enters the war after the Japanese attack on Pearl Harbor

POLITICS

• **3–5 Jan:** British and Australian troops capture Bardia (in Libya) from the Italians.

• **22 Jan:** The Italians surrender Tobruk to British and Australian troops.

• **30 Jan:** South African troops drive the Italians out of Kenya.

• **12 Feb:** As Commonwealth troops advance steadily in Libya, German general Erwin Rommel arrives with reinforcements.

• **30 Mar:** The German counter-offensive in North Africa begins. By 10 Apr, British and Australian troops are besieged in Tobruk.

• **6 Apr:** Germany invades Yugoslavia and Greece.

• **13 Apr:** The USSR and Japan sign a neutrality pact.

• **17 Apr:** Yugoslavia surrenders.

• **17 Apr:** British troops enter Iraq where pro-Axis Rashid Ali rules.

The Star of David worn by all Jews over the age of six in Nazi-occupied territory.

• **22 Apr:** Greece surrenders to Germany.

• **25 Apr:** Germany invades Egypt.

• **7 May:** A German weather ship is captured off Iceland, revealing secret documents on the German coding machine, *Enigma*.

• **9 May:** a captured U-boat yields the Allies a cipher machine and code books.

• **10 May:** Rudolf Hess, deputy leader of the Nazi party, flies to Scotland claiming to bring peace proposals. He is treated as a prisoner of war.

• **10 May:** Germany drops thousands of incendiary bombs on London and destroys the Chamber of the House of Commons.

• **20 May – 1 Jun:** Germany invades Crete forcing an Allied evacuation.

• **23 – 27 May:** Britain destroys Germany's battleship, the *Bismarck*.

• **31 May:** Iraq signs an armistice.

• **8 Jun:** British and Free French forces invade Syria to prohibit Axis activity.

• **22 Jun – 5 Dec:** Germany invades the USSR without warning.

• **25 Jun:** Finland declares war on the USSR and invades Karelia.

• **6 Jul:** The Russians abandon Poland and the Baltic states in the face of rapid German advance.

• **27 Jul:** Japan forces France to accept a joint protectorate over Indochina.

• **9 – 12 Aug:** Churchill and Roosevelt meet to establish postwar principles in the Atlantic Charter.

• **25 Aug – 9 Sept:** Britain and the USSR invade Iran securing oil supplies.

• **8 Sept:** In the USSR, the siege of Leningrad begins (relieved Jan 1944).

• **15 Oct:** As German forces approach Moscow, the Russian government transfers to Kubishev.

• **18 Nov:** British and Commonwealth troops launch a counteroffensive in North Africa (10 Dec Tobruk is relieved).

• **27 Nov:** The Russians launch a successful counteroffensive.

• **27 Nov:** Britain declares war on Finland, Hungary and Romania.

• **5 Dec:** as winter encroaches, Hitler abandons his invasion of the USSR.

• **7 Dec:** The Japanese attack the US Pacific Fleet at anchor in Pearl Harbor.

• **7 Dec:** The US and UK declare war on Japan 8 Dec.

• **11 Dec:** Germany and Italy declare war on the United States.

CULTURE

• Utility clothing and furniture is introduced in Britain.

• The artist Henry Moore draws Londoners taking refuge from the Blitz.

• Olivier Messaien writes *Quatuor pour la fin du temps* while a prisoner of war.

• Dmitri Shostakovich writes his *Seventh Symphony* under siege in Leningrad.

• **Jul:** The BBC begins broadcasts to European resistance movements prefaced by the Morse Code signal for V and the slogan "V for Victory".

• **Sept:** Germany orders all Jews over the age of six to wear a Star of David.

• **Dec:** In US, the Manhattan Project begins to develop an atomic bomb.

THE TIDE
BEGINS TO TURN

US troops enter the European war;
the Allies make progress on all fronts

POLITICS

• **1 JAN:** Representatives of 26 nations meet in Washington, D.C. and issue a declaration not to make separate peace treaties with the Axis powers.

• **5 JAN–31 MAR:** The Russians launch a winter offensive on all fronts.

• **20 JAN:** In Germany, Nazi leaders discuss the Jewish question; Reinhard Heydrich's "final solution" is mass extermination in concentration camps.

• **21 JAN:** Rommel launches a new offensive in North Africa.

• **25 JAN:** The Japanese force a British retreat from Kuala Lumpur (Malaya) to Singapore, and move to invade Burma.

• **26 JAN:** The first United States troops arrive in the UK.

• **15 FEB:** With Singapore City under siege, Britain surrenders to the Japanese. 130,000 troops become prisoners of war.

• **19 FEB:** Japanese planes bomb Darwin, Australia.

US military intervention costs heavy losses.

• **28 FEB:** Java is invaded by Japan.

• **7 MAR:** Japanese land on New Guinea.

• **9 APR:** US and Filipino forces on the Bataan Peninsula surrender to Japan.

• **18 APR:** American B25 bombers carry out a raid on Tokyo.

• **23–30 APR:** The "Baedeker" raids, German bombers hit historic British cities.

• **1 MAY:** British withdraw from Burma.

• **4–7 MAY:** The Battle of the Coral Sea is fought between the US and Japan off southern New Guinea.

• **27 MAY:** In North Africa, Rommel's forces begin a drive that leads to the recapture of Tobruk on 21 Jun.

• **30 May:** The first British "thousand bomber" raid is carried out by the RAF on Cologne in Germany.

• **31 May:** Three Japanese midget submarines raid Sydney Harbor, Australia, 19 seamen die.

• **3–7 Jun:** US victory in the Battle of Midway in the Pacific shifts the balance of naval power away from Japan.

• **10 Jun:** Nazis destroy the Czecho-slovakian village of Lidice in revenge for the murder of Reinhard Heydrich.

• **1 Jul:** In Russia, the Germans finally capture Sevastopol.

• **7 Aug:** 19,000 US marines land on Guadalcanal, Gavatu and Tulagi in the Solomon Islands.

• **19 Aug:** British and Canadian troops raid Dieppe in France testing the possibility of an invasion.

• **19 Aug:** The Battle of Stalingrad begins. German troops attack in the face of fierce Russian resistance.

• **2 Sept:** German SS troops destroy the Jewish ghetto in Warsaw, Poland, killing 50,000 Jews.

• **23 Oct–4 Nov:** The Second Battle of El Alamein. The British, led by Gen. Montgomery ("Monty"), finally retake Tobruk on 13 Nov.

• **7 Nov:** US general, Dwight D. Eisenhower, leads a combined Anglo-American invasion force in N. Africa.

• **11 Nov:** The Germans occupy the whole of France.

• **12 Nov:** The US navy wins the Battle of Guadalcanal and establishes naval superiority in the Pacific.

• **19 Nov:** The Russian counter-offensive at Stalingrad surrounds the besieging German army.

CULTURE

• The first jet fighter, the German Messerschmidt Me262, goes on its maiden flight.

• In the UK, Gilbert Murray founds the charity OXFAM.

• The first gold disk is awarded to band leader Glenn Miller (USA) for *Chattanooga Choo-Choo*.

• **Feb:** In Britain, "plimsoll lines" appear on baths in hotels and public places in response to fuel shortages.

• **May:** The portable rocket launcher "Bazooka" is tested by the US army.

• **Dec:** In the US, Enrico Fermi creates the first controlled chain reaction in the first nuclear reactor.

• **Dec:** In Britain, the Beveridge Report presages the postwar welfare state.

THE ALLIES TASTE VICTORY

*Germany retreats and
Russia pushes westward*

POLITICS

• **14–24 JAN:** Winston Churchill
and Franklin D. Roosevelt meet at the
Casablanca Conference to discuss war
strategy; they agree that Germany and
Japan must surrender unconditionally.

• **18 JAN–16 JUN:** Japanese submarines are deployed off the eastern
coast of Australia.

• **23 JAN:** In N. Africa, British troops
recapture Tripoli. The Germans retreat
destroying many installations.

• **21 FEB:** Allied armies in N. Africa
are placed under US general Dwight
Eisenhower's supreme command.

• **5 MAR:** British and US bombers
begin a series of raids over the Ruhr,
Germany's industrial heartland.

• **20 MAR:** In N. Africa, Gen.
Montgomery's troops break through the
Mareth Line into southern Tunisia.

• **19 APR:** In Poland, an uprising in
the Warsaw ghetto is brutally crushed
killing at least 10,000 Jews.

Bogart wrestles with the morals of wartime.

• **26 APR:** The Germans discover a
mass grave of 4,000 Polish officers at
Katyn near Smolensk in the USSR.

• **7 MAY:** Allied forces capture Tunis
and Bizerta in N. Africa giving the Allies
control of Mediterranean shipping.

• **13 MAY:** German and Italian forces
in N. Africa surrender.

• **17 MAY:** The British RAF breach two
huge dams in the Ruhr and Eder valleys
in Germany using the bouncing bomb.

• **3 JUN:** The French Committee of
National Liberation is formed.

• **1 JUL:** Twin US offensives in central
Pacific begin.

1 9 4 3

- **5–20 JUL:** Germany attacks along a 170-mile front in the Kursk area (USSR). The Russians defeat them in the largest tank engagement of World War II.

- **10 JUL:** The Allies launch an invasion of Italy.

- **19 JUL:** US bombers attack Rome.

- **25 JUL:** In Italy, King Victor Emmanuel dismisses Mussolini and asks Marshal Badoglio to form a government.

- **27 JUL:** The Allies drop incendiaries on Hamburg, creating the first firestorm.

- **3 SEPT:** Allied troops land on mainland Italy.

- **4 SEPT:** US and Australian troops land on northeast New Guinea and overrun Japanese strongholds.

- **8 SEPT:** The Italians surrender unconditionally.

- **10 SEPT:** The Germans slowly withdraw in southern Italy, moving to occupy Rome and Milan.

- **12 SEPT:** Mussolini is rescued from house arrest by the Germans.

- **15 SEPT:** Mussolini proclaims a puppet Social Republic on Lake Garda in German-occupied Italy.

- **13 OCT:** Italy declares war on Germany.

- **1 Nov:** US forces land on Bougainville in the Solomon Islands.

- **20–24 Nov:** US forces recapture the Gilbert Islands in the face of fanatical Japanese resistance.

- **29–30 Nov:** In Yugoslavia, the congress at Jajce announces a new Federal Republic under Marshal Tito.

- **1 DEC:** In the Cairo Declaration, Roosevelt, Churchill, Stalin and Jiang Jieshi agree a postwar policy for the Far East with the unconditional surrender of Japan a necessary prerequisite.

- **24 DEC:** The Russians launch offensives in the Ukraine, Crimea and northern Russia.

CULTURE

- The jitterbug becomes the new dance craze in the United States.

- *Casablanca*, starring Humphrey Bogart and Ingrid Bergman wins the Academy Award for the Best Picture.

- Rogers and Hammerstein's musical *Oklahoma* is a hit in the United States.

- Alan Turing (UK) develops the first electronic computer, known as *Colossus*. It is used for breaking German ciphers.

- The world's first nuclear reactor is activated at Oak Ridge, Tennessee.

VICTORY IS IN SIGHT

D-Day invasions; US forces annihilate the Japanese fleet

French troops lead the Allies into liberated Paris.

POLITICS

• **22 JAN:** Allied forces land at Anzio in southern Italy but are trapped by German forces.

• **26 JAN:** Leningrad is relieved by Soviet forces after a two-year siege.

• **29 JAN:** US forces in the Pacific begin an offensive to take the Marshall Islands, the Carolines and the Marianas.

• **6 MAR:** US bombers begin daylight raids on Berlin.

• **2 APR:** Soviet troops enter Romania.

• **8–10 APR:** Soviet troops take Odessa, beginning the liberation of the Crimea.

• **9 APR:** Charles de Gaulle becomes commander of the Free French forces.

• **11–25 MAY:** The Allies break through the German defenses at Anzio.

• **4 JUN:** Allied forces take Rome.

• **6 JUN:** Operation Overlord (D-Day) launches a massive Allied invasion of northern France at Normandy.

• **10 JUN:** German SS troops massacre 642 people at Oradour-sur-Glane in central France in reprisal for the capture of an SS officer.

• **10–15 JUN:** Soviet forces drive the Finns from the Karelian isthmus.

• **13 JUN:** The first German V-1 flying bomb hits London.

• **19–20 JUN:** At the Battle of the Philippine Sea, the Japanese navy loses 400 aircraft.

• **30 JUN:** US troops take Cherbourg in northern France.

• **1–22 JUL:** Delegates from 44 nations meet at Bretton Woods, New Hampshire, and agree to set up an International Monetary Fund.

• **3 Jul:** Soviet troops take Minsk, capturing 100,000 German prisoners.

• **18 Jul:** Gen. Tojo resigns as Japanese chief of staff and prime minister.

• **20 Jul:** In Germany, Klaus von Stauffenberg fails to assassinate Hitler.

• **23 Jul:** Soviet troops enter Poland.

• **1 Aug:** The citizens of Warsaw revolt against German rule.

• **15 Aug:** The Allies invade the south of France.

• **21 Aug–7 Oct:** Delegates from the major powers meet at Dumbarton Oaks to discuss an international organization to promote peaceful arbitration.

• **24 Aug:** French resistance fighters recapture most of Paris.

• **25 Aug:** US troops march into Paris.

• **30 Aug:** The French government returns to the capital.

• **4 Sept:** Allied forces liberate Antwerp.

• **11 Sept:** US troops enter Germany near Trier but meet fierce resistance.

• **17 Sept:** British troops fail to capture Arnhem bridge in Holland.

• **20 Aug–8 Sept:** Soviet forces attack Romania and the country changes sides declaring war on Germany.

• **Oct:** The Russians enter Slovakia, Hungary and Yugoslavia.

• **9–20 Oct:** Winston Churchill and UK foreign secretary Anthony Eden visit Moscow to agree postwar spheres of influence with Stalin.

• **14 Oct:** Allied troops liberate Athens.

• **23–26 Oct:** At the Battle of Leyte Gulf, the Japanese fleet is routed by the United States navy.

• **7 Nov:** Franklin D. Roosevelt wins a fourth term as United States president.

• **16 Dec:** The Germans launch a last major offensive in the Ardennes, known as the Battle of the Bulge.

CULTURE

• The first automatic general-purpose digital computer, the *Mark-1,* is built in Harvard University.

• The first part of Sergei Eisenstein's film *Ivan the Terrible* is released in the Soviet Union.

• Aaron Copland's ballet *Appalachian Spring,* choreographed by Martha Graham, premières in Washington D.C.

• In Britain, Francis Bacon's painting *Three Figures at the Base of a Crucifixion* provokes outrage.

• **16 Dec:** Glenn Miller's aircraft goes missing, he is presumed dead.

WORLD WAR II IS OVER

The Allies rejoice as Germany and Japan surrender

POLITICS

• **10–28 JAN:** The Allies eliminate the German "bulge" in the Ardennes.

• **13 JAN:** Soviet forces take Budapest, and Warsaw on 17 Jan.

• **27 JAN:** The Red Army liberates Auschwitz death camp.

• **4–11 FEB:** Churchill, Roosevelt and Stalin meet at Yalta in the Crimea to discuss postwar strategy.

• **13–14 FEB:** The Allies carry out a massive firebomb raid on Dresden.

• **19 FEB–16 MAR:** US marines take Iwo Jima island after fierce fighting.

• **7 MAR:** Allied forces reach the Rhine and establish a bridgehead at Cologne.

• **9 MAR:** The US Air Force begins bombing raids on Japanese cities.

• **1 APR:** US armies encircle the Ruhr and take nearly 400,000 prisoners.

• **1 APR–22 JUN:** US marines capture Okinawa from the Japanese.

Winston Churchill's famous V for Victory.

• **12 APR:** US president Roosevelt dies; vice-president Harry Truman takes over the reins of government.

• **16 APR–2 MAY:** Red Army troops led by Georgi Zhukov capture the city of Berlin.

• **25 APR–26 JUN:** At a conference in San Francisco, 48 countries meet to negotiate the United Nations charter.

• **28 APR:** Mussolini and his mistress are killed by Italian partisans.

• **30 APR:** Hitler shoots himself in his bunker in Berlin.

• **4 MAY:** Hitler's successor, Admiral Dönitz, surrenders the Netherlands, Denmark and northwest Germany to Field Marshall Montgomery.

• **8 May:** Germany surrenders unconditionally; victory in Europe (VE-Day) is celebrated in Britain and the United States.

• **27 May:** Chinese troops take Nanjing from the Japanese.

• **11 Jun:** Liberals under Mackenzie King win the Canadian general election.

• **22 Jun:** The US, USSR, Britain and France partition Germany.

• **5 Jul:** John Curtin, prime minister of Australia, dies; Joseph Chifley takes over.

• **7 Jul–2 Aug:** Stalin, Truman, Churchill and Attlee meet at Potsdam to plan the occupation of Germany.

• **26 Jul:** The Labor party wins a landslide victory at the British general election; Clement Attlee becomes prime minister.

• **2 Aug:** British troops liberate Burma from Japanese occupation. Civilian government is restored in Oct.

• **6 Aug:** The US drops an atomic bomb on Hiroshima in Japan, killing 78,000 people. A second atomic bomb is dropped on Nagasaki three days later.

• **8 Aug:** The Soviet Union declares war on Japan and invades Manchuria.

• **15 Aug:** Japan unconditionally surrenders to the Americans.

• **25 Aug:** Ho Chi Minh proclaims a republic of Vietnam.

• **2 Sept:** Following the surrender of Japanese forces in Korea, the country is divided into Soviet and American spheres of influence.

• **21 Oct–13 Nov:** In the French general elections, Charles de Gaulle becomes head of the government.

• **24 Oct:** The United Nations is founded with 51 member states.

• **29 Nov:** Communist leader Tito proclaims a Yugoslavian republic.

• **20 Nov:** The Nuremberg trials of Nazi war criminals begin.

C U L T U R E

• Charlie Parker, founder of bebop jazz, establishes his first band.

• In the UK, the Home Service and Light Program are set up to broaden the scope of BBC radio broadcasting.

• **12 Mar:** Anne Frank, the 15-year-old Jewish Dutch diarist, dies in Belsen concentration camp.

• **16 Jul:** The world's first nuclear explosion takes place at Alamogordo air base, New Mexico.

• **5 Dec:** New Zealand introduces new welfare state legislation.

JUSTICE AND REVENGE

The UN sets up headquarters as the "iron curtain" descends over Europe

POLITICS

• **20 Jan:** French president Charles de Gaulle resigns.

• **29 Jan:** The United Nations chooses Norwegian delegate Trygve Lie as its first secretary-general.

• **31 Jan:** The new Yugoslav constitution sets up six constituent republics with a powerful central authority.

• **1 Feb:** Hungary is declared an independent republic.

• **21–22 Feb:** Violent demonstrations take place in India against British rule.

• **24 Feb:** Juan Perón becomes president of Argentina.

• **25 Feb:** In China, Mao Zedong and Jiang Jieshi agree to found a National Army that includes both Communists and Nationalists.

• **2 Mar:** Ho Chi Minh is elected president of the Democratic Republic of Vietnam; France recognizes it as an autonomous state within Indochina.

Nazi leaders stand trial at Nuremberg.

• **5 Mar:** In a speech in Fulton, Missouri, Winston Churchill coins the phrase "iron curtain" to describe the division of Europe between Communism and the West.

• **21 Mar:** Nazi leader Hermann Goering denies any knowledge of the "final solution" to the Jewish problem.

• **18 Apr:** The League of Nations is formally dissolved; having been superseded by the United Nations.

• **27 Apr:** Opening of the war crimes tribunal in Japan, at which charges are brought against Hideki Tojo and others.

• **9 May:** Italy votes by referendum to become a republic.

• **16 May:** The British announce a plan for Indian independence.

• **25 May:** Transjordan is proclaimed independent.

• **4 Jul:** The Philippines become independent from the United States.

• **22 Jul:** Zionist terrorists bomb the British Palestine Army Command at the King David Hotel in Jerusalem.

• **29 Jul:** The All-India Muslim League demands a separate, sovereign state of Pakistan.

• **19 Aug:** Civil war breaks out in China between Communists and Nationalists.

• **1 Sept:** The Greek monarchy is restored by referendum, civil war ensues.

• **8 Sept:** Bulgaria votes to become a republic.

• **30 Sept:** The Nuremberg trial ends; 12 Nazi leaders are sentenced to death and five others to life imprisonment.

• **Oct:** A Japanese "Peace Constitution" renounces war, abolishes feudalism and declares Emperor Hirohito and his successors to be constitutional monarchs.

• **13 Oct:** The French vote for the new constitution of the Fourth Republic, with reduced presidential powers.

• **15 Oct:** Nazi war criminal Hermann Goering kills himself shortly before his execution.

• **6 Nov:** The National Health Service Act is passed in Britain.

• **23 Nov:** The French bomb Hanoi in northeast Vietnam, effectively beginning the French Indochinese war.

• **5 Dec:** Millionaire John D. Rockefeller jr. (USA) donates US$8.5 million for UN permanent headquarters to be set up in New York city.

• **28 Dec:** The French declare martial law throughout Indochina.

C U L T U R E

• A craze for jukebox music begins in the United States and Britain.

• Benjamin Spock's *Common Sense Book of Baby and Child Care* is published in the United States.

• US scientists win all the Nobel prizes awarded in 1946.

• **14 Feb:** *ENIAC,* the first genuine electronic computer, goes into operation at the University of Pennsylvania, USA.

• **5 Jul:** The first bikinis are revealed at a Paris fashion show.

• **25 Jul:** The United States carries out the first subsurface atomic explosion, at Bikini Atoll.

• **22 Nov:** The ballpoint pen goes on sale in the United States.

DIOR'S "NEW LOOK"

Colonial powers continue to lose their imperial possessions

POLITICS

• **1 Jan:** Britain grants Nigeria limited self-government.

• **1 Jan:** In Britain, the coal industry is nationalized.

• **16 Jan:** In France, Vincent Auriol is elected president.

• **21 Jan:** J. C. Smuts, prime minister of South Africa, refuses to put Southwest Africa under UN trusteeship.

• **31 Jan:** British women and children are evacuated from Palestine as Jewish terrorists become increasingly violent.

• **10 Feb:** Italy agrees to pay reparations to the Allies and cede territory to Greece, Yugoslavia and France. Finland, Hungary and Romania relinquish territory to the USSR.

• **20 Feb:** Britain announces its intention to quit India by June 1948.

• **5 Mar:** The USSR rejects Western proposals for the international control of atomic research.

Glamor after years of wartime austerity.

• **12 Mar:** US president Harry S Truman enunciates the "Truman doctrine" to suppress communism.

• **14 Mar:** The US leases military bases on the Philippines for 99 years.

• **14 Apr:** Gen. Charles de Gaulle founds the Rassemblement du Peuple Français (RPF).

• **23 May:** In Britain, the Cabinet agrees to partition India into two states, one Hindu (India) and one Muslim (Pakistan).

• **5 Jun:** US secretary of state, George Marshall, proposes the Marshall Plan to enable Europe's postwar recovery.

- **10 Jun:** President Truman becomes the first US president to visit Canada.

- **23 Jun:** The US Congress passes the antilabor union Taft-Hartley Act.

- **6 Jul:** Spain makes a constitutional change to restore the monarchy after Franco's death.

- **15 Jul:** West European countries, with exception of Czechoslovakia, Poland and Finland, accept the Marshall Plan. The USSR rejects the plan.

- **20 Jul:** In Indonesia, Dutch troops launch "police action" against Indonesian nationalists.

- **Aug—Sept:** An estimated 10,000 people are killed in clashes on the Punjab border. Indian and Pakistani governments halt refugee traffic.

- **3 Aug:** The Dutch and Indonesian governments comply with a UN request to call a ceasefire in Indonesia.

- **15 Aug:** India and Pakistan proclaim their independence under prime ministers Jawaharlal Nehru (India) and Liaqat Ali Khan (Pakistan).

- **1 Sept:** The Communist party wins a general election in Hungary.

- **29 Oct:** The Benelux Customs Union (Belgium, the Netherlands and Luxembourg) is established.

- **30 Oct:** The General Agreement on Tariffs and Trade (GATT) is signed by 23 countries.

- **27 Nov:** Australian banks are nationalized.

- **29 Nov:** The UN votes to partition Palestine and set up a Jewish state; fighting erupts between Arabs and Jews.

- **14 Dec:** The USSR devalues its currency.

- **30 Dec:** Conflict over Kashmir, India is referred to the UN.

- **30 Dec:** King Michael of Romania is forced to abdicate by Communists.

CULTURE

- French fashion designer Christian Dior presents his "New Look," hailed as a post-war morale boost for women.

- President Truman sets up the CIA (Central Intelligence Agency) in the US.

- The first UFO (unidentified flying object) is recorded over Kansas.

- The "Dead Sea Scrolls" are discovered in a cave in Jordan.

- The first microwave cookers go on sale in the United States.

- **14 Oct:** US test pilot, Chuck Yeager, becomes the first person to fly through the sound barrier.

THE COLD WAR SETS IN

Eastern Europe is dominated by the USSR

Gandhi is murdered by a Hindu extremist.

POLITICS

• **1 JAN:** In Britain, the railways are nationalized.

• **4 JAN:** Burma becomes independent.

• **30 JAN:** Indian leader Mahatma Gandhi is assassinated by a Hindu extremist, Nathuram Godre.

• **1 FEB:** The Federation of Malaya is proclaimed by Britain.

• **4 FEB:** Ceylon becomes independent.

• **25–27 FEB:** In Czechoslovakia, the Communists take over power led by prime minister Klement Gottwald.

• **10 MAR:** Jan Masaryk, Czech foreign minister and opponent of communism, falls to his death from a high window.

• **17 MAR:** A 50-year mutual defense treaty is signed between Britain, France and the Benelux countries.

• **20 MAR:** Soviet delegates to the Allied Central Council walk out following accusations that the West is conspiring against the USSR.

• **30 MAR–30 APR:** The Pan-American conference draws up the Charter of Organization of American States.

• **1 APR:** In Berlin, the USSR imposes strict checks on traffic leaving the city from the Western zones.

• **16 APR:** Organization for European Economic Cooperation (OEEC) is set up.

• **14 MAY:** The Jewish state of Israel is proclaimed with Dr. Chaim Weizmann as president and David Ben-Gurion as prime minister.

• **17 MAY:** The Arab League nations invade Israel.

• **26 MAY:** The South African coalition government is defeated by the pro-apartheid Nationalist Afrikaaner party.

• **7 Jun:** After the implementation of a Soviet-style constitution in Czechoslovakia, President Benes resigns and is replaced by Klement Gottwald.

• **24 Jun:** The USSR, fearing a merger of Western occupation zones in Germany, blockades all surface traffic between Berlin and West Germany.

• **5 Jul:** In Britain, the National Health Service, together with other welfare schemes, comes into effect.

• **30 Jul:** The president of Hungary, Zoltán Tildy, resigns over the proposed collectivization of agriculture.

• **1 Aug:** France, Britain and the USA merge occupation zones in Germany.

• **2 Aug:** In the US, the Un-American Activities Committee investigates alleged Communist infiltration of government.

• **15 Aug:** The Republic of Korea is proclaimed in Seoul.

• **4 Sept:** Queen Wilhelmina of the Netherlands abdicates in favor of her daughter Juliana.

• **9 Sept:** North Korea claims independence for the entire country as the Democratic People's republic of Korea. Kim Il Sung becomes leader.

• **17 Sept:** The ruler of Hyderabad surrenders his state to Indian forces.

• **17 Sept:** In Israel, Count Folke Bernadotte, a UN mediator, is murdered by Jewish terrorists.

• **22 Oct:** The British Commonwealth is renamed the Commonwealth of Nations.

• **30 Oct:** In China, Mao Zedong's communist forces capture Manchuria.

• **3 Nov:** In the US, Democrat Harry S Truman wins a second term as president.

• **15 Nov:** In Canada, Liberal prime minister W. L. Mackenzie King retires and is succeeded by Louis St. Laurent.

• **9 Dec:** The UN General Assembly adopts the declaration of human rights.

• **29 Dec:** The Dutch occupy Jakarta in Indonesia and arrest the government.

CULTURE

• The board game Scrabble is launched in the United States.

• In the US, Richard and Maurice McDonald open a drive-in hamburger restaurant, the first of what was to become a massive international chain.

• US artist Jackson Pollock exhibits "action painting".

• The Kinsey report into sexual mores, *Sexual behavior of the Human Male*, causes a stir in the US.

BERLIN: THE DIVIDED CITY

COMECON and NATO are established

POLITICS

• **JAN:** The Council for Mutual Economic Assistance (COMECON) is set up by the Eastern bloc countries.

• **22 JAN:** In the Chinese civil war, Beijing falls to the Communists. Nationalist leader, Jiang Jieshi resigns the presidency and calls for a ceasefire.

• **25 JAN:** The first Israeli elections are won by David Ben-Gurion's Labor Party.

• **1 FEB:** Postwar clothes rationing ends in Britain.

• **24 FEB:** Israel and Egypt agree an armistice. Further armistices with Lebanon, Transjordan and Syria follow in the ensuing months.

• **31 MAR:** Newfoundland joins the Dominion of Canada as tenth province.

• **4 APR:** The North Atlantic Treaty Organization (NATO) is founded.

• **8 APR:** Britain, France and the US reach agreement on the establishment of a new German state (West Germany).

Berliners welcome the Allied airlift.

• **18 APR:** Éire leaves the Commonwealth of nations and becomes the Republic of Ireland.

• **5 MAY:** Ten European nations sign the Statute of the Council of Europe.

• **11 MAY:** Israel is admitted to the UN.

• **11 MAY:** Siam becomes Thailand again (first renamed 1939).

• **11 MAY:** The British parliament passes the Ireland Bill recognizing the independence of the Republic of Ireland with special status for Irish citizens.

• **12 MAY:** The USSR lifts the Berlin blockade. The city is formally divided into eastern and western sectors.

• **23 May:** The Federal Republic of Germany is proclaimed, consisting of US, British and French, but not Soviet zones.

• **26 May:** In China, Shanghai falls to Mao Zedong's Communist forces.

• **2 Jun:** Transjordan is renamed the Hashemite kingdom of Jordan.

• **14 Jun:** The French establish a Vietnamese government in Saigon with Bao Dai as head of state.

• **27 Jun:** The Liberal party, led by Louis St. Laurent wins the Canadian general election.

• **25 Jun:** The South African Citizenship Act lays the foundations of apartheid.

• **19 Jul:** Laos becomes a semi-autonomous state within French Indochina.

• **14 Aug:** First elections held in the Federal Republic of Germany result in Christian Democrats forming a government led by Konrad Adenauer.

• **1 Oct:** The Chinese Communist leader Mao Zedong proclaims the People's Republic of China.

• **7 Oct:** The German Democratic Republic is proclaimed in East Germany.

• **16 Oct:** In Greece, the civil war ends in defeat for the Communists.

• **Nov:** The National Party is elected in New Zealand ending 14 years of Labor government.

• **8 Nov:** Cambodia becomes a semi-autonomous state within French Indochina.

• **8 Dec:** Chinese nationalists led by Jiang Jieshi set up a Republic of China on the island of Formosa (Taiwan).

• **14 Dec:** The Israeli capital moves from Tel Aviv to Jerusalem.

• **17 Dec:** A new coalition government is formed in Australia headed by Liberal Robert Menzies.

• **28 Dec:** Ahmed Sukarno is elected president of the newly-independent Republic of Indonesia.

CULTURE

• Arthur Miller wins the Pulitzer Prize for *Death of A Salesman*.

• The US music magazine *Billboard* starts a Country and Western chart and introduces the term "rhythm and blues"

• George Orwell's *Nineteen Eighty Four* is published in Britain.

• Cape Canaveral is established as a rocket testing ground in Florida.

• **Feb:** In Peru, a mob burns down a radio station after H. G. Well's story *The War of the Worlds* causes mass panic.

THE COLD WAR ESCALATES

The US, USSR and China all become involved in conflict in Korea

POLITICS

• **10 Jan:** The Soviet envoy to the UN Security Council walks out in protest at the presence of Nationalist China.

• **31 Jan:** President Truman orders the US Atomic Energy Commission to research and build a hydrogen bomb.

• **2 Feb:** France recognizes the independence of Cambodia and Laos.

• **7 Feb:** The UK and US recognize the government in south Vietnam; the USSR has already recognized Ho Chi Minh's government in Hanoi in the north.

• **9 Feb:** Joseph McCarthy launches a campaign against Communist infiltration of US federal government.

• **14 Feb:** Mao Zedong and Stalin sign a 30-year friendship pact in Moscow.

• **23 Feb:** In Britain, the Labor government wins a second term of office.

• **3 Mar:** British nuclear scientist Klaus Fuchs is convicted of selling secrets to the Soviet Union.

Mitzi Gaynor and Rossano Brazzi in South Pacific.

• **14 Apr:** In Greece, the Venizelos government falls and is replaced by one led by Gen. Nikolaos Plastiras.

• **24 Apr:** Jordan annexes Arab Palestine to include the West Bank in its territory.

• **1 May:** China outlaws infanticide, polygamy and child marriages.

• **26 May:** Petrol rationing ends in the United Kingdom.

• **20 Jun:** France, Germany, Belgium, Netherlands, Luxembourg and Italy meet to discuss the Schuman Plan for future European economic integration.

• **25 Jun:** North Korean forces invade South Korea. The South Korean capital, Seoul, falls on 28 Jun.

• **26–27 Jun:** The UN intervenes in

Korea; US forces arrive in Pusan on
1 Jul, led by Gen. Douglas MacArthur.

• **22 Jul:** Leopold III returns to
Belgium from exile; he transfers his
authority to his son Baudouin.

• **26–27 Jul:** Britain and France
decide to send troops to Korea; Australia
commits its troops on 1 Aug.

• **3 Aug:** Communist China is denied
entry to the United Nations.

• **18 Sept:** The Viet Minh take Dong
Khe from the French.

• **25 Sept:** UN forces recapture Seoul
after a surprise landing at Inchon.

• **1 Oct:** South Korean forces invade
North Korea.

• **21 Oct:** Chinese troops invade Tibet.

• **26 Oct:** South Korean and UN troops
take the North Korean capital Pyongyang
and reach the Chinese border.

• **16 Nov:** King Farouk of Egypt calls
for the evacuation of the British from
the Suez Canal, and the unification of
Egypt with the Sudan.

• **24–27 Nov:** Chinese troops drive the
UN from the Chinese border with Korea.

• **5 Dec:** The UN flees from Pyongyang.

• **24 Dec:** Chinese troops cross from
North to South Korea.

CULTURE

• Diners' Club cards (the first modern
charge cards) are issued in New York.

• Cyclamate is introduced as an
artificial sweetener.

• Antihistamines become popular as a
cure for colds and allergies.

• French architect Le Corbusier begins
work on the chapel at Ronchamp
(completed 1955).

• **Apr:** In the US, John von Neumann,
using the computer *ENIAC,* makes the
first 24-hour computerized weather
forecast.

• **1 May:** The musical *South Pacific*
(Rodgers and Hammerstein) wins the
Pulitzer Prize.

• **7 Jul:** The first successful color
television broadcasts are made in the
United States.

• **2 Oct:** The *Charlie Brown* cartoon
by Charles Schultz appears in the US.

• **1 Nov:** Pope Pius XII officially
declares that the bodily ascension of the
Virgin Mary is a Catholic doctrine.

• **24 Nov:** The musical *Guys and
Dolls* opens on Broadway, New York.

• **25 Dec:** Scottish nationalists steal
the coronation stone (Stone of Scone)
from Westminster Abbey, London.

THE UN MAKES PEACE IN KOREA

The advent of the long-playing record brings music to a wider audience

POLITICS

• **1–4 Jan:** North Korean and Chinese forces capture the capital city of Seoul.

• **26 Jan:** UN forces launch a counter offensive in Korea.

• **5 Feb:** The Gold Coast's first general election is won by the Convention People's Party led by Kwame Nkrumah.

• **14 Feb:** In Israel, David Ben-Gurion's government resigns over religious education policies.

• **18 Feb:** A national dock strike begins in New Zealand (resolved in Jun).

• **26 Feb:** An amendment to the US constitution limits presidents to two terms of office.

• **7 Mar:** The Iranian prime minister, Gen. Ali Razmura, is murdered by a religious extremist.

• **8 Mar:** The Iranian parliament votes to nationalize the oil industry.

• **14 Mar:** The UN and South Korean forces recapture Seoul.

A South Korean soldier searches for communists.

• **5 Apr:** Julius and Ethel Rosenberg (USA) are sentenced to death for selling atomic secrets to the USSR.

• **11 Apr:** US president Truman dismisses Gen. Douglas MacArthur as commander of the UN forces in Korea for advocating a policy of war with China. Gen. Matthew Ridgway succeeds.

• **3 May:** The Festival of Britain is opened in London by King George VI.

• **14 May:** In South Africa, the Afrikaner Nationalist government votes to disenfranchise "colored" people.

• **14 May:** China grants Tibet religious freedom if it severs ties with the West.

• **20 May:** The Iranian government orders the Anglo-Iranian Oil Co. to leave the country. Britain appeals to the International Court of Justice.

• **1 Jun:** Éamon de Valera's Fianna Fáil party win the Irish elections.

• **7 Jun:** British diplomats, Guy Burgess and Donald Maclean disappear while under suspicion of espionage.

• **17 Jun:** The French elections result in victory for the Gaullists.

• **26 Jun:** The Soviet UN delegate calls for a ceasefire in the Korean war.

• **5 Jul:** The International Court finds in Britain's favor in its dispute with Iran. Iran rejects the finding.

• **8 Jul:** UN and Communist representatives meet to discuss terms for a ceasefire in the Korean war.

• **20 Jul:** King Abdullah of Jordan is assassinated; his son Talal succeeds.

• **1 Sept:** USA, Australia and New Zealand sign a mutual defense treaty (the ANZUS pact).

• **8 Sept:** Japan signs a peace treaty with 48 other countries that opposed her in World War II, some refuse to sign.

• **27 Sept:** Iranian troops take over the Anglo Iran Oil Co.'s refinery at Abadan.

• **16 Oct:** Pakistani prime minister Ali Khan is assassinated.

• **19 Oct:** British troops seize control of the Suez Canal following Egyptian complaints about British presence.

• **27 Nov:** A truce line is agreed between North and South Korea.

• **24 Dec:** The former Italian colony of Libya (now a UK-French protectorate) proclaims its independence.

CULTURE

• US motor manufacturer Chrysler pioneers power steering.

• In Australia, rural communities receive education via radio broadcasts.

• Deutsche Grammophon markets the first 33 r.p.m. long-playing record.

• The US novelist Dashiell Hammett is jailed for six months after refusing to testify before the McCarthy Commission.

• Avant-garde musician John Cage (USA) composes *Imaginary Landscape No 4* using 12 randomly tuned radios.

• J. D. Salinger's *Catcher in the Rye* sums up teenage experience in the US.

• **5 Sept:** 16-year-old US tennis star Maureen Connolly ("Little Mo") becomes the youngest-ever winner of the ladies' US championships.

• **10 Dec:** Benjamin Britten's opera *Billy Budd* premières in London.

H-BOMB ROCKS THE WORLD

A severe polio epidemic in the US leads to the development of a vaccine

POLITICS

• **JAN:** Australia suffers a severe drought not relieved until 1953.

• **9 JAN:** British prime minister, Winston Churchill agrees to permit US military bases in Britain.

• **14 JAN:** The UN Security council refuses Tunisia's appeal to present its case for autonomy, sparking off riots.

• **18–27 JAN:** Anti-British riots in Egypt end with the dismissal of the government by King Farouk.

• **24 JAN:** Canadian Vincent Massey is appointed governor general of Canada.

• **6 FEB:** King George VI of Britain dies, Elizabeth II succeeds.

• **18 FEB:** Greece and Turkey are admitted to NATO.

• **1 MAR:** Pandit Nehru's Congress party wins 364 of the 489 National Assembly seats in India's first national elections.

• **10 MAR:** Gen. Fulgencio Batista, in exile since 1944, seizes power in Cuba.

"Operation Mike" the H-bomb explodes.

• **10 MAR:** The USSR proposes 4-power talks on unification and rearmament of Germany. UK, France and USA oppose it.

• **21 MAR:** In the Gold Coast, Kwame Nkrumah becomes the first African prime minister south of the Sahara.

• **22 APR:** In South Africa, prime minister Dalan introduces a bill making parliament a high court to prevent the supreme Court from invalidating apartheid race legislation.

• **25 APR:** French troops attack the Vietminh strategic base at Tay Ninh.

• **28 APR:** Japan regains sovereignty.

• **1 JUN:** The United People's party wins the Ceylon general election.

• **22 Jul:** The International Court of Justice rules that it has no jurisdiction in the dispute between the Anglo-Iranian Oil Co. and the Iranian government.

• **23 Jul:** Gen. Muhammad Neguib seizes power in Egypt. King Farouk abdicates in favor of his 9-month-old son Fuad II on 26 Jul.

• **26 Jul:** In Argentina, Eva ("Evita") Perón, wife of President Perón, dies.

• **11 Aug:** Prince Hussein is proclaimed king of Jordan.

• **24 Aug:** The Kenyan government imposes a curfew to curtail the nationalist Mau Mau secret society.

• **11 Sept:** Eritrea, a former Italian colony in North Africa administered by the UK, is federated with Ethiopia.

• **3 Oct:** The UK explodes its first atomic bomb, on the Monte Bello islands off northwest Australia.

• **22 Oct:** Iran breaks off diplomatic relations with Britain.

• **31 Oct:** The US explodes the world's first thermonuclear device, the hydrogen bomb, at Eniwetok Atoll in the Pacific. The team that developed it was led by Edward Teller, a Hungarian-American.

• **5 Nov:** Republican Dwight D. Eisenhower wins the US presidency.

• **19 Nov:** The Vietminh launch an offensive against the French in Vietnam.

• **25 Nov:** In Kenya, 2,000 members of the Kikuyu tribe are arrested as the Mau Mau begin to revolt against British rule.

CULTURE

• A polio epidemic in the US strikes over 47,500 people.

• In Britain, a winter smog in London leads to over 2,000 deaths.

• "Acrilan", an acrylic fiber, is first manufactured in the United States.

• A phosphorated hesperidin oral contraceptive is developed.

• The first pocket-sized transistor radio is marketed by Sony in Japan.

• A British doctor, Douglas Bevis, develops the amniocentesis test.

• Jonas Salk (USA) produces a killed-virus vaccine against polio.

• Gene Kelly directs, acts and sings in the hit movie *Singing in the Rain*.

• The world's first sex-change operation is carried out by K. Hamburger, in Denmark, on George Jorgenson, afterward known as Christine.

• **8 Mar:** In the US, a Pennsylvania hospital pioneers the use of an artificial heart. The patient lives for 80 minutes.

DNA IS A DOUBLE HELIX

The Kinsey Report makes public the secrets of the bedroom

POLITICS

• **14 JAN:** Marshal Tito is elected as the first president of Yugoslavia.

• **3 FEB:** Over 1,000 people die in floods in the Netherlands.

• **5 MAR:** Joseph Stalin dies, he is succeeded as premier and first secretary of the Communist party by Georgi Malenkov.

• **5 MAR:** King Norodom Sihanouk proclaims Cambodian independence.

• **31 MAR:** Dag Hammerskjold is chosen to succeed Trygve Lie as Secretary General of the United Nations.

• **8 APR:** Jomo Kenyatta is imprisoned for Mau Mau activities in Kenya.

• **11 APR:** France announces that Vietminh forces have invaded Laos.

• **15 APR:** The National party wins a clear victory in the South African elections.

• **18 APR:** Muhammad Ali forms a new government in Pakistan.

Queen Elizabeth II is crowned, 2 Jun.

• **4 MAY:** More than 2,000 people flee from East Berlin to West, following food shortages in the Soviet zone.

• **17 JUN–12 JUL:** Martial law is imposed in East Berlin following anti-Soviet uprisings.

• **18 JUN:** Gen. Neguib proclaims a republic in Egypt.

• **19 JUN:** Convicted spies Julius and Ethel Rosenberg go to the electric chair, despite widespread doubts of their guilt.

• **5 JUL:** Imre Nagy forms a new government in Hungary, promising cultural and economic freedoms.

• **10 JUL:** Lavrenti Beria, head of internal security in the Soviet Union, is dismissed (later convicted and executed).

• **27 JUL:** The armistice ending the Korean war is signed.

• **14 AUG:** The Soviet Union announces it has tested a hydrogen bomb.

• **20 AUG:** Premier Mousasddiq of Iran is deposed; the shah returns 22 Aug.

• **6 SEPT:** Konrad Adenauer's Christian Democrats win power in West Germany.

• **12 SEPT:** Nikita Khrushchev is appointed first secretary of the Communist party in the Soviet Union.

• **30 OCT:** Austria protests against continued Allied occupation.

• **2 Nov:** Pakistan is declared an Islamic state within the Commonwealth.

• **24 Nov:** Senator Joseph McCarthy accuses former US president Truman of aiding suspected Communists.

• **29 Nov:** French paratroopers capture Dien Bien Phu from the Vietminh.

• **7 DEC:** David Ben-Gurion resigns as prime minister of Israel.

• **23 DEC:** Robert Oppenheimer, US nuclear physicist and "father of the bomb", has his security pass withdrawn for suspected Communist sympathies.

• **24 DEC:** Julius Nyerere is elected president of the Tanganyika African Association.

CULTURE

• Alfred Kinsey produces his report *Sexual Behavior in the Human Female*, revealing an unexpectedly high degree of unfaithfulness.

• US scientists show that the tars from tobacco can cause cancer in mice.

• The disease myxomatosis spreads across Western Europe, killing millions of rabbits.

• Ossip Zadkine's bronze monument: *To a Destroyed City*, commemorates the 1940 bombing of the port of Rotterdam.

• **17 APR:** Charlie Chaplin, accused of communism by Senator McCarthy, leaves the US for Switzerland.

• **25 APR:** Francis Crick (UK) and James Watson (USA) announce that they have discovered the double-helix structure of DNA.

• **29 MAY:** New Zealander Edmund Hillary and Sherpa Tenzing Norgay are the first to conquer the summit of Mount Everest.

• **2 JUN:** The coronation of Queen Elizabeth II takes place in Westminster Abbey, London. UK sales of televisions soar before the event.

• **2 Nov:** In Britain, Rev. Chad Varah sets up the Samaritans, an organization to assist depressed or suicidal people.

REDS UNDER THE BEDS

Senator McCarthy unleashes anti-communist paranoia in the US

POLITICS

• **25 Jan:** The foreign ministers of France, Britain, US and USSR meet in west Berlin to discuss the German and Austrian peace treaties. The USSR rejects proposals for German reunification.

• **3 Feb:** Queen Elizabeth II arrives in Sydney for the first visit to Australia by a reigning British monarch.

• **25 Feb:** In Egypt, Col. Gamal Abdel Nasser forces president Neguib to resign. After popular demonstrations, Neguib is restored.

• **14 Mar:** The Vietminh begin a siege of French forces in Dien Bien Phu.

• **13 Apr:** Soviet diplomat Vladimir Petrov is granted asylum in Australia, following exposure of a Soviet spy ring.

• **18 Apr:** In Egypt, Col. Nasser ousts Neguib again, though Neguib is restored to a nominal presidency.

• **24 Apr:** In Kenya, British forces begin a major operation against the nationalist Mau Mau movement.

Roger Bannister sets a new world record.

• **25 Apr:** Juan Perón is re-elected president of Argentina and promptly arrests four opposition leaders.

• **7 May:** In Vietnam, the French surrender the fortress at Dien Bien Phu. The Vietminh call for freedom for Vietnam, Laos and Cambodia.

• **13 May–22 Jun:** A five-power subcommittee of the UN discusses an inspection system and a possible ban on nuclear testing.

• **29 May:** Thailand complains to the UN Security Council that Communists in Indochina threaten her security.

• **29 May:** In Australia, the coalition government of the Liberal and County parties is re-elected.

• **Jun:** Senator Joseph McCarthy alleges Communist infiltration of the CIA and nuclear weapons plants. President Eisenhower moves to stop McCarthy investigating the CIA.

• **2 Jun:** John Costello heads a coalition government in Ireland.

• **12 Jun:** The French government is defeated in the National Assembly. Pierre Mendès-France becomes premier.

• **29 Jun:** The Potomac Charter, a six-point declaration of Western policy, is released in the US.

• **20 Jul:** An armistice divides Vietnam along the 17th parallel. Communists control the north; a French-backed nationalist regime controls the south.

• **10 Aug:** The Netherlands and Indonesia sever their last links.

• **17 Aug:** President Eisenhower says the US will act to stop China invading Formosa (Taiwan) after Chinese gunboats are sunk off the island.

• **8 Sept:** Creation of SEATO, the Southeast Asia Treaty Organization: a defensive alliance of the US, UK, France, Australia, New Zealand, the Philippines, Pakistan and Thailand.

• **23 Oct:** A nine-power agreement on Western European Union allows West Germany to rearm and enter NATO.

• **1 Nov:** Terrorist raids begin the war of independence in Algeria.

• **17 Nov:** In Egypt, Nasser places Naguib under house arrest and becomes head of state.

• **1 Dec:** The US signs a pact of mutual security with Nationalist China.

• **14 Dec:** In Greece, supporters of a Cypriot-Greek union riot in Athens.

CULTURE

• In Britain, "Teddy Boys" appear on the streets.

• Marlon Brando wears denim jeans and a leather jacket in Laslo Benedek's film, *The Wild One*.

• Japanese director Akira Kurosawa's *The Seven Samurai* becomes one of the first Japanese films to make an impact on Western culture.

• Jonas Salk's anti-polio vaccine is released for general use.

• **Mar:** Canada's first subway line opens in Toronto.

• **6 May:** 25-year-old British medical student, Roger Bannister, breaks the four-minute-mile barrier (3 min. 59.4 sec.).

• **13 May:** The St. Lawrence Seaway Bill authorizes its construction, to improve navigation between the Atlantic and the Canadian Great Lakes.

THE WARSAW PACT

Apartheid in South Africa draws international criticism

POLITICS

• **18 JAN:** In Kenya, Mau Mau nationalists are offered an amnesty.

• **25 JAN:** Jacques Soustelle is appointed governor-general of Algeria after riots protesting against French rule.

• **5 FEB:** Pierre Mendès-France resigns as French premier after a vote of no confidence in his government's handling of Algerian demands for independence. Edgar Fauré forms a Radical ministry.

• **8 FEB:** In USSR, Georgi Malenkov resigns over arms policy and is replaced as premier by Nikolai Bulganin.

• **10 FEB:** In South Africa, police carry out a military-style operation to displace 60,000 Africans from their township near Johannesburg which has been designated a white residential area.

• **24 FEB:** Turkey and Iraq sign the anti-Communist Baghdad Pact. Iran, Pakistan and Britain join months later.

• **2 MAR:** Egypt and Syria sign a defensive agreement.

Screen goddess Marilyn Monroe poses for photos.

• **6 APR:** Winston Churchill, 80, resigns as British prime minister.

• **18–27 APR:** At the Bandung conference in Indonesia, delegates from 29 African and Asian countries call for an end to colonialism and racism.

• **18 APR:** Hungarian premier Imre Nagy is dismissed for "deviation", Andras Hegedüs takes over.

• **5 MAY:** West Germany becomes a sovereign state as US occupation ends.

• **7 MAY:** In retaliation for ratification of the 1954 agreement on Western European Union, the USSR annuls agreements with Britain and France.

• **9 MAY:** West Germany joins NATO.

• **14 May:** The USSR, Albania, Bulgaria, Czechoslovakia, Hungary, Poland, Romania and East Germany sign the Warsaw Pact, a 20-year mutual defense treaty.

• **15 May:** Austrian sovereignty is restored by a treaty signed by the UK, US, France and USSR.

• **26 May:** Soviet premier Bulganin and First Secretary Khrushchev visit Yugoslavia and sign a treaty of friendship between the two countries.

• **16 Sept:** Gen. Eduardo Lonardi leads a revolt ousting President Perón of Argentina. Perón goes into exile.

• **24 Oct:** After a referendum in South Vietnam, Emperor Bao Dai is deposed and a republic is proclaimed under Ngo Dinh Diem.

• **24 Oct:** The South African delegate walks out of a UN debate on racial conflict in South Africa.

• **16 Nov:** South Africa leaves the UN.

• **16 Nov:** The deposed sultan of Morocco returns, agreeing to set up a constitutional government and negotiate independence with France.

CULTURE

• After the US increases immigration controls, many West Indian immigrants go to Britain instead.

• Fashion guru Mary Quant opens her shop *Bazaar* on London's King's Road.

• British scientist Dorothy Hodgkin discovers the composition of vitamin B12, treatment for pernicious anemia.

• Velcro is patented in Switzerland.

• Marilyn Monroe stars in *The Seven Year Itch*, the movie success of the year.

• Tight denim jeans become fashionable in the US and UK.

• Lego is first produced by Danish former carpenter Ole Kirk Christiansen.

• **Mar:** Floods in Australia leave 44,000 people homeless.

• **12 Mar:** In the US, jazz saxophonist Charlie Parker, originator of bebop, dies aged 34.

• **18 May:** The Wimpy Hamburger chain opens its first store in London, introducing the hamburger to Europe.

• **Jul:** Disneyland opens at Anaheim, California, USA.

• **22 Sept:** In Britain, Independent Television begins broadcasting.

• **30 Sept:** In the US, film star James Dean, age 24, dies in a car crash.

• **31 Oct:** In Britain, Princess Margaret announces her decision not to marry Captain Peter Townsend, a divorcee.

COMMUNISM'S IRON FIST

The Suez crisis blackens Britain's reputation across the world

POLITICS

• **1 Jan:** Sudan is proclaimed an independent democratic republic.

• **12 Jan:** More British troops are sent to Cyprus following the murder of a Turkish policeman by EOKA terrorists.

• **19 Jan:** Sudan joins the Arab League.

• **1 Feb:** US president Eisenhower and UK prime minister Anthony Eden issue the Declaration of Washington, warning Asia and African countries against accepting aid from the USSR.

• **14–20 Feb:** Soviet premier Nikita Khrushchev denounces Stalin's policies.

• **2 Mar:** Morocco achieves independence from France.

• **20 Mar:** Tunisia gains independence from France.

• **23 Mar:** Pakistan becomes the world's first Islamic republic, but remains in the British Commonwealth.

• **22 Apr:** China appoints the Dalai Lama chairman of a committee to

Hungarian nationalists riot in the streets.

prepare Tibet for regional autonomy within the Chinese People's Republic.

• **10 May:** UN Secretary-General, Dag Hammarskjöld, arranges an unconditional ceasefire between Israel, Egypt, Jordan, Syria and Lebanon.

• **13 Jun:** British forces evacuate the Suez Canal zone in Egypt.

• **24 Jun:** Col. Nasser is elected as president of Egypt, unopposed.

• **28 Jun:** Anti-Communist riots in Poland are violently suppressed.

• **19 Jul:** The US and UK refuse to finance the Aswan High Dam because of Egyptian connections with the USSR.

• **26 JUL:** President Nasser of Egypt seizes the Suez Canal, to use canal revenues to finance the Aswan Dam.

• **16–23 AUG:** At the Suez Conference, London, 22 countries discuss the crisis.

• **22 SEPT:** President Somoza of Nicaragua is assassinated and succeeded by his son Luis.

• **23 SEPT:** Britain and France refer the Suez dispute to the UN Security Council.

• **23 OCT:** An uprising in Hungary demanding democratic government and withdrawal of Soviet troops is brutally put down by Soviet forces.

• **24 OCT:** Egypt, Jordan and Syria set up joint command of their armed forces.

• **29 OCT:** Israeli troops invade Egyptian land on the Sinai peninsula.

• **30 OCT:** Egypt rejects an ultimatum for a ceasefire. The UK and France bomb Egyptian airfields, for which they are internationally condemned.

• **2 NOV:** The Hungarian government appeals to the Western powers for assistance against the USSR.

• **4 NOV:** Soviet forces attack Budapest and crush the rebellion.

• **7 NOV:** The UN demands a ceasefire in Egypt; its terms are accepted by the UK and France.

• **21 NOV:** The UN General Assembly censures the USSR over Hungary.

• **2 DEC:** Fidel Castro begins a revolt against the Cuban government.

CULTURE

• Wilkinson Sword markets long-life stainless steel razor blades in the UK.

• *Heartbreak Hotel* tops the US charts and Elvis Presley emerges as a teen idol.

• Jørn Utzon's Opera House goes into construction in Sydney, Australia.

• John Osborne's *Look Back in Anger* premières in London.

• The Bell Telephone Co. in the US develops a "visual telephone" capable of transmitting pictures simultaneously with sound.

• FORTRAN, the first computer programming language is developed in the US.

• **MAR:** The first mass trial of birth control pills takes place in Puerto Rico.

• **APR:** The US Supreme court rules that racial segregation in public transportation is unconstitutional.

• **19 APR:** Prince Rainier of Monaco marries movie star Grace Kelly.

• **22 NOV:** The Summer Olympic Games open in Melbourne, Australia.

RACIST DRAMA AT LITTLE ROCK

*The space race begins as the Soviet
Union puts Sputnik into orbit*

POLITICS

• **10 Jan:** Harold Macmillan becomes
British prime minister following
Anthony Eden's resignation, 9 Jan.

• **31 Jan:** The French military is sent
into Algeria in the face of a growing
independence movement.

• **5 Feb:** Éamon de Valera becomes
prime minister of Ireland following a
Fianna Fáil victory at the polls.

• **18 Feb:** A US grand jury indicts
playwright Arthur Miller for un-
American activities.

• **6 Mar:** The Gold Coast becomes the
Republic of Ghana, but remains within
the British Commonwealth.

• **25 Mar:** The Treaty of Rome is
signed by representatives of six
European nations, setting up the
European Economic Community (EEC).

• **9 Apr:** The Suez canal is reopened.

• **14 Apr:** King Hussein of Jordan
survives a coup attempt.

Elvis Presley in Jailhouse Rock.

• **15 May:** The United Kingdom
explodes its first hydrogen bomb at
Christmas Island in the Pacific.

• **10 Jun:** The Conservative party wins
the Canadian general election; John
Diefenbaker becomes prime minister.

• **20 Jun:** British prime minister
Harold Macmillan claims that "most of
our people have never had it so good".

• **3 Jul:** Nikita Khrushchev foils an
attempted coup in the Soviet Union;
three leading members of the Politburo,
Molotov, Shepilov and Malenkov are
expelled the following day.

- **26 Aug:** The USSR announces the successful test of an intercontinental ballistic missile.

- **31 Aug:** Malaya gains independence from Britain.

- **4 Sept:** In the US, black students are barred from an all-white school at Little Rock, Arkansas.

- **22 Sept:** François "Papa Doc" Duvalier is elected president of Haiti.

- **23 Sept:** President Eisenhower orders US federal troops to enforce desegregation at Central High School, Little Rock.

- **4 Oct:** The Soviet Union launches *Sputnik 1*, a satellite orbiting 500 mi (800 km) above the earth.

- **10 Oct:** A severe leakage of radioactivity occurs after a fire at the British nuclear establishment at Windscale, in northwest England.

- **3 Nov:** The Soviet Union sends a dog, Laika, into Earth orbit, in *Sputnik II*.

- **30 Nov:** The Labor party under Walter Nash wins the New Zealand general election by one seat.

- **7 Dec:** The first US space flight fails; the rocket explodes on takeoff.

- **18 Dec:** The first US atomic power plant, at Shippingport, Pennsylvania, begins to produce electricity.

CULTURE

- The Crickets (with Buddy Holly) cut their first hit single, *That'll be the Day*.

- **14 Jan:** Movie star Humphrey Bogart dies, age 58.

- **5 Feb:** Rock 'n' rollers Bill Haley and the Comets tour Britain.

- **4 May:** First primetime rock-music TV network special, in the USA.

- **1 June:** The first British Premium Bond winners are selected by a random number generator known as ERNIE.

- **4 Sept:** The Wolfenden Report recommends that homosexual acts between consenting adults should be decriminalized in the UK.

- **26 Sept:** Leonard Bernstein's *West Side Story* opens on Broadway.

- **24 Oct:** French couturier Christian Dior dies.

- **29 Nov:** David Lean's *The Bridge on the River Kwai* premières in London.

- **4 Dec:** The British government rejects the Wolfenden Report.

- **20 Dec:** Elvis Presley stars as an ex-convict pop singer in *Jailhouse Rock*.

- **25 Dec:** Queen Elizabeth II broadcasts her first televised Christmas message to the Commonwealth.

COLONIAL EMPIRES CRUMBLE

NASA is established to direct the United States space program

POLITICS

• Mao Zedong launches the radically modernizing but economically disastrous "Great Leap Forward" in China.

• **13 Jan:** Nine thousand scientists from 43 nations petition the UN to ban tests of nuclear bombs.

• **1 Feb:** Egypt and Syria form the United Arab Republic.

• **3 Feb:** The Netherlands, Luxembourg & Belgium form the Benelux Economic Union, which allows free movement of persons, goods, services and capital.

• **8 Feb:** The French bomb a Tunisian village in retaliation for an alleged destruction of an aircraft.

• **22 Feb:** Following the restoration of the 1853 constitution, Arturo Frondizi is elected president of Argentina.

• **27 Mar:** Nikolai Khrushchev succeeds Bulganov as Soviet premier.

• **5 Apr:** Fidel Castro proclaims "total war" against the Cuban Batista regime.

Sir Edmund Hillary at the South Pole.

• **1 May:** President Nasser of Egypt commits his country to support the Soviet Union.

• **23 May:** The Comecon countries agree to closer economic integration; Communist China, North Korea, North Vietnam and Mongolia integrate their economies with Comecon.

• **1 Jun:** Charles de Gaulle is recalled as French premier to lead a government of national safety in the Algerian crisis.

• **17 Jun:** Execution of former Hungarian prime minister Imre Nagy.

• **14 Jul:** King Faisal of Iraq and his heir are assassinated; Abdul Karim el-Kassem becomes premier, and adopts anti-Western policies.

• **31 Jul:** "Papa Doc" Duvalier acquires dictatorial powers in Haiti.

• **23 Aug:** Mainland China begins to bombard the Nationalist-controlled island of Quemoy in the Taiwan Straits.

• **27 Aug:** The National Aeronautics and Space Agency (NASA) is set up to direct US space exploration.

• **28 Sept:** In a referendum, the French approve an extension of presidential powers in the country's Fifth Republic.

• **28 Oct:** Giuseppe Roncalli becomes Pope John XXIII, following the death of Pius XII.

• **27 Nov:** The USSR demands that West Berlin should become a demilitarized free city.

• **28 Nov:** Mali, Mauritania, Senegal, Chad, Gabon and Congo-Brazzaville proclaim their independence.

• **3 Dec:** Dutch commercial concerns, including oil companies, are nationalized in Indonesia.

• **16 Dec:** The Allies reject Soviet demands for the demilitarization of West Berlin.

• **21 Dec:** Charles de Gaulle is elected president of France with 78 % of the popular vote.

CULTURE

• The beatnik movement begins in California, and spreads to Europe.

• The hula-hoop craze begins in the United States.

• A link is detected between the drug thalidomide, given to pregnant women, and severe birth defects.

• The use of ultrasound scanning techniques to examine unborn babies is pioneered by I. Donald in Britain.

• In the US, Du Pont markets Lycra, an artificial elastic.

• The first bifocal contact lenses appear.

• Boris Pasternak's *Dr Zhivago* is first published in translation in Italy, since the Soviet authorities refuse to allow its publication in the USSR.

• The submarine USS *Nautilus* passes under the North Pole.

• **3 Jan:** Sir Edmund Hillary, with a New Zealand expedition, reaches the South Pole, beating a rival British expedition by 17 days.

• **6 Feb:** Eight of the Manchester United football team – the "Busby Babes" – are killed in an aircraft crash in Munich.

• **29 Jun:** As Brazil win football's World Cup for the first time, Pelé becomes a world-famous star.

CASTRO BECOMES CUBAN PREMIER

*Alaska and Hawaii join
the United States of America*

POLITICS

• **1 JAN:** In the US, Alaska becomes the 49th state of the Union.

• **2 JAN:** After Cuban dictator Batista flees, Fidel Castro becomes premier.

• **8 JAN:** Gen. Charles de Gaulle is inaugurated as president of the Fifth Republic of France.

• **17 JAN:** The Federal State of Mali is formed by the union of the newly created republics of Senegal and Sudan.

• **20 FEB:** Political disturbances in Nyasaland (E. Africa) lead to the arrest of Dr. Hastings Banda and others.

• **28 FEB:** Britain and Egypt settle claims arising from the Suez crisis.

• **13–27 MAR:** In Tibet, a revolt is crushed by the Chinese and the Dalai Lama flees to India.

• **14 MAR:** De Gaulle refuses to put one-third of France's naval forces under NATO command.

Khrushchev addresses the press on a US tour.

• **24 MAR:** Iraq withdraws from the Baghdad Pact and the Anglo-Iraqi agreement of 1956 lapses.

• **4 APR–30 MAY:** The Ivory coast forms the Sahel-Benin Union with Niger, Haute Volta and Dahomey.

• **11 MAY–5 AUG:** The US, UK, France and the USSR discuss the reunification of Germany at a Conference in Geneva.

• **22 MAY:** Canada and the US sign an agreement to cooperate on the use of atomic energy for mutual defense.

• **30 MAY:** Iraq terminates military assistance agreements with the US.

• **3 JUN:** Singapore becomes a self-governing state within the British Commonwealth.

• **4 Jun:** In Cuba, US-owned sugar mills and plantations are expropriated.

• **17 Jun:** Éamon de Valera becomes president of the Republic of Ireland.

• **21 Aug:** In the US, Hawaii becomes the 50th state of the Union.

• **20 Aug:** In South Africa, the anti-apartheid Progressive party is founded.

• **15 Sept:** Soviet premier Nikita Khrushchev arrives in Washington D.C. for an official tour of the US.

• **22 Sept:** UN votes against admitting the People's Republic of China.

• **25 Sept:** The prime minister of Ceylon, Solomon Bandaranaike, is assassinated by a Buddhist monk.

• **8 Nov:** The United Arab Republic and Sudan agree to share Nile water after construction of the Aswan High Dam.

• **20 Nov:** The European Free Trade Association (EFTA) is founded by Britain, Austria, Denmark, Norway, Sweden, Portugal and Switzerland.

C U L T U R E

• The first Xerox copier is introduced.

• The world's first geothermal power station is installed in New Zealand.

• Sony market the first portable transistorized television in Japan.

• **2 Jan:** The USSR launches the space-ship *Lunik I* which flies past the Moon and on to orbit the Sun

• **3 Feb:** American singer and teen idol Buddy Holly dies in a plane crash.

• **13 Feb:** The Barbie doll, in a zebra-stripe swimsuit, is launched in the US.

• **25 Apr:** In Canada, the 400 mi (650 km) St. Lawrence Seaway opens.

• **16 May:** Francois Truffaut wins best director at the Cannes Film Festival for *Les Quatre cent coups*. It is part of the French "New Wave" seeking to escape the conventions of Hollywood.

• **25 May:** The US launches a space-craft that takes two monkeys to a height of 360 mi (580 km) above the earth.

• **25 Jul:** The hovercraft *SRN-1* makes its maiden flight from Britain to France.

• **18 Aug:** In Britain, Alec Issigonis designs the Mini for the British Motor Corporation.

• **14 Sept:** The USSR's *Lunik II* crashes on the moon.

• **4 Oct:** *Lunik III* is launched; it goes on to take the first photographs of the dark side of the moon.

• **1 Dec:** The Antarctic Treaty is signed by 12 countries reserving the region for peaceful scientific research.

THE SWINGING SIXTIES

The contraceptive pill and the pacemaker make their debut

POLITICS

• **1 JAN:** French Cameroon becomes the Republic of Cameroon with Ahmadun Ahidjo as its first president.

• **18 JAN:** Argentina, Brazil, Mexico, Paraguay, Peru and Uruguay establish the Latin American Free Trade Association (LAFTA).

• **19 JAN:** USA and Japan sign a treaty of mutual cooperation and security.

• **24 JAN:** In Algeria, French settlers riot in response to President de Gaulle's sacking of commander Jacques Massu.

• **3 FEB:** In South Africa, British prime minister Harold Macmillan makes his famous "wind of change" speech in Capetown urging South Africa to abandon its policy of apartheid.

• **15–16 MAR:** Syngman Rhee wins his fourth presidential election in South Korea. (Allegations of fraud lead to Rhee's resignation weeks later).

• **21 MAR:** Demonstrations against the South African pass laws erupt into riots

The novel accused of depravity and corruption.

at Sharpeville when police open fire on a crowd and kill 67 black Africans.

• **25 MAR:** All black political organizations are banned in South Africa.

• **21 APR:** Brasília replaces Rio de Janeiro as the capital of Brazil.

• **27 APR:** French Togoland becomes the Republic of Togo.

• **28 APR:** Martial law is proclaimed in Turkey following student riots in Ankara and Istanbul.

• **5 MAY:** The USSR announces it has shot down a US U-2 aircraft on 1 May. The US denies that it was a spy plane.

• **8 MAY:** Leonid Brezhnev becomes president of the Soviet Union.

• **14–17 MAY:** A Summit meeting in Paris between USSR, USA, Britain and France breaks up after President Eisenhower refuses to apologize to the USSR for the U-2 affair.

• **27 MAY:** In Turkey, premier Adnan Menderes is ousted in a military coup.

• **26 JUN:** British Somaliland becomes independent.

• **26 JUN:** Madagascar becomes independent as the Malagasy Republic.

• **30 JUN:** The Belgian Congo becomes independent under President Youlou.

• **1 JUL:** Italian Somaliland joins British Somaliland to form the new independent Republic of Somalia.

• **6 JUL:** In the Congo Republic, the army mutinies against the government; UN peacekeeping troops are called in.

• **12 JUL:** France grants independence to Benin, Niger, Burkina Faso, the Central African Republic and Congo.

• **21 JUL:** In Ceylon, Mrs. Sirimavo Bandaranaike becomes the world's first woman prime minister.

• **7 AUG:** In Cuba, Castro nationalizes all US-owned property in retaliation for "US economic aggression".

• **16 AUG:** Cyprus gains independence with Archbishop Makarios as president.

• **19 AUG:** The pilot of the U-2 plane, Gary Powers, is sentenced to 10 years' imprisonment by the Soviets.

• **6 OCT:** A referendum in South Africa favors the establishment of a republic.

• **19 OCT:** The US imposes an embargo on shipments to Cuba.

• **9 NOV:** John F. Kennedy wins the US presidential election for the Democrats.

• **28 NOV:** French Mauritania becomes the Islamic Republic of Mauritania.

CULTURE

• Häagen-Dazs ice-cream is developed.

• In Britain, the first pacemaker is developed for patients with heart disease.

• **APR:** The movie *Ben Hur,* starring Charlton Heston, wins 10 Oscars.

• **1 APR:** The US launches the first weather satellite, *Tiros 1.*

• **9 MAY:** The Food and Drug Administration in Washington D.C. approves the contraceptive pill for use.

• **19 AUG:** A Soviet spacecraft carrying two dogs makes 17 orbits of the Earth before returning safely.

• **8 SEPT:** UK publisher Penguin Books is tried for publishing D. H. Lawrence's banned novel *Lady Chatterley's Lover.* (Found not guilty of obscenity 2 Nov).

KENNEDY'S "NEW FRONTIER"

Miniskirts hit the catwalks and the Twist becomes all the rage

POLITICS

• **3 Jan:** The US severs diplomatic relations with Cuba.

• **20 Jan:** John F. Kennedy is inaugurated 35th president of the United States. He promises the American people they "stand on the edge of a new frontier."

• **Feb:** Patrice Lumumba, deposed premier of the newly independent state of Congo, is murdered in suspicious circumstances in Katanga.

• **8–12 Mar:** At the Tananarive Conference, Congolese leaders make a tentative agreement to form a confederation of 18 states.

• **9 Mar:** The Dalai Lama appeals to the UN to restore Tibetan independence.

• **7 Apr:** The UN votes unanimously to censure South Africa's apartheid policy.

• **17 Apr:** A force of Cuban exiles, backed by the CIA, attempts an invasion of Cuba at the Bay of Pigs.

• **21 Apr:** A military revolt in Algeria

Yuri Gagarin, the first man to orbit the Earth.

is suppressed after President de Gaulle declares a state of emergency.

• **27 Apr:** Sierra Leone becomes independent within the Commonwealth.

• **26 May:** Amnesty International, a campaigning organization on behalf of political prisoners, is set up in London.

• **31 May:** South Africa becomes independent and leaves the Commonwealth.

• **25 Jun:** Iraq lays claim to the former British protectorate of Kuwait.

• **Jul:** Fears of a Communist crackdown on contact between East and West Berlin leads to a flood of refugees to the West.

• **1 Jul:** Britain sends troops to Kuwait (withdrawn 13 Aug).

• **10 Aug:** Britain applies to join the Common Market, also known as the European Economic Community (EEC).

• **13 Aug:** East Germany closes the border between East and West Berlin.

• **17–18 Aug:** The Berlin Wall is constructed.

• **1–6 Sept:** The Non-Aligned Nations Conference calls for complete disarmament and an end to nuclear testing.

• **5 Sept:** The US announces the resumption of nuclear tests.

• **13 Sept:** UN forces attempt to overthrow Moise Tshombe's secessionist regime in Katanga.

• **18 Sept:** UN Secretary-General Dag Hammarskjöld is killed in an air crash in Northern Rhodesia while on his way to meet Moise Tshombe of Katanga.

• **24 Nov:** The UN General Assembly adopts a resolution that Africa should be respected as a denuclearized zone.

• **9 Dec:** Tanganyika becomes an independent republic within the Commonwealth of Nations.

• **9 Dec:** In Southern Rhodesia, Joshua Nkomo forms the Zimbabwe African People's Union (ZAPU).

• **9 Dec:** The USSR breaks off diplomatic relations with Albania.

• **15 Dec:** The UN General Assembly rejects a Soviet proposal to admit the People's Republic of China.

• **21 Dec:** President Tshombe of Katanga province agrees to end secession from the Congo Republic.

CULTURE

• Chubby Checker's pop single *The Twist* starts a dance craze.

• The first haute couture miniskirts are presented to the fashion press by Marc Bohan at Dior and André Courrèges.

• New Zealand introduces compulsory selective national service.

• The Pill becomes available in Britain.

• **1 Mar:** President Kennedy establishes a Peace Corps for young Americans to serve overseas.

• **12 Apr:** Cosmonaut Yuri Gagarin, in his Soviet spacecraft *Vostok I,* becomes the first man to orbit the Earth.

• **16 Jun:** Russian ballet dancer, Rudolf Nureyev, defects to the West.

• **Sept:** The first Weight Watchers group is founded by Jean Nidetch of the Queens district in New York.

• **17 Sept:** In Britain, the biggest yet "ban-the-bomb" march in London ends in violent clashes with police, leading to nearly 1,000 arrests.

NUCLEAR WAR THREATENS

*Bob Dylan and
The Beatles rise to fame*

POLITICS

• **3 Jan:** Indonesia declares the Dutch colony of West New Guinea to be an Indonesian province (official May 63).

• **14 Jan:** The European Economic Community incorporates its Common Agricultural Policy.

• **10 Feb:** Gary Powers, the pilot in the U-2 affair of 1960, is released by the USSR in return for the spy, Rudolf Abel.

• **26 Feb:** The Irish Republican Army (IRA) suspends its campaign of violence against the British government, begun in 1956.

• **18 Mar:** A ceasefire is agreed in the war in Algeria.

• **6 May:** Nam Tha falls to the Pathet Lao forces, giving rise to fears of a new Communist threat in Indochina.

• **1 Jul:** Britain institutes controls on immigration from the Commonwealth.

• **1 Jul:** Rwanda and Burundi achieve full independence.

British CND members protest against US policy.

• **6 Aug:** Jamaica becomes independent within the Commonwealth of Nations.

• **31 Aug:** Trinidad and Tobago become independent within the Commonwealth.

• **2 Sept:** The Soviet Union agrees to supply arms to Cuba.

• **24 Sept:** Soviet president Leonid Brezhnev visits Yugoslavia; relations between the two nations improve.

• **9 Oct:** Uganda becomes independent within the Commonwealth.

• **20 Oct:** The Chinese invade India, following a border dispute.

• **22 Oct:** US president Kennedy reveals that Soviet missiles have been supplied to Cuba.

• **24 Oct:** The US imposes a naval quarantine on Cuba to prevent military supplies reaching the country.

• **26 Oct:** Soviet premier Khrushchev offers to withdraw Soviet missiles from Cuba if the US will also withdraw their missiles from Turkey.

• **27 Oct:** Kennedy insists that work on Cuban missile bases must stop before negotiations begin.

• **28 Oct:** Khrushchev announces that the Cuban missiles are to be withdrawn.

• **30 Oct:** The UN General Assembly rejects a Soviet proposal to admit Communist China.

• **6 Nov:** The UN General Assembly condemns South Africa for its apartheid policy and recommends member states to take economic sanctions.

• **14 Nov:** Eritrea votes to become a province of Ethiopia.

• **21 Nov:** The Chinese halt their advance into India.

• **30 Nov:** The Burmese delegate U Thant is elected UN secretary general.

• **9 Dec:** Tanzania becomes independent within the Commonwealth.

• **19–21 Dec:** President Kennedy agrees to supply Britain with Polaris nuclear missiles.

CULTURE

• US singer Bob Dylan records *Blowin' in the Wind*.

• Silicone breast implants are developed by the Dow Corning Corp. Midland, Mich.

• British pop group The Beatles makes its first single, *Love Me Do*.

• The first tab-opening all-aluminum beer can is test-marketed in Virginia by Iron City Beer, Pittsburgh, Pennsylvania.

• British artists Peter Blake and David Hockney, and New York artist Andy Warhol, create Pop Art, a movement based on images from the graphic arts.

• In his book *The Gutenberg Galaxy*, US author Marshall McLuhan coins the term "global village".

• **30 May:** The "King of Swing" Benny Goodman plays a concert in Moscow.

• **10 Jul:** The communications satellite, Telstar, allows transmission of TV images across the Atlantic.

• **5 Aug:** Film star Marilyn Monroe is found dead in Los Angeles following a drug overdose.

• **29 Nov:** The UK minister for aviation and the French ambassador to Britain sign the *Concorde* agreement in London to cooperate to build the world's first supersonic airliner.

ASSASSINATION OF A PRESIDENT

Martin Luther King declares "I have a dream..."

POLITICS

• **14 JAN:** President de Gaulle of France publicly objects to Britain's attempt to enter the European Common Market.

• **15 JAN:** In the Congo Republic, Moise Tshombe of Katanga finally accepts a UN plan ending secession.

• **22 JAN:** France and Germany sign a treaty of cooperation.

• **8 FEB:** Premier Abdul Kassem Karim is assassinated in a military coup in Iraq; Col. Abdas Saläm Arif succeeds.

• **14 FEB:** Harold Wilson takes over the leadership of the British Labor party after the death of Hugh Gaitskell.

• **8 MAR:** The Syrian government is overthrown by a third military coup.

• **8 APR:** The Liberals win a general election in Canada. (Lester B. Pearson forms a ministry on 17 Apr).

• **12 APR:** Martin Luther King is arrested for leading a civil rights march in the southern US state of Alabama.

Robert, Jacqueline and Edward Kennedy at the state funeral of JFK in Washington, D.C.

• **MAY:** The South Vietnamese government led by Ngo Dinh Diem begins a systematic persecution of Buddhists.

• **11 MAY:** In the USSR, Greville Wynne, a British businessman, is implicated in the trial of Soviet intelligence officer Oleg Penkovsky and is sentenced to eight years for espionage.

• **18 MAY:** Federal troops are sent in by President Kennedy to quell race riots in Alabama.

• **22–26 MAY:** A conference of African heads of state at Addis Ababa spawns the Organization for African Unity (OAU).

• **5 JUN:** In Britain, cabinet minister

John Profumo resigns after a scandal links his name to model Christine Keeler.

• **11 Jun:** In Greece, the opposition party led by George Papandreou questions the legitimacy of the 1961 election. Prime minister Constantine Karamanlis resigns.

• **26 Jun:** US president Kennedy visits West Berlin and makes his famous anti-communist speech declaring *"Ich bin ein Berliner"*.

• **5 Aug:** USA, USSR and Britain sign a nuclear test ban treaty.

• **28 Aug:** Large-scale civil rights demonstrations take place in Washington, D.C. Martin Luther King proclaims: "I have a dream...that all men are created equal."

• **1 Oct:** Nigeria becomes an independent republic.

• **10 Oct:** Harold Macmillan resigns as British prime minister following a report censuring the government's handling of the Profumo affair. He is succeeded by Sir Alec Douglas-Home.

• **15 Oct:** In West Germany, chancellor Konrad Adenauer resigns and is succeeded by Dr. Ludwig Erhard.

• **1–2 Nov:** Ngo Dinh Diem, leader of South Vietnam is killed in a US-supported military coup.

• **22 Nov:** US president John F. Kennedy is assassinated during a visit to Dallas, Texas. Lyndon B. Johnson is sworn in as the next president.

• **12 Dec:** Kenya wins independence.

CULTURE

• The new Beatles' single *I want to hold your hand* sells a million copies pre-release.

• Carbon fiber is developed in the UK.

• The hologram is developed by Emmett Leith and Julius Upatnicks at the University of Michigan.

• Friction welding is invented in the Soviet Union.

• Color Polaroid film is introduced by the Polaroid Corporation, Boston.

• **Jan–Feb:** The *Mona Lisa* is seen by nearly two million people at exhibitions in Washington, D.C. and New York city.

• **Jan:** *Whisky-à-Go-Go,* the world's first discotheque, opens in Los Angeles.

• **3 Jun:** Pope John XXXIII dies and is succeeded by Paul VI.

• **16 Jun:** The world's first female astronaut, Valentina Tereshkova (USSR), is launched into space.

• **10 Sept:** The American Express charge card is launched in Britain.

CIVIL RIGHTS IN THE US

African states continue to establish independent governments

POLITICS

• **13–17 JAN:** The Arab League countries decide to set up a unified military command.

• **6 FEB:** The British and French governments agree to build a Channel Tunnel.

• **11 MAR:** The US and British embassies in Phnom Penh, Cambodia, are attacked.

• **APR:** A UN peacekeeping force arrives in Cyprus to quell fighting between Greek and Turkish Cypriots.

• **13 APR:** Ian Smith becomes prime minister of Southern Rhodesia.

• **27 APR:** Zanzibar merges with Tanganyika to form the Republic of Tanganyika and Zanzibar (renamed Tanzania on 29 Oct).

• **4 MAY:** The "Kennedy round" of GATT talks begins.

• **27 MAY:** Indian prime minister Jawaharlal Nehru dies.

The Beatles land in London after their US tour.

• **JUN:** The Palestinian Liberation Organization (PLO) is set up in Jerusalem.

• **11 JUN:** In South Africa, Nelson Mandela and seven other members of the African National Congress receive life sentences for sabotage.

• **26 JUN:** Moise Tshombe, leader of the Katangan province, is recalled from exile to join the Congolese government.

• **2 JUL:** President Johnson signs the US Civil Rights Act (equal rights to blacks).

• **6 JUL:** Nyasaland becomes independent as Malawi, with Dr. Hastings Banda as prime minister.

• **2–3 AUG:** US Navy ships are attacked off the North Vietnamese coast.

• **7 Aug:** US Congress gives President Johnson authority to commit large forces to US intervention in Vietnam.

• **3 Sept:** A state of emergency is declared in Malaysia after a series of warlike acts by Indonesia.

• **21 Sept:** Malta becomes an independent state within the Commonwealth.

• **5 Oct:** 57 people escape from East Berlin by crawling through a tunnel.

• **15 Oct:** In the Soviet Union, Nikita Khrushchev is replaced by Leonid Brezhnev as Communist party leader, and by Aleksey Kosygin as premier.

• **15 Oct:** The British general election brings the Labor party to power for the first time in 13 years, with Harold Wilson as prime minister.

• **24 Oct:** Northern Rhodesia becomes independent as Zambia, with Kenneth Kaunda as president.

• **25 Oct:** Harold Wilson warns Southern Rhodesia that a unilateral declaration of independence would lead to economic sanctions.

• **Nov:** The Vietcong launch a major attack on a US base at Bien Hoa.

• **2 Nov:** King Saud of Saudi Arabia is deposed and Prince Faisal becomes king.

• **3 Nov:** Democrat Lyndon B. Johnson wins a sweeping victory in the US presidential elections.

• **21 Dec:** The British House of Commons votes to abolish the death penalty for murder.

CULTURE

• Mary Quant, fashion designer, and Vidal Sassoon, hairdresser, set up shops in the London of the "swinging sixties".

• Astronomers Arno Penzias and R.W. Wilson detect "cosmic background radiation", providing decisive evidence of the "Big Bang" origin of the Universe.

• G.I. Joe (later called Action Man) goes on sale in the US

• **8 Feb:** British pop idols the Beatles receive a rapturous reception on their first visit to New York.

• **25 Feb:** Boxer Cassius Clay becomes heavyweight champion of the world and changes his name to Muhammad Ali.

• **24 Aug:** The first Catholic mass is said in English (rather than Latin).

• **Oct:** French writer and philosopher Jean-Paul Sartre refuses the Nobel Prize for Literature.

• **21 Nov:** The Verrazano Narrows suspension bridge over New York harbor is officially opened. It becomes the longest suspension bridge in the world.

WAR IN VIETNAM

Space technology leaps forward and high-speed trains go into service

POLITICS

• **2 Jan:** Indonesia withdraws from the United Nations.

• **24 Jan:** Former British prime minister Winston Churchill dies aged 91.

• **7 Feb:** After Vietcong attacks on US areas in South Vietnam, US aircraft begin bombing raids on North Vietnam.

• **18 Feb:** Gambia becomes an independent state within the Commonwealth of Nations.

• **21 Feb:** Malcolm X, the founder of the US pro-violence Black Nationalist group, is assassinated.

• **19 Mar:** Nicolae Ceaucescu becomes first secretary of the Romanian Communist party.

• **31 Mar:** US president Johnson sends 3,500 troops to North Vietnam following a bomb attack that wrecks the US embassy in Saigon.

• **9 Apr:** Indian and Pakistani troops clash on the Kutch-Sind border.

US marines on combat duty in Vietnam.

• **29 Apr:** President de Gaulle of France condemns foreign intervention in Vietnam. Australia announces that troops are to be sent to South Vietnam.

• **30 Apr:** A military junta seizes power in the Dominican Republic; the US sends in troops to protect its citizens.

• **7 May:** In Southern Rhodesia, Ian Smith's pro-white Rhodesian Front Party wins a sweeping victory.

• **12 May:** West Germany establishes diplomatic relations with Israel; 10 Arab states break off relations in response.

• **19 Jun:** Algerian president Ahmed Ben Bella is deposed in a bloodless coup. Col. Houari Boumédienne takes over.

• **28 Jul:** President Johnson announces the deployment of another 50,000 troops in Vietnam. The US is on the offensive.

• **11–16 Aug:** Race riots in the Watts district of Los Angeles, California, leave 34 dead and over 800 injured.

• **6 Sept:** India launches a full-scale invasion of Pakistan.

• **20 Sept:** The US House of Representatives approves the use of force to resist communism.

• **15–18 Oct:** Demonstrations against the war in Vietnam are held in the US and London.

• **11 Nov:** Ian Smith, prime minister of Southern Rhodesia, makes a Unilateral Declaration of Independence. Britain declares the regime illegal and imposes economic sanctions.

• **25 Nov:** In the Congo Republic, Gen. Mobotu imposes five years' army rule.

• **5 Dec:** In the French presidential elections, Gen. de Gaulle narrowly beats his socialist rival François Mitterrand on the second ballot.

• **9 Dec:** Nikolai Podgorny replaces Anastas Mikoyan as president of USSR.

• **18 Dec:** Nine African states break off diplomatic relations with Britain for not using force against Rhodesia.

CULTURE

• Miniskirts become popular.

• The millionth Mini car is produced in the UK.

• **8 Feb:** Cigarette advertising is banned from commercial television in Britain.

• **18 Mar:** Soviet cosmonaut Aleksey Leonov makes the first "space walk," leaving *Voskhod II* for 20 minutes.

• **2 May:** The world's first commercial communications satellite, Early Bird, is launched linking the US, Canada, UK and Europe.

• **3 Jun:** US astronaut Edward White leaves *Gemini 4* for a 20-minute walk in space.

• **15 Jul:** US spaceprobe *Mariner 4* sends back the first detailed photographs of Mars.

• **21–29 Aug:** *Gemini 5* with Gordon Cooper and Charles Conrad jr. aboard makes 120 orbits of the Earth.

• **1 Nov:** In Japan, the high-speed train begins a scheduled service from Tokyo to Osaka (321 mi [516 km] in 3hr 10 min).

• **26 Nov:** France launches its first satellite.

• **15 Dec:** *Gemini 7* makes a rendezvous with *Gemini 6* in orbit around the Earth.

HAPPENINGS AND FLOWER POWER

Mao Zedong's Red Guards purge "bourgeois reactionary thinking"

POLITICS

• **1 JAN:** Pope Paul VI appeals for peace in Vietnam.

• **1 JAN:** In Central African Republic, Col. Jean-Bedel Bokassa seizes power.

• **8 JAN:** US troops launch a major offensive against the "Iron Triangle," a Viet Cong stronghold near Saigon.

• **11 JAN:** India's prime minister Lal Bahadur Shastri dies. Mrs. Indira Gandhi comes to power.

• **15 JAN:** The Nigerian army led by Gen. Ironsi seizes control of the country.

• **20 JAN:** Australian prime minister Robert Menzies retires after 17 years in office; Harold Holt succeeds.

• **1 FEB:** China protests to Britain about US warships in Hong Kong.

• **7–8 FEB:** US president Johnson meets South Vietnamese leaders in Honolulu.

• **21 FEB:** President de Gaulle of France calls for NATO to be dismantled.

Twiggy, the face of the decade.

• **22 FEB:** Milton Obote, prime minister of Uganda, seizes power and two days later suspends the constitution.

• **24 FEB:** In Ghana, President Kwame Nkrumah's government is overthrown while he is on an official visit to China.

• **8 MAR:** Australia announces that it will triple its forces in Vietnam.

• **10 MAR:** France requests removal of NATO bases from French territory.

• **11 MAR:** President Sukarno of Indonesia is stripped of office and army commander Gen. Suharto takes power.

• **3 MAY:** The US admits shelling Cambodia.

- **26 Jun:** A major civil rights rally is held in Jackson, Mississippi.

- **29 Jun:** US bombers attack the North Vietnamese cities Hanoi and Haiphong. The UK government disassociates itself from the bombing of populated areas.

- **1 Jul:** France withdraws from NATO.

- **1 Aug:** Col. Yakubu Gowon seizes power in another Nigerian coup.

- **11 Aug:** Indonesia and Malaysia end three years of undeclared war.

- **13 Aug:** Cultural revolution begins in China with a mass rally in Peking.

- **6 Sept:** South African prime minister Hendrik Verwoerd is assassinated. He is succeeded by B. J. Vorster.

- **30 Sept:** Bechuanaland becomes independent as Botswana.

- **4 Oct:** Basutoland becomes independent as Lesotho.

- **5 Oct:** Spain closes the land frontier with Gibraltar (except for pedestrians).

- **24–25 Oct:** Australia, New Zealand, the Philippines, Thailand, South Korea and South Vietnam pledge aid and political self-determination to South Vietnam at the Manila Conference.

- **13 Nov:** Israeli forces attack the Hebron area of Jordan.

- **22 Nov:** In Spain, Gen. Franco introduces a new constitution.

- **30 Nov:** Barbados becomes an independent state within the Commonwealth.

- **22 Dec:** Southern Rhodesia is declared a republic.

CULTURE

- Ultra-thin model Twiggy (Lesley Hornby) launches her career.

- Australia adopts decimal currency.

- Barclaycard becomes Britain's first credit card.

- The TV science fiction serial *Star Trek* begins in the US.

- The Beatles record *Eleanor Rigby* and *Day Tripper* and give their last concert at Candlestick Park, San Francisco.

- **3 Feb:** The unmanned Soviet spacecraft *Luna 9* makes the first soft landing on the Moon.

- **16 Mar:** US *Gemini 8* carries out the first docking operation in space.

- **21 Oct:** A slag heap at Aberfan, South Wales, slips and engulfs a school killing 116 children and 28 adults.

- **Nov:** Severe floods in northern Italy put two-thirds of Florence under water and damage many works of art.

THE SIX-DAY WAR

General de Gaulle encourages French separatism in Quebec

POLITICS

• **JAN:** In China, the People's Liberation Army is mobilized to support worker-peasants against the Red Guards.

• **27 JAN:** A UN treaty limiting the use of outer space for military purposes is signed by 62 nations including the USSR and USA.

• **26 FEB:** In Vietnam, US and South Vietnamese forces launch Operation Junction City, the biggest offensive so far.

• **28 MAR:** U Thant, Secretary General of the UN, proposes a Vietnam peace plan which is accepted by the US but rejected by North Vietnam.

• **1 APR:** A new constitution comes into effect in South Vietnam.

• **15 APR:** Large-scale protests against the Vietnam War take place in New York and San Francisco.

• **21 APR:** A military coup in Greece imposes the regime of "Greek Colonels."

• **27 APR–29 OCT:** "Expo '67" in

Israeli troops advance into battle.

Canada marks the centenary of Canadian confederation.

• **18 MAY:** The UN withdraws its peacekeeping force from the Israeli border at the request of the UAR.

• **22 MAY:** The UAR closes the Gulf of Aqaba to Israeli shipping.

• **30 MAY:** The Ibo region of Nigeria secedes as Biafra under Col. Odumegwu Ojukwu, starting a civil war.

• **5 JUN:** The Six-Day War breaks out between Israel and the Arab states. Preemptive strikes by Israel cripple the Arab air forces.

• **6–7 JUN:** Israeli troops advance

taking control of the Gaza Strip, Jericho and the West Bank.

• **10 Jun:** The UAR and its allies accept a ceasefire.

• **18 Jul:** Britain announces a drastic reduction in its forces east of Suez.

• **24 Jul:** President de Gaulle, on a visit to Montreal angers the Canadian government by shouting *"Vive le Québec libre"* ("Long live free Quebec").

• **27 Jul:** Paratroopers have to be brought in to restore order as race riots flare in Detroit, Michigan.

• **8 Aug:** ASEAN (Association of Southeast Asian Nations) is established by Thailand, Indonesia, Singapore, the Philippines and Malaysia.

• **11 Aug:** US planes intensify attacks on North Vietnam, bombing within 10 miles of the Chinese border.

• **11–14 Sept:** Border clashes erupt between Chinese and Indian troops on Tibet-Sikkim border.

• **9 Oct:** The Revolutionary guerrilla Che Guevara, former confidant of Fidel Castro, is executed by the Bolivian army.

• **21 Oct:** The Israeli destroyer *Eilat* is sunk by the Egyptian navy.

• **24 Oct:** Israeli artillery destroys Suez oil refineries.

• **7 Dec:** Nicolae Ceaucescu becomes Romanian head of state.

• **17 Dec:** Australian prime minister Harold Holt dies in an accident.

CULTURE

• "Flower power" rallies for love and peace dominate the US and Europe.

• **4 Jan:** In Britain, Donald Campbell dies attempting to break the world water speed record in his boat *Bluebird*.

• **6 Jan:** The Angostura bridge opens over the Orinoco river.

• **27 Jan:** Three US astronauts die in a fire in an *Apollo* spacecraft during tests at Cape Kennedy.

• **18 Mar:** The Liberian tanker *Torrey Canyon* runs aground off Land's End, UK creating an enormous oil slick.

• **18 Jun:** In US, the first large pop festival is held at Monterey, featuring Jimi Hendrix, Janis Joplin and the Who.

• **Oct:** In Britain, breathalyzer tests are introduced for drivers to determine how much alcohol they have consumed.

• **18 Oct:** The Soviet spaceprobe *Venera 4* softlands on Venus.

• **3 Dec:** In South Africa, the world's first heart transplant is performed by Christiaan Barnard on Louis Washkansky (who dies on 21 Dec).

RIOTS AND REVOLUTION

Alexander Dubcek introduces "Communism with a human face"

POLITICS

• **4 JAN:** The number of US troops in South Vietnam reaches 486,000.

• **9 JAN:** John Grey Gorton becomes prime minister of Australia.

• **21 JAN:** North Korean raiders invade Seoul and attempt to kill the South Korean president Pak Chung Hee.

• **31 JAN:** In Vietnam, the Vietcong launch the Tet (New Year) offensive.

• **16 MAR:** US troops massacre the hamlet of My Lai, South Vietnam.

• **17 MAR:** Demonstrators against the Vietnam War attempt to storm the American embassy in London.

• **4 APR:** Martin Luther King is shot dead in Memphis, Tennessee, triggering violence in cities throughout the US.

• **5 APR:** Czech premier Alexander Dubcek begins the process of liberalization known as the "Prague Spring".

• **6 APR:** Pierre Elliott Trudeau becomes prime minister of Canada.

Student riot in Paris during May.

• **11 APR:** In West Berlin, the attempted assassination of student leader, Rudi Dutschke triggers student riots across Europe.

• **MAY:** In France, up to 30,000 students fight with police in the streets of Paris. The rioting students are supported by workers throughout the country who strike and occupy factories.

• **13 MAY:** The US and North Vietnam begin peace talks in Paris.

• **5 JUN:** Robert Kennedy is shot in Los Angeles after winning the California primary election. (He dies the next day.)

• **11 JUN:** West Germans need to apply for visas to cross to East Germany.

• **12 Jun:** The French government bans open-air demonstrations.

• **27 Jun:** The Czechoslovak National Assembly abolishes censorship and Czech intellectuals produce "2,000 words": an appeal to speed democracy.

• **1 Jul:** 61 nations, including Britain, the US and USSR sign a nuclear non-proliferation treaty.

• **15 Jul:** Soviet, East German, Hungarian, Polish and Bulgarian leaders declare Czechoslovakian reforms unacceptable.

• **30 Jul:** Dubcek, Brezhnev and other Eastern Bloc leaders meet to discuss the Czechoslovakian reforms.

• **15 Aug:** Nigeria refuses to allow International Red Cross supplies to be flown in to starving Biafrans.

• **20–21 Aug:** Soviet and allied forces invade Czechoslovakia to restore strict communism. Government leaders are arrested.

• **6 Sept:** The former British colony of Swaziland becomes independent.

• **12 Sept:** Albania abandons the Warsaw Pact.

• **4 Oct:** Czechoslovak leaders accede to Soviet demands to dismantle liberal reforms.

• **31 Oct:** President Johnson halts bombing of North Vietnam.

• **5 Nov:** Republican Richard Nixon is elected 37th US president.

CULTURE

• Calvin Klein starts his own fashion business in the US.

• In Britain, the Beatles form the Apple Corporation including shops, a film company and a recording company.

• In Britain, sextuplets are born after the mother receives new fertility drugs.

• After the effects of the drug thalidomide are discovered, a regulatory body, the Committee on Safety of Medicines, is established.

• **Apr:** Abortion becomes lawful in Britain if the pregnancy is harmful to the physical or mental health of the woman or child.

• **29 Jul:** Pope Paul VI issues the encyclical *Humanae Vitae* denouncing the use of artificial contraception.

• **24 Aug:** France explodes its first hydrogen bomb in the South Pacific.

• **27 Sept:** The musical *Hair* opens on the London stage.

• **21 Dec:** US astronauts J. A. Lovell, W. Anders and F. Borman complete the first flight around the Moon in *Apollo 8*.

A GIANT LEAP FOR MANKIND

British troops are sent to quell riots in Northern Ireland

Apollo 11's *Buzz Aldrin walks on the moon.*

POLITICS

• **16 JAN:** Czech student Jan Palach burns himself to death in protest at the Soviet occupation of his country.

• **18 JAN:** South Vietnamese and National Liberation Front delegations join the Paris peace talks.

• **20 JAN:** Richard Nixon is inaugurated the 37th US president.

• **3 FEB:** Yassir Arafat is elected chairman of the Palestine Liberation Organization (PLO).

• **18 FEB:** An Israeli airliner is attacked by Arab terrorists at Zurich airport.

• **2 MAR:** Chinese and Soviet troops clash on the Ussuri river border.

• **7 MAR:** Golda Meir becomes prime minister of Israel.

• **17 APR:** Alexander Dubcek is replaced as Czech leader by Gustav Husak.

• **28 APR:** After defeat in a referendum on regional reforms, Gen. de Gaulle resigns as French president.

• **JUN:** Fears grow of mass starvation in the breakaway Nigerian province of Biafra, following a government ban on Red Cross relief flights.

• **15 JUN:** Georges Pompidou is elected president of France.

• **8 JUL:** The US embarks on a policy of "Vietnamization" of the war and a gradual withdrawal of US troops.

• **19 JUL:** Mary Jo Kopechne is drowned in a car accident involving Senator Edward Kennedy at Chappaquiddick Island, Massachusetts.

• **23 JUL:** Prince Juan Carlos is selected to succeed as head of state in Spain on the retirement of General Franco.

• **12 AUG:** Protestant–Catholic unrest

breaks out in Northern Ireland. The British government takes responsibility for security in Ulster.

• **13 Aug:** Soviet troops cross the border into Xinjiang province, China.

• **1 Sept:** Following a military coup, Muammar Qadhafi become head of the new Socialist Libyan Arab Republic.

• **16 Sept:** US president Nixon announces the withdrawal of another 35,000 troops from Vietnam.

• **3 Oct:** The Greek government restores civil liberties.

• **11 Oct:** Fresh rioting breaks out in Belfast, and the British government sends in more troops the next day.

• **15 Oct:** Massive anti-war protests take place in Washington D.C.

• **21 Oct:** Social Democrat Willy Brandt becomes chancellor of West Germany.

• **17 Nov:** The US and USSR begin strategic arms limitation talks (SALT) in Helsinki. A nuclear nonproliferation treaty is ratified 24 Nov.

• **24 Nov:** The US Army announces William Calley will be court martialed for the My Lai massacre in May 1968.

• **25 Nov:** The US agrees to destroy all stocks of germ warfare weapons.

CULTURE

• The Bulgarian artist Christo completes *Wrapped Coast*, an Australian island covered in plastic sheeting and rope.

• Australian tennis star Rod Laver wins his second grand slam in the year that he wins the Wimbledon men's singles title for the fourth time.

• The United States and Canada both ban the use of the insecticide DDT.

• **9 Feb:** The Boeing 747 jumbo jet has its maiden flight.

• **13 Feb:** Scientists in Cambridge, UK, announce the first successful *in vitro* fertilization of a human embryo.

• **Mar:** Beatle John Lennon and his wife Yoko Ono stage a "love-in" for world peace in the Hilton Hotel, Amsterdam.

• **2 Mar:** Concorde's maiden flight from Toulouse, France.

• **20 Jul:** The *Apollo 11* spacecraft lands on the Moon.

• **Aug:** Some 400,000 rock fans attend the festival of music held at Woodstock, New York state.

• **9 Aug:** In Los Angeles, cult leader Charles Manson kills actress Sharon Tate and four others.

• **14 Nov:** *Apollo 12* takes Charles Conrad and Al Bean to the Moon.

US TROOPS ENTER CAMBODIA

Student anti-war protestors are shot dead in the United States

POLITICS

• **12 Jan:** Biafran leader, Gen. Ojukwu flees to the Ivory Coast and Biafra surrenders unconditionally to Nigeria.

• **16 Jan:** Col. Muammar Qadhafi becomes premier of Libya.

• **12 Feb:** An Israeli air raid on Cairo kills 70 civilians.

• **23 Feb:** Guyana becomes a republic within the Commonwealth.

• **2 Mar:** Rhodesia declares itself a republic, dissolving ties with Britain.

• **11 Mar:** Iraq recognizes Kurdish autonomy ending nine years' war.

• **18 Mar:** Prince Sihanouk of Cambodia is ousted in a military coup led by right wing, pro-US Lon Nol.

• **19 Mar:** First-ever meeting of East and West German heads of government (Willi Stoph and Willy Brandt) at Erfurt, East Germany.

• **21 Mar:** In Czechoslovakia, Dubcek is expelled from the Communist party.

Margaret Court (Australia) wins Wimbledon.

• **2 Apr:** Israeli and Syrian troops fight their worst battle since the Six-Day War.

• **16 Apr:** Clifford Dupont becomes first president of the Republic of Rhodesia.

• **19 Apr:** Communist forces advance toward Phnom Penh in Cambodia. Cambodian premier Lon Nol appeals to the United States for assistance.

• **30 Apr:** US and Vietnamese troops attack Communist areas in Cambodia.

• **4 May:** Four students at Kent State University in Ohio are shot dead by troops while taking part in an anti-war demonstration.

• **18 Jun:** In Britain, the Conservatives unexpectedly win a general election; Edward Heath becomes prime minister.

• **25 Jun:** The US presents a new peace plan for Middle East. Egypt, Jordan and Israel accept over the next few months.

• **16 Jul:** In Britain, a state of emergency is declared as dockers (longshoremen) call a national strike over their wages.

• **7 Aug:** A 90-day truce begins between Israel, Egypt and Jordan (renewed 5 Nov for a further 90 days).

• **4 Sept:** Socialist Salvador Allende becomes president of Chile and the world's first elected Marxist leader.

• **6 Sept:** Palestinian guerrillas hijack four passenger aircraft and obtain the release of Palestinians held in Israel, Switzerland, West Germany and Britain.

• **16 Sept:** King Hussein of Jordan proclaims martial law but fighting between the army and Palestinian guerrillas escalates into civil war.

• **27 Sept:** King Hussein and Yassir Arafat sign a ceasefire.

• **28 Sept:** President Nasser of Egypt dies of a heart attack; he is succeeded by Anwar Sadat.

• **9 Oct:** Cambodia declares itself to be the Khmer Republic.

• **10 Oct:** Fiji becomes independent within the Commonwealth of Nations.

• **10 Oct:** In Canada, Quebec minister of labor, Pierre Laporte, is kidnapped by the *Front de Libération du Québec* and is found murdered 7 days later.

• **8 Nov:** Egypt, Libya and Sudan agree to federate; joined by Syria on 27 Nov.

• **8 Dec:** In Pakistan, the first free elections since 1948 result in victory in West Pakistan for Bhutto's People's party and in East Pakistan for the pro-independence Awami League.

CULTURE

• Robert Altman's movie *M.A.S.H.* examines attitudes to the Vietnam war.

• In US and UK, discrimination on grounds of sex becomes illegal.

• **22 Jan:** The first "jumbo jet", the Boeing 747, enters transatlantic service.

• **9 Apr:** Paul McCartney issues a high court writ against the other Beatles.

• **24 Apr:** China launches its first satellite.

• **7 Jun:** The Who perform their rock opera *Tommy* at New York's Metropolitan Opera House.

• **4 Jul:** Australian tennis player Margaret Court wins the Wimbledon Ladies' Singles title.

• **18 Sept:** US rock singer Jimi Hendrix dies of a drugs overdose, aged 27.

CIVIL WAR IN PAKISTAN

A military coup in Uganda is followed by a reign of terror

POLITICS

• **5 Jan:** Israel, Egypt and Jordan resume indirect peace talks with UN mediator Gunnar Jarring.

• **25 Jan:** In Uganda, army officers led by Major-Gen. Idi Amin oust president Milton Obote in a military coup.

• **10 Mar:** In Northern Ireland, three off-duty British soldiers are murdered.

• **10 Mar:** William MacMahon replaces John Gorton as Australian premier.

• **12 Mar:** In Turkey, a bloodless military coup leads to the resignation of premier Suleyman Demirel.

• **23 Mar:** Brian Faulkner replaces Major Chichester Clark as prime minister of Northern Ireland.

• **26 Mar:** Civil war erupts in Pakistan; the Awami League declares autonomy for East Pakistan (as Bangladesh).

• **7 Apr:** US president Nixon announces the withdrawal of 100,000 troops from Vietnam by December.

Idi Amin takes the oath of office, 5 Feb.

• **19 Apr:** Sierra Leone becomes a republic within the Commonwealth.

• **21 Apr:** In Haiti, François (Papa Doc) Duvalier dies and is succeeded by his son, Jean-Claude, aged 19 and known as "Baby Doc".

• **23 Apr:** Anti-Vietnam war protests take place in Washington D.C.

• **May:** Several million refugees flee into India to escape the war in Pakistan.

• **27 May:** Egypt and the USSR sign a 15-year treaty of friendship.

• **9 Jul:** In Londonderry, Northern Ireland, two civilians are shot dead by British troops. The British government refuses to hold an inquiry.

• **13 Jul:** The Jordanian army begins a campaign to remove Palestinian guerrillas from bases in north Jordan. Iraq and Syria close borders with Jordan in protest.

• **11 Aug:** In Northern Ireland, 300 suspected terrorists are arrested and interned provoking rioting.

• **18 Aug:** New Zealand and Australia announce the withdrawal of combat forces from Vietnam by December.

• **24 Sept:** Britain expels 90 Russian diplomats for alleged spying.

• **25 Oct:** The UN General Assembly votes to admit Communist China and expel Taiwan.

• **27 Oct:** The Republic of Congo changes its name to Zaire.

• **12 Nov:** President Nixon proclaims the end of the US offensive in Vietnam and announces the withdrawal of 45,000 troops by Feb 1972.

• **24 Nov:** Britain signs a draft agreement on Rhodesian independence.

• **28 Nov:** Palestinian guerrillas assassinate the Jordanian prime minister. King Hussein rules out further talks.

• **3 Dec:** After numerous border clashes, India sends troops into Pakistan in support of Bangladesh.

• **6 Dec:** India recognizes the independence of Bangladesh.

• **17 Dec:** Pakistan surrenders after two week-war with India.

• **20 Dec:** Zulfikar Ali Bhutto becomes president of Pakistan.

• **22 Dec:** Mujibur Rahman becomes president of Bangladesh.

• **31 Dec:** Kurt Waldheim becomes UN secretary-general.

CULTURE

• "Hot pants" become the latest fashion craze in the US and UK.

• Disney World opens in Orlando, Florida.

• In the US, Texas Instruments introduces the first pocket calculator.

• Britain passes legislation restricting Commonwealth immigration.

• **Jan:** In Britain, divorce is permitted by consent after two-year separation.

• **5 Feb:** US spacecraft *Apollo 14* lands on the Moon; two moonwalks are made and samples collected.

• **19 Apr:** USSR launches the *Salyut 1* space station.

• **Nov:** US space probe *Mariner 9* orbits Mars and transmits numerous photographs of the planet.

NIXON RIDES HIGH

Arab guerrillas strike at the Olympic Games

POLITICS

• **9 JAN:** In Britain, a national coal strike begins which leads to large-scale power cuts.

• **22 JAN:** Britain, Ireland and Denmark sign the treaty of accession to the EEC – membership to commence from 1 Jan 1973.

• **30 JAN:** "Bloody Sunday" in Londonderry, Northern Ireland, 13 civilians are killed by British troops during riots against internment.

• **30 JAN:** Pakistan withdraws from the Commonwealth in protest against the imminent recognition of Bangladesh by Britain, Australia and New Zealand.

• **2 FEB:** Anti-British demonstrators in the Irish Republic burn down the British Embassy in Dublin.

• **7 FEB:** In New Zealand, Sir Keith Holyoake retires as prime minister; succeeded by John Marshall.

• **21–28 FEB:** Nixon visits Beijing, the first visit of a US president to China.

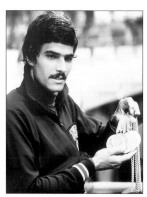

Swimmer Mark Spitz wins gold for the US.

• **13 MAR:** Britain resumes relations with China after a 22-year break.

• **30 MAR:** Britain imposes direct rule on Northern Ireland with William Whitelaw as secretary of state.

• **15 APR:** The North Vietnamese launch a new offensive and the US carries out bombing raids on Haiphong.

• **22 MAY:** Nixon becomes first United States president to visit the USSR.

• **22 MAY:** Ceylon becomes the independent republic of Sri Lanka within the Commonwealth.

• **26 MAY:** Soviet premier Brezhnev and US president Nixon sign a treaty limiting strategic arms.

• **1–15 JUN:** In West Germany, police arrest the Baader-Meinhof urban guerrilla group.

• **17 JUN:** In the US, five intruders are arrested while trying to install eaves-dropping equipment in the Democratic National Committee's HQ in Washington – the Watergate break-in.

• **21 JUL:** In Northern Ireland, 22 bombs explode in Belfast, killing 13 people and injuring 130.

• **6 AUG:** Ugandan military dictator Idi Amin gives Asians of non-Ugandan citizenship 90 days to leave Uganda. Many attempt to flee to Britain.

• **11 AUG:** The last American combat unit is withdrawn from South Vietnam. In North Vietnam, US air raids continue against the Communist offensive.

• **5 SEPT:** Arab terrorists murder 11 Israeli athletes in the Olympic village near Munich, West Germany.

• **29 SEPT:** Japan and China agree to end the state of war existing since 1937.

• **3 OCT:** The US and USSR sign final SALT accords limiting their armory of nuclear missiles.

• **29 OCT:** Arab terrorists hijack a Lufthansa flight and secure the release of three Palestinians being held in West Germany for the Olympic massacre.

• **6 NOV:** The British government imposes a 90-day freeze on wages, prices and rents in a bid to curb inflation.

• **7 NOV:** Richard Nixon is reelected US president by a huge majority.

• **25 NOV:** Norman Kirk becomes prime minister of New Zealand after the Labor party wins a sweeping victory.

• **2 DEC:** Gough Whitlam becomes Australian prime minister after the Australian Labor party wins the general election.

CULTURE

• In Britain, women are allowed to compete as professional racehorse jockeys.

• American artist Carl André's collection of prefabricated bricks is bought by the Tate Gallery in London provoking a storm of protest.

• **JUL:** Launch of *Landsat I,* the first Earth resources technology satellite.

• **26 AUG:** US swimmer Mark Spitz wins a record seven Olympic gold medals.

• **1 SEPT:** Bobby Fischer becomes the first US world chess champion beating Boris Spassky of the USSR.

• **7 DEC:** *Apollo 17* is launched, the last spacecraft of that series.

EGYPT AND ISRAEL AT WAR

The Arabs cut oil supplies to the United States

POLITICS

• **9 JAN:** Southern Rhodesia closes its border with Zambia after terrorist attacks.

• **17 JAN:** President Marcos proclaims a new constitution in the Philippines under which he rules indefinitely.

• **27 JAN:** The US, North and South Vietnam and the Vietcong sign an agreement to end the Vietnam war.

• **21 FEB:** Israeli fighter planes shoot down a Libyan Boeing 727 over Sinai.

• **21 FEB:** A ceasefire between the government and the Pathet Lao ends 20 years of war in Laos.

• **27 FEB–8 MAY:** In the US, American Indians occupy Wounded Knee, South Dakota, demanding an investigation of the federal treatment of Indians.

• **2 MAR:** Palestinian terrorists murder the US ambassador to Sudan.

• **8 MAR:** In a Northern Ireland referendum, voters choose to remain in the UK, but only 59% of citizens vote.

Egypt attacks Israel to start the Yom Kippur war.

• **11 MAR:** The Peronista candidate Hector J. Campora wins the Argentinian presidential campaign. He later resigns to make way for Juan Perón.

• **29 MAR:** The last US troops leave Vietnam.

• **6 APR:** The finance ministers of the EEC countries establish a European fund for monetary cooperation.

• **10 APR:** In Lebanon, Israeli commandos land in Beirut and kill three Palestinian guerrilla leaders.

• **30 APR:** In the US, President Nixon accepts responsibility for bugging the Watergate building but denies personal involvement.

• **24 JUN:** Soviet premier Brezhnev attends a summit conference in the US.

• **21 Jul:** France begins a series of nuclear tests at Mururoa Atoll despite protests from Australia and New Zealand.

• **31 Jul:** The first session of the new Northern Ireland legislature ends in uproar when militant Protestants disrupt the proceedings.

• **6 Aug:** US bombers accidentally bomb a friendly village in Cambodia.

• **11 Sept:** In Chile, a military junta headed by Gen. Pinochet seizes power in a bloody coup during which President Allende is killed.

• **23 Sept:** Juan Perón and his third wife Isabel return from exile as president and vice-president of Argentina.

• **6 Oct:** Egypt and Syria attack Israel starting the Yom Kippur war.

• **12 Oct:** US Court of Appeal orders Nixon to hand over the Watergate tapes.

• **17 Oct:** Eleven Arab states agree to cut oil production and raise prices in protest at US support for Israel.

• **24 Oct:** Syria accepts UN ceasefire.

• **25 Oct:** US forces go on the alert as fears rise of USSR involvement in the Middle East conflict.

• **11 Nov:** Egypt and Israel accept a US plan for a ceasefire.

• **25 Nov:** A military coup in Greece ousts the government of President Papadopoulos.

• **9 Dec:** Britain, Northern Ireland and the Irish Republic agree to establish a Council of Ireland.

• **17 Dec:** In Britain, Prime Minister Edward Heath initiates a three-day industrial week in response to crippling disputes in the coal, railway and power sectors.

CULTURE

• Bar codes are introduced for stock control and pricing in supermarkets.

• The craze for skateboarding gets under way in the United States.

• Drinks cans with push-through tabs are manufactured in the United States.

• Israeli Uri Geller claims paranormal abilities to bend spoons by mind-power.

• **22 Jan:** The Supreme Court legalizes abortion in the United States.

• **14 May:** NASA launches the first US space station, *Skylab*.

• **8 Oct:** Britain's first commercial radio station, the London Broadcasting Company, goes on the air.

• **20 Oct:** Sydney Opera House is officially opened.

HEADS ROLL IN GOVERNMENT

Nixon, Brandt, Heath, Golda Meir and Tanaka resign

POLITICS

• **4 Jan:** US president Nixon refuses to comply with subpoenas calling for him to hand over White House documents.

• **18 Jan:** Egypt and Israel agree to end their 5-month conflict by separating their forces along the Suez Canal.

• **2 Feb:** China launches a new Cultural Revolution in a campaign against the teachings of Confucius and the policies of Lin Piao.

• **7 Feb:** Grenada becomes independent within the Commonwealth.

• **10 Feb:** British coalminers begin a full strike for a large pay increase.

• **2 Mar:** Military rule in Burma ends as General Ne Win becomes president.

• **4 Mar:** Edward Heath resigns as British prime minister and Labor party leader Harold Wilson forms a new government in Britain.

• **28 Mar:** In Romania, Nikolae Ceaucescu is elected president.

Nixon resigns in fear of impeachment, 9 Aug.

• **2 Apr:** French president Georges Pompidou dies in office.

• **10 Apr:** Israeli premier Golda Meir resigns in the aftermath of the Yom Kippur war. She remains in power until June as head of a caretaker government.

• **25 Apr:** An almost bloodless coup in Portugal overthrows Dr. Caetano.

• **8 May:** Willy Brandt resigns as chancellor of West Germany, following a spy scandal. Helmut Schmidt replaces him on 16 May.

• **27 May:** Valéry Giscard d'Estaing is sworn in as president of France.

• **31 May:** Israel and Syria agree to disengage their territorial dispute in the Golan Heights.

• **4 Jun:** Yitzhak Rabin becomes premier of Israel.

• **17 Jun:** An IRA bomb explodes in the British Houses of Parliament.

• **15 Jul:** President Makarios of Cyprus is overthrown in a Greek-engineered coup.

• **20 Jul:** Turkey invades Cyprus.

• **23 Jul:** The Greek military junta resigns and Constantin Karamanlis returns from exile.

• **26 Jul:** The US House Judiciary Committee recommends that the House of Representatives impeach Nixon.

• **30 Jul:** A ceasefire is agreed in Cyprus.

• **9 Aug:** US president Nixon resigns; Gerald Ford is sworn in as president.

• **8 Sept:** Gerald Ford gives Nixon an unconditional pardon.

• **12 Sept:** Emperor Haile Selassie of Ethiopia is deposed in a left-wing military coup.

• **10 Oct:** At the second British general election of the year, Labor wins a narrow majority.

• **14 Oct:** The United Nations recognizes the PLO as the representative of the Palestinian people.

• **17 Nov:** At the first democratic election in Greece for 10 years, the New Democracy party of Karamanlis wins decisively.

• **21 Nov:** Twenty-one people die in bombs planted by the IRA in two public houses in Birmingham, UK.

• **26 Nov:** Japanese prime minister Tanaka resigns following a corruption scandal.

C U L T U R E

• Scientists warn of the danger to the ozone layer posed by the release of chlorofluorocarbons (CFCs) into the atmosphere.

• The Swedish pop group Abba become internationally successful following their victory in the Eurovision Song Contest with *Waterloo*.

• **5 Feb:** US spaceprobe *Mariner 10* sends back pictures of Venus from as close as 26,000 miles.

• **13 Feb:** Russian novelist Alexander Solzhenitsyn is deported from the Soviet Union after publication of *The Gulag Archipelago*.

• **30 Jul:** French becomes the official language of Quebec, in Canada.

• **12 Nov:** British aristocrat Lord Lucan disappears following the murder of his children's nanny.

COMMUNISM RULES THE EAST

*The governments of
South Vietnam and Laos fall*

POLITICS

• **1 Jan:** Four aides of former US president Nixon are convicted of Watergate offences.

• **11 Feb:** Margaret Thatcher is elected leader of the British Conservative party.

• **13 Feb:** Turkish Cypriots declare the northern part of the island independent.

• **25 Mar:** King Faisal of Saudi Arabia is assassinated by his nephew; crown prince Khalid ibn Abdul Aziz succeeds.

• **30 Mar:** North Vietnamese troops take Da Nang as South Vietnamese resistance collapses.

• **13 Apr:** Civil war erupts between Christian Falangists and Muslims in Beirut, Lebanon.

• **17 Apr:** The Cambodian government surrenders to the Khmer Rouge.

• **30 Apr:** South Vietnam surrenders to North Vietnam (the last US helicopter left the previous day); Saigon is renamed Ho Chi Minh City.

China's underground army is unearthed.

• **5 Jun:** At Britain's first ever referendum, the people vote to stay in the European Economic Community.

• **5 Jun:** The Suez Canal is reopened for all but Israeli shipping.

• **7 Jun:** The Greek parliament adopts a new constitution.

• **12 Jun:** Indian prime minister Indira Gandhi is found guilty of corrupt electoral practices; she refuses to resign.

• **25 Jun:** Mozambique gains its independence from Portugal.

• **26 Jun:** The Indian government declares a state of emergency; opposition leaders are imprisoned and press censorship is imposed.

• **29 Jul:** A bloodless military coup deposes General Gowon as head of state in Nigeria.

• **4 Sept:** Egypt and Israel sign a military disengagement treaty concerning the Sinai peninsula.

• **16 Sept:** Papua New Guinea achieves independence within the Commonwealth of Nations.

• **15 Oct:** The "cod war" breaks out between Britain and Iceland.

• **30 Oct:** Crown prince Juan Carlos takes over power in Spain.

• **2 Nov:** The first Israeli ship uses the Suez Canal.

• **10 Nov:** Angola achieves independence from Portugal, but immediately plunges into civil war.

• **11 Nov:** After the Australian Senate rejects financial legislation, Governor General John Kerr dismisses the prime minister, Gough Whitlam, and appoints Malcolm Fraser to form a Liberal-Country party coalition.

• **22 Nov:** Juan Carlos is proclaimed king of Spain following Franco's death two days earlier.

• **29 Nov:** After New Zealand's general election, National Party leader Robert Muldoon becomes prime minister.

• **3 Dec:** Laos becomes a People's Democratic Republic with Prince Souphanouvong as president.

CULTURE

• The tomb of the Chinese emperor Shi Huangdi, is excavated. It contains over 6,000 figures in military formation. The media christen it the "terracotta army."

• Disco music and reggae both become popular.

• Liquid crystal displays (LCDs) for use in watches and calculators are marketed for the first time in the United States.

• The Indian government undertakes an active birth control policy, advocating widespread sterilization and abortion.

• In Britain, the Sex Discrimination Act and the Equal Opportunities Act both come into force, to end discrimination in employment against women.

• The rock group Queen releases the first significant rock video to accompany its single *Bohemian Rhapsody*.

• **18 Sept:** US heiress Patti Hearst, kidnapped the previous year by the revolutionary Symbionese Liberation Army, is arrested during a bank robbery.

• **9 Oct:** Nuclear scientist and Soviet dissident, Andrei Sakharov, is awarded the Nobel Prize for Peace for his advocacy of civil liberties.

SOWETO SHOCKS THE WORLD

Basic constitutional rights are suspended in India

Punk takes to the streets in Britain.

POLITICS

• **6 JAN:** Following 15 sectarian murders within a week in Northern Ireland, the British government sends in the elite SAS (Special Air Service).

• **8 JAN:** The Indian government postpones parliamentary elections and announces the indefinite continuation of the state of emergency first imposed in June 1975.

• **8 JAN:** Chinese prime minister Zhou En Lai dies; succeeded by Hua Guofeng.

• **14 FEB:** In Angola, the Soviet-backed MPLA (Popular Movement for the Liberation of Angola) gains control of all key points in Angola.

• **19 FEB:** Iceland breaks off diplomatic relations with Britain over the "cod war."

• **16 MAR:** In Britain, prime minister Harold Wilson resigns suddenly. James Callaghan takes over.

• **24 MAR:** A bloodless military coup deposes president Isabel Perón of Argentina (widow of Juan Perón).

• **4 APR:** Khieu Samphan of the Khmer Rouge takes over from Prince Sihanouk as head of state of Cambodia.

• **25 APR:** In Portugal, the first free elections for 50 years result in a minority socialist government led by Mario Soares.

• **13–19 MAY:** Fighting between Muslim and Christian forces breaks out again in Lebanon as the civil war ceasefire collapses.

• **1 JUN:** Britain and Iceland agree terms to end the "cod war."

• **16 JUN:** In South Africa, during race riots in the black township of Soweto, the police open fire on demonstrators killing six and injuring 60. By the end of June, 176 black Africans have died.

• **25 Jun:** President Idi Amin becomes president of Uganda for life.

• **27 Jun:** Palestinian terrorists hijack an Air France plane and force it to fly to Entebbe, Uganda.

• **29 Jun:** Communist party leaders meet in East Berlin and endorse the independence of each national Communist party.

• **2 Jul:** North and South Vietnam are reunited as one nation, the Socialist Republic of Vietnam.

• **3–4 Jul:** Israeli commandos storm the hijacked plane in Uganda freeing most of the hostages.

• **1 Aug:** Trinidad and Tobago become independent within the Commonwealth.

• **18 Aug:** Jacques Chirac, prime minister of France resigns, Raymond Barre takes over as premier.

• **9 Sept:** Mao Zedong, chairman of the Chinese Communist party dies at the age of 82. Hua Guofeng succeeds.

• **20 Sept:** In Sweden, a general election results in defeat for the Social Democratic party after 44 years in power.

• **24 Sept:** Southern Rhodesian leader Ian Smith stuns white Rhodesians as he announces a two-year plan for transition to black majority rule.

• **23 Oct:** In China, the "Gang of Four" are arrested and imprisoned.

• **6 Oct:** The army seizes power in Thailand in a bloody coup.

• **2 Nov:** Democrat Jimmy Carter is elected 39th United States president.

• **24 Dec:** Takeo Fukuda becomes prime minister of Japan.

CULTURE

• Apple Computers is founded in the US by Steve Jobs and Stephen Wozniak.

• In the US, Shere Hite publishes *The Hite Report: a nationwide study on female sexuality*.

• In Britain, punk music and style emerges.

• The first cases of Legionnaire's disease are diagnosed in the US.

• **3 Jul:** Swedish tennis player Bjorn Borg, aged 20, wins the Wimbledon men's singles tennis title.

• **10 Jul:** The town of Seveso near Milan in northern Italy is devastated by the release of poisonous dioxin gas from a nearby pesticide plant.

• **17 Jul:** The Olympic Games open in Montreal, Canada. Subsequently 14-year-old Romanian gymnast Nadia Comaneci scores the first 10 out of 10 ever awarded in her sport.

MIDDLE EAST BREAKTHROUGH

President Sadat breaks ranks among Arab nations and visits Israel

POLITICS

• **3 FEB:** Lt.-Col. Mengistu Haile Mariam becomes leader of Ethiopia after Brig.-Gen. Teferi Benti is murdered.

• **16 FEB:** In Uganda, Archbishop Janani Luwum, a civil rights activist, is murdered by security forces.

• **7 MAR:** Zulfikar Ali Bhutto claims a massive victory in the Pakistani general election.

• **11–23 MAR:** Violent protests erupt in Pakistan against vote-rigging.

• **20 MAR:** Elections in India result in victory for the Janata party. Morarji Desai becomes prime minister.

• **17 MAY:** The Labor party is defeated in Israeli elections for the first time in 29 years.

• **15 JUN:** Adolfo Suarez becomes prime minister after the first free elections in Spain since 1936.

• **16 JUN:** In the USSR, Leonid Brezhnev becomes head of state.

Refugees flee Vietnam's Communist regime.

• **17 JUN:** In the Irish Republic, the Fianna Fáil party wins a large victory.

• **21 JUN:** Menachim Begin, leader of the Likud party, becomes prime minister of Israel.

• **27 JUN:** French Somaliland becomes the Republic of Dijbouti.

• **5 JUL:** Gen. Zia ul-Huq arrests Prime Minister Bhutto and seizes power in Pakistan.

• **22 JUL:** In China, the "Gang of Four" are expelled from the Chinese Communist Party and Deng Xiapong is reinstated as deputy prime minister.

• **23 JUL:** Somali forces invade Ethiopia in a dispute over the Ogaden area.

• **31 Aug:** Ian Smith's Rhodesian Front party wins an overwhelming victory in the general election.

• **7 Sept:** The US and Panama sign a treaty transferring the Panama Canal to full Panamanian control in 1999.

• **12 Sept:** Black South African leader Steve Biko is killed while in police custody.

• **28 Sept:** Cambodian leader Pol Pot arrives in Beijing to discuss Chinese aid.

• **18 Oct:** German commandos storm a hijacked Lufthansa plane in Mogadishu killing three of the four Palestinian hijackers.

• **4 Nov:** The United Nations Security Council imposes an arms embargo on South Africa.

• **9 Nov:** President Sadat of Egypt indicates that he is willing to negotiate peace terms with Israel.

• **21 Nov:** Sadat visits Israel and addresses the Knesset.

• **Dec:** Refugees ("boat people") begin to flee the Communist regime in Vietnam.

• **5 Dec:** President Sadat breaks off diplomatic ties with Syria, Iraq, Libya, Algeria and South Yemen for opposition to his peace moves toward Israel.

C U L T U R E

• Skateboarding becomes popular in Britain.

• The Apple II is the first personal computer available in assembled form and the first to be really successful.

• Amnesty International wins the Nobel Peace Prize.

• Blockbuster movie *Star Wars,* written and directed by George Lucas is released in the United States.

• Steven Spielberg's blockbusting movie *Close Encounters of the Third Kind* costs $20 million in special effects.

• The soundtrack album from the film *Saturday Night Fever,* starring John Travolta, becomes a worldwide bestseller.

• In the US, two homosexual men are diagnosed as having the rare cancer Karposi's sarcoma; they are probably New York's first AIDS victims.

• **8 Feb:** Soviet spacecraft *Soyuz 24* links with orbiting space lab *Salyut 5.*

• **11 May:** The US government announces that within 2 years CRC's will be banned as propellants in aerosols.

• **16 Aug:** Rock star Elvis Presley dies aged 42.

• **14 Oct:** Singer and movie star Bing Crosby dies aged 73.

THE YEAR OF THREE POPES

Islamic fundamentalism stirs in Iran

POLITICS

• **JAN:** Cambodia and Vietnam continue their border conflict.

• **3 MAR:** Southern Rhodesian leader Ian Smith signs an agreement for power sharing with three moderate black leaders. However Nkomo and Mugabe denounce the agreement and the UN Security Council describes it as illegal.

• **14 MAR:** Israel invades southern Lebanon in response to a PLO attack which killed 11 Israeli civilians.

• **15 MAR:** Somalia accepts defeat in the Ogaden War and withdraws troops.

• **16 MAR:** Former Italian prime minister Aldo Moro is kidnapped by Red Brigade terrorists.

• **18 MAR:** Former Pakistani prime minister Zulfikar Ali Bhutto is sentenced to death.

• **28 MAR:** In Rhodesia, guerrilla warfare increases as the Patriotic Front attempts to persuade moderate black Africans to reject the settlement of 3 Mar.

Cleaning up after the Amoco Cadiz *oilspill.*

• **27 APR:** A Soviet-backed military coup in Afghanistan establishes an Islamic government.

• **9 MAY:** In Italy, Aldo Moro is found dead after the Italian government refuses to capitulate to his captors.

• **11 MAY:** Islamic fundamentalists riot in Tehran calling for the removal of Shah Muhammad Reza Pahlavi.

• **15 JUN:** Italian president Giovanni Leone resigns after allegations of fiscal misconduct.

• **24 JUN:** The president of North Yemen is killed by a bomb.

• **26 JUN:** The president of South Yemen is killed by the same faction that murdered the North Yemeni president.

- **Jul:** China withdraws aid from Vietnam and Albania.

- **7 Jul:** The Solomon Islands gain independence from British rule.

- **22 Aug:** In Nicaragua, Sandinista guerrillas seize the parliament building in Managua and take 1,500 hostages.

- **5–17 Sept:** Talks between Egypt, the US and Israel at Camp David lead to the Camp David Accords, which end 30 years of hostility between Egypt and Israel.

- **8 Sept:** In Tehran, demonstrations against the Shah's modernization lead to the imposition of martial law.

- **29 Sept:** In South Africa, P. W. Botha becomes prime minister and B. J. Vorster accepts the post of president.

- **27 Oct:** The UN military command in South Korea discover an invasion tunnel beginning in North Korea.

- **31 Oct:** Iranian oil workers hold anti-Shah strikes.

- **6 Nov:** The shah of Iran appoints a military government after violent riots.

- **19 Dec:** Indira Gandhi is expelled from the Indian Parliament and imprisoned on charges of conspiracy and electoral misconduct.

- **25 Dec:** Vietnam begins a full-scale invasion of Cambodia.

CULTURE

- Discos become popular in Europe and the United States.

- Compact disks are first demonstrated in West Germany.

- In Britain, David Hockney designs the Glyndebourne production of Mozart's *The Magic Flute*.

- **16 Mar:** The supertanker *Amoco Cadiz* runs aground off Brittany, France, spilling over 220,000 tonnes of oil and contaminating the coastline.

- **25 Jul:** In Britain, the world's first "test-tube" baby, Louise Brown, is born in Manchester.

- **6 Aug:** Pope Paul VI dies.

- **26 Aug:** Cardinal Albino Luciani of Italy is elected as Pope John Paul I.

- **28 Sept:** Pope John Paul I dies.

- **16 Oct:** Cardinal Karol Wojtyla of Poland becomes John Paul II, the first non-Italian Pope since 1523.

- **29 Oct:** In China, Mao Zedong's *Little Red Book* is denounced by the Communist party.

- **10 Dec:** President Anwar Sadat of Egypt and prime minister Menachim Begin of Israel jointly win the Nobel Peace Prize.

WINTER OF DISCONTENT

*The Thatcher revolution
begins in Britain*

POLITICS

• **1 JAN:** China and the United States establish diplomatic relations.

• **7 JAN:** Vietnamese troops and Cambodian rebels capture Phnom Penh and overthrow the Pol Pot regime.

• **16 JAN:** The shah of Iran and his family flee to Egypt.

• **30 JAN:** In Southern Rhodesia, a referendum of white Rhodesians votes overwhelmingly for black majority rule.

• **31 JAN:** In Britain, public sector workers strike in response to the government's 5% limit on pay rises. The period becomes known as "the winter of discontent."

• **1 FEB:** Religious leader Ayatollah Khomeini returns to Iran from exile.

• **8 FEB:** The US withdraws aid to the Somoza regime in Nicaragua in protest at human rights violations.

• **17 FEB–5 MAR:** China makes punitive invasions into Vietnam.

Ayatollah Khomeini returns to Iran.

• **22 FEB:** The island of St. Lucia becomes independent.

• **23 FEB–16 MAR:** War breaks out between North and South Yemen.

• **8 MAR:** In Tehran, Iranian women march in protest at their loss of freedom under Islamic laws.

• **12 MAR:** In Grenada, a bloodless coup establishes a people's revolutionary government headed by Maurice Bishop.

• **26 MAR:** President Sadat of Egypt and Prime Minister Begin of Israel sign a peace treaty in Washington D.C.

• **29 MAR:** Ugandan dictator Idi Amin is driven from the country by nationalist troops and Tanzanian soldiers. He is forced to live in exile.

• **30 Mar:** In Britain, an IRA bomb kills Airey Neave, Conservative spokesman on Northern Ireland.

• **1 Apr:** Iran is declared an Islamic Republic by Ayatollah Khomeini.

• **4 Apr:** In Pakistan, former president Zulfikar Ali Bhutto is executed after being convicted of conspiracy to murder.

• **3 May:** After a British general election, Conservative party leader Margaret Thatcher becomes the first woman prime minister in Europe.

• **22 May:** The Progressive Liberal party wins the Canadian general election; Joseph Clark becomes prime minister.

• **28 May:** Britain agrees to take in 982 Vietnamese "boat people" refugees on the South China Sea.

• **2 Jun:** Pope John Paul II begins a tour of his native Poland.

• **4 Jun:** South African president Vorster resigns after a financial scandal.

• **7–10 Jun:** European electors vote for the first European Parliament.

• **18 Jun:** The arms limitation treaty SALT II is signed by US president Carter and Soviet premier Brezhnev in Vienna.

• **16 Jul:** Saddam Hussein becomes president of Iraq.

• **20 Jul:** President Anastasio Somoza of Nicaragua flees the country.

• **27 Aug:** Earl Mountbatten of Burma is killed in Ireland by an IRA bomb.

• **26 Oct:** President Park Chung Hee of South Korea is assassinated.

• **4 Nov:** Iranian militants storm the US embassy in Tehran, initially taking more than 100 hostages.

• **15 Nov:** British art historian Professor Anthony Blunt is revealed as a Soviet spy.

• **20–23 Nov:** Armed militants seize the Grand Mosque in Mecca.

• **25 Dec:** The Soviet Union begins an invasion of Afghanistan in support of a Marxist regime.

CULTURE

• Albanian-born Mother Teresa wins the Nobel Peace Prize for her work with slum-dwellers in Calcutta.

• Canada becomes the first country to operate a satellite TV broadcasting service.

• **28 Mar:** An accident at Three Mile Island nuclear plant in Pennsylvania threatens a serious release of radiation.

• **Oct:** The World Health Organization declares smallpox to be eradicated after a 22-year campaign.

IRANIAN HOSTAGE CRISIS

Polish shipyard workers demand democratic rights

POLITICS

• **7 Jan:** Indira Gandhi is reelected as prime minister of India.

• **8 Jan:** Soviet troops are reported to be in control of most of Afghanistan.

• **22 Jan:** Dissident Russian physicist Andrei Sakharov is stripped of honors and exiled from Moscow after criticizing the Soviet invasion of Afghanistan.

• **25 Jan:** Abolhassan Bani Sadr is the first elected president of Iran.

• **18 Feb:** In Canada, Pierre Trudeau wins a second term as prime minister.

• **22 Feb:** Martial law is declared in Kabul, capital of Afghanistan, following protests against the Soviet invasion.

• **7 Apr:** US president Carter breaks off diplomatic relations with Iran and bans trade between the two countries.

• **18 Apr:** Britain's last colony in Africa, Southern Rhodesia, becomes independent as Zimbabwe, led by Prime Minister Robert Mugabe.

Mount St. Helens erupts, 18–19 May.

• **25 Apr:** A US commando mission to rescue the embassy hostages in Tehran (taken 4 Nov 1979) fails with the loss of eight soldiers. US secretary of state, Cyrus Vance, resigns.

• **30 Apr:** Princess Beatrix is crowned queen of the Netherlands.

• **30 Apr:** Terrorists seize the Iranian embassy in London, demanding the release of political prisoners in Iran.

• **May:** Fernando Terry becomes president of Peru ending 12 years of military rule.

• **4 May:** President Tito of Yugoslavia dies; a rotating presidency succeeds him.

- **5 MAY:** The SAS successfully storms the Iranian embassy in London.

- **18–19 MAY:** The long-dormant volcano on Mount St. Helens (USA) erupts causing widespread destruction.

- **12 JUN:** Japanese prime minister Masayoshi Ohira dies. Zenko Suzuki succeeds on 17 Jul.

- **23 JUN:** In India, Indira Gandhi's son and political heir-apparent, Sanjay, dies in an air crash.

- **29 JUN:** Vigdis Finnbogadottir of Iceland becomes Europe's first elected female head of state.

- **30 JUL:** The Israeli Knesset proclaims a united Jerusalem as capital of Israel.

- **2 AUG:** Right-wing terrorists plant a bomb in Bologna railway station in Italy killing 84 people and injuring hundreds.

- **14 AUG:** In Poland, workers at the Gdansk shipyard go on strike for the right to have free trade unions.

- **30 AUG:** Lech Walesa signs an agreement with the Polish government allowing the formation of independent trade unions.

- **12 SEPT:** After a military coup in Turkey, Gen. Evren takes power.

- **22 SEPT:** *Solidarnosc* (Solidarity) is formed in Poland.

- **24 SEPT:** Iraq invades Iran to gain control of the Shatt-al-Arab waterway.

- **4 NOV:** Republican Ronald Reagan is elected as the 40th US president.

- **20 NOV:** In China, the trial begins of the "Gang of Four".

- **11 DEC:** NATO leaders warn the USSR not to intervene in Poland's affairs.

- **15 DEC:** Milton Obote becomes president of Uganda.

CULTURE

- Sony of Japan launch the "Walkman" a portable, personal tape recorder.

- **JAN:** US scientists announce the production of interferon, a disease-fighting protein.

- **MAR:** The world conservation strategy is published, following three years of research by 450 government agencies.

- **5 JUL:** Bjorn Borg of Sweden becomes the first tennis player to win five successive men's singles titles at Wimbledon.

- **19 JUL–3 AUG:** The Olympic Games in Moscow are boycotted by 65 nations protesting the invasion of Afghanistan.

- **12 NOV:** US spaceprobe *Voyager 1* passes within 77,000 miles of Saturn.

- **8 DEC:** Rock star John Lennon is shot dead in New York.

THE FAIRYTALE WEDDING

*Unrest swells again
in the Middle East*

POLITICS

• **JAN:** The European Monetary Fund (EMF) is set up and the European Currency Unit (ECU) is introduced.

• **1 JAN:** Greece becomes the 10th member of the EEC.

• **20 JAN:** Ronald Reagan is inaugurated as the 40th US president.

• **21 JAN:** Iran releases all 52 US hostages who have been held in Tehran since Nov 1979.

• **25 JAN:** Jiang Qing, widow of Mao Zedong, and Zhang Chunqiao receive death sentences suspended for two years; the other two members of the "Gang of Four" receive long jail sentences.

• **29 JAN:** Adolfo Suarez resigns as prime minister of Spain.

• **3 FEB:** Gro Harlem Brundtland is Norway's first woman prime minister.

• **9 FEB:** Polish prime minister Josef Pinkowski resigns and is replaced by Gen. Wojciech Jaruzelski.

The Prince and Princess of Wales on their wedding day, 29 July.

• **23 FEB:** In Spain, Col. Terejo Monila storms the Cortes with 200 civil guards and attempts a coup.

• **2 MAR:** Four senior British politicians leave the Labor party and set up a new centrist Social Democratic party (SDP).

• **30 MAR:** Ronald Reagan survives an attempt on his life in Washington D.C.

• **1 APR:** Heavy fighting breaks out between the Christian Druze and the Syrian peacekeeping forces in Beirut.

• **10–12 APR:** Many police and civilians are injured in race riots in Brixton, South London.

• **5 MAY:** In Northern Ireland, Bobby Sands (IRA member of parliament for

Fermanagh and South Tyrone) dies after a hunger strike in the Maze prison.

• **10 May:** François Mitterrand is the first socialist president of France since the foundation of the Fifth Republic.

• **13 May:** Pope John Paul II is seriously wounded in an assassination attempt in St. Peter's Square, Rome.

• **30 May:** President Zia ur-Rahman of Bangladesh is assassinated.

• **7 Jun:** Israeli aircraft bomb a nuclear power plant being built near Baghdad.

• **4–15 Jul:** Riots break out in Toxteth, Liverpool, and other parts of the UK including London.

• **25 Jul:** Rugby fans clash with anti-apartheid demonstrators in New Zealand during a tour by the South African team.

• **7 Aug:** Over one million Solidarity members strike in Poland over food shortages.

• **19 Aug:** US aircraft shoot down two Libyan jets over the Gulf of Sirte.

• **11 Sept:** The Soviet Union warns the Polish government about its loss of control and concessions to protesters.

• **6 Oct:** President Anwar Sadat of Egypt is assassinated by Muslim fundamentalist soldiers; he is succeeded by Hosni Mubarak four days later.

• **18 Oct:** In Greece, the first socialist government is elected under Andreas Papandreou.

• **14 Nov:** Senegal and Gambia form a confederation known as Senegambia.

• **13 Dec:** Gen. Jaruzelski imposes martial law in Poland; Solidarity is banned and Lech Walesa, its leader, is placed under arrest.

• **22 Dec:** Leopoldo Galtieri becomes president of Argentina.

CULTURE

• France introduces the *Train à Grand Vitesse* (TGV), a high speed train.

• IBM launches its personal computer (with 64 Kb of memory and a single floppy disk drive) running the Microsoft disk-operating system (MS-DOS). It later becomes the industry standard for PCs.

• Acquired Immune Deficiency Syndrome (AIDS) is recognized by the American Center for Disease Control.

• **12 Apr:** Launch of the first US Space Shuttle *Columbia*.

• **11 May:** Death of Jamaican reggae star Bob Marley.

• **29 Jul:** The wedding of the Prince of Wales and Lady Diana Spencer is watched on television by over 700 million people worldwide.

WAR IN THE FALKLANDS

Britain's "Iron Lady"
fights one last colonial battle

POLITICS

• **JAN:** Unemployment in Britain reaches three million.

• **31 JAN:** Israel agrees to a UN peace-keeping force in Sinai.

• **17 FEB:** In Zimbabwe, Joshua Nkomo is dismissed from government.

• **11 MAR:** The British government announces its intention to buy the US Trident 2 system to replace Polaris.

• **24 MAR:** Gen. H. M. Ershad seizes power in a military coup in Bangladesh.

• **25 MAR:** President Ortega suspends the Nicaraguan constitution.

• **2 APR:** Argentine troops invade the Falkland Islands (Malvinas).

• **3 APR:** The UN Security Council demands an Argentine withdrawal.

• **4 APR:** The first ships of the Royal Navy task force leave for the Falklands.

• **17 APR:** A new Canadian constitution is proclaimed severing links with Britain.

British troops hoist the Union flag and White Ensign on South Georgia in the Falklands.

• **25 APR:** British forces recapture South Georgia.

• **25 APR:** Israel completes its withdrawal from Sinai.

• **30 APR:** President Reagan pledges US support for Britain against Argentina.

• **2 MAY:** A British submarine sinks the *General Belgrano,* 360 crew die.

• **21 MAY:** British troops land at Port San Carlos on the Falklands Islands.

• **24 MAY:** In the Iran–Iraq war, Iranian troops recapture Khorramshahr.

• **6 JUN:** After the Israeli ambassador to the UK is shot by Palestinian terrorists, Israel invades Lebanon.

• **14 JUN:** Argentine forces surrender at Port Stanley ending the Falklands War.

• **17 JUN:** President Galtieri of Argentina is ousted and replaced by Gen. Alfredo Saint Jean.

• **22 JUN:** New Zealand announces a 12-month freeze on prices and wages.

• **29 JUN:** As Israeli troops encircle Beirut, prime minister Begin offers to allow the PLO leave with their weapons.

• **13 AUG:** In Poland, clashes between police and demonstrators as thousands of workers march through Gdansk.

• **21 AUG:** The PLO begins to withdraw from Beirut according to a US plan.

• **28–30 AUG:** In Beirut, war breaks out between the Muslim Druse militia and the Lebanese army.

• **15 SEPT:** Israeli troops push into west Beirut.

• **18 SEPT:** Over 800 Palestinians die when Christian Phalangist militiamen enter the refugee camps of Sabra and Chatila in West Beirut.

• **1 OCT:** After the collapse of Helmut Schmidt's government, Christian democrat Helmut Kohl is elected chancellor of West Germany.

• **28 OCT:** Socialist Felipe Gonzalez wins the Spanish general elections.

• **10 NOV:** Soviet president Leonid Brezhnev dies; he is succeeded by Yuri Andropov two days later.

• **22 NOV:** President Reagan decides to employ 100 MX intercontinental ballistic missiles in Wyoming.

• **12 DEC:** Over 20,000 women circle the US air base at Greenham Common, UK, to protest against the deployment of US Cruise missiles.

CULTURE

• Rap music becomes popular in the UK and USA.

• The first commercially available compact disk players are on sale.

• The first computer-controlled artificial limb is designed by Jerrold Petrovsky in the USA.

• *ET – The Extra Terrestrial*, directed by Stephen Spielberg, is a smash-hit movie on both sides of the Atlantic.

• **7 JUL:** In Britain, a burglar breaks into Buckingham Palace and enters the Queen's bedroom.

• **10 SEPT:** The European rocket *Ariane* crashes shortly after takeoff on its first operational mission.

• **11 OCT:** The hull of the *Mary Rose*, Henry VIII's flagship wrecked in the Solent in 1545, is raised to the surface.

MILITARY COUP IN GRENADA

The US develops a new missile shield nicknamed "Star Wars"

POLITICS

• **18 Jan:** South Africa reimposes direct rule on Namibia.

• **11 Feb:** An inquiry into the Beirut massacre of Palestinian refugees in Sept 1982 results in the resignation of Ariel Sharon, Israeli defense minister.

• **15 Feb:** The Lebanese government regains control of Beirut.

• **5 Mar:** Robert Hawke (Labor) becomes Australian prime minister.

• **6 Mar:** In West Germany, the Green party wins 24 seats in the election.

• **23 Mar:** US president Reagan proposes a "Star Wars" defense system.

• **1 Apr:** In Britain, anti-nuclear protesters form a 14-mile human chain. Similar protests take place in Italy, the Netherlands and West Germany.

• **18 Apr:** The US embassy in Beirut is bombed, killing over 30 people.

• **17 May:** Israel and Lebanon agree on the withdrawal of Israeli troops.

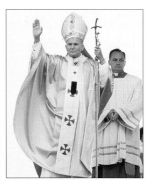

Pope John Paul II visits his native Poland.

• **9 Jun:** In Britain, Margaret Thatcher wins a second term in office.

• **16-23 Jun:** The Pope visits Poland, meets Lech Walesa and states that the right to join a free trade union is "given by the Creator".

• **24 Jun:** Syria expels PLO leader Yassir Arafat and Syrian tanks lay siege to his guerrilla bases in Lebanon.

• **21 Jul:** Martial law in Poland is lifted after 19 months.

• **4 Aug:** Bettino Craxi becomes Italy's first Socialist prime minister.

• **6 Aug:** US sends aircraft to support Chad against Libyan-backed rebels.

• **21 Aug:** Philippine opposition leader

Benigno Aquino is assassinated at Manila airport on his return from exile.

• **1 Sept:** A South Korean passenger plane is shot down by a Soviet war plane in Soviet territory. All 269 people on board are killed. The USSR makes unsupported accusations of spying.

• **3–4 Sept:** Civil war breaks out in Lebanon following Israeli withdrawal.

• **15 Sept:** Israeli prime minister Menachem Begin resigns, and is succeeded by Yitzhak Shamir on 10 Oct.

• **19 Sept:** The Caribbean islands of St. Kitts-Nevis become independent.

• **26 Sept:** A ceasefire is agreed in Lebanon.

• **20 Oct:** In Grenada, a left-wing military coup deposes prime minister Maurice Bishop.

• **23 Oct:** In Beirut, suicide bombers kill 242 US and 62 French troops.

• **25 Oct:** US marines invade Grenada to depose the left-wing government at the request of the governor-general.

• **22–23 Nov:** Breakdown of US-USSR arms reduction talks. NATO and USSR announce an increase in nuclear forces.

• **17 Dec:** In Britain, an IRA car bomb explodes outside Harrods department store in London killing six people.

CULTURE

• Pop star Madonna storms to fame.

• The Australian yacht *Australia II* wins the America's Cup for the first time since the race began in the 1870's.

• Large areas of Ethiopia are reported to be suffering in the worst drought since 1973 bringing famine to millions.

• The HIV retrovirus, from which AIDS can result, is identified.

• Bulgarian-born artist Christo wraps 11 islands in Biscayne Bay, Miami, Florida, with pink polypropylene fabric.

• **16–19 Feb:** In South Australia, bush fires burn 6,700 sq km (2,590 sq mi) killing 71 people and injuring 1,000 more.

• **29 Mar:** The first laptop computer is launched in the US.

• **24 Apr:** 80,000 Canadians in various cities protest against the proposed testing of US Cruise missiles in Alberta.

• **25 May:** The film *Return of the Jedi* grosses $6.2 million on its opening day.

• **13 Jun:** US *Pioneer 10* crosses the orbit of Neptune, the first spacecraft to travel beyond known planets.

• **7–14 Aug:** The first official World Athletics championships are held in Helsinki.

BAND AID RAISES FUNDS

Assassination of Indira Gandhi escalates racial conflict in South Asia

POLITICS

• **1 JAN:** Brunei becomes independent.

• **1 JAN:** In Nigeria, a 19-member Supreme Military Council under Gen. Muhammad Buhari takes office.

• **6 FEB:** In Lebanon, civil war erupts in West Beirut between Sh'ite Muslims and Druse militias. President Gemayel orders a 24-hour curfew.

• **9 FEB:** Soviet premier Yuri Andropov dies; Konstantin Chernenko succeeds.

• **29 FEB:** In Canada, prime minister Pierre Trudeau resigns.

• **1 MAR:** A joint South African-Angolan commission supervises the withdrawal of South African troops from Angola.

• **12 MAR:** In Britain, mineworkers strike in over 100 pits in protest against layoffs and mine closures.

• **23 MAR:** In Britain, civil servant Sarah Tisdall, is jailed for six months for passing on classified information about US Cruise missiles to a daily newspaper.

Sikh separatists occupy their holiest shrine, the Golden Temple at Amritzar.

• **17 APR:** In Britain, policewoman Yvonne Fletcher is killed and 11 others are injured when a gunman fires from inside the Libyan embassy.

• **6 JUN:** In India, hundreds of Sikh extremists die when troops storm the Golden Temple at Amritsar.

• **14 JUL:** In New Zealand, the Labor party defeats the ruling National party in a general election.

• **3 AUG:** Upper Volta is renamed Burkina Faso.

• **31 AUG:** In Israel, Yitzhak Shamir and Shimon Peres agree to form a government of national unity and alternate the post of prime minister.

• **3 Sept:** In South Africa, 14 die in rioting in Sharpeville and other black townships around Johannesburg.

• **4 Sept:** In Canada, Brian Mulroney (Conservative) becomes prime minister.

• **17 Sept:** France and Libya agree to withdraw from Chad by mid-Nov.

• **17 Sept:** In South Africa, the first multiracial cabinet is sworn in with prime minister Botha as president.

• **20 Sept:** In Lebanon, an Islamic suicide bomber explodes at the US embassy in Beirut killing 20 people.

• **26 Sept:** China and Britain sign a draft agreement for the return of Hong Kong to China in 1997.

• **12 Oct:** In Britain, an IRA bomb explodes at the Grand Hotel in Brighton during a Conservative party conference, killing five people.

• **28 Oct:** In China, the Communist party announces economic reforms allowing a measure of free enterprise.

• **30 Oct:** In Poland, pro-Solidarity priest Fr. Popieluszko is found murdered after being kidnapped by the police.

• **31 Oct:** Indian prime minister Indira Gandhi is assassinated by two Sikh bodyguards. Her son Rajiv Gandhi is sworn in as her successor.

• **5 Nov:** Daniel Ortega is re-elected president of Nicaragua.

• **6 Nov:** Ronald Reagan is reelected as US president in a landslide victory.

C U L T U R E

• In Britain, BMX bikes become a craze amongst youngsters.

• Katherine Hamnett's fashion collection is inspired by antinuclear protests at Greenham Common, UK.

• Michael Jackson's album *Thriller* sells over 37 million copies in the US.

• Apple launch the Macintosh computer with graphical user interface and mouse.

• **10 Apr:** First birth from a frozen embryo, Monash university, Australia.

• **28 Jul–12 Aug:** The Los Angeles Olympics are boycotted by the USSR and other Eastern European countries.

• **Oct:** The Ethiopian government appeals for help to save an estimated 6.4 million facing starvation.

• **Dec:** Band Aid organized by Bob Geldof produces a chart-topping single to raise money for famine relief.

• **Dec:** A toxic gas leakage at the US chemical company Union Carbide in Bhopal, India, causes at least 2,500 deaths and serious side-effects to a further 200,000 people.

MILLIONS STARVE IN ETHIOPIA

Scientists discover a hole in the ozone layer over Antarctica

POLITICS

• **2 Jan:** The USA officially withdraws from UNESCO.

• **14 Jan:** The Israeli cabinet decides on a three-stage withdrawal from occupied Lebanon, beginning in Feb.

• **25 Jan:** In South Africa, President Botha opens a three-chamber parliament for whites, Indians and coloreds.

• **5 Feb:** Libya releases four detained UK nationals after negotiations by the archbishop of Canterbury's envoy Terry Waite.

• **7 Feb:** In Poland, four secret police officers are convicted of the murder of Fr. J. Popieluszko.

• **3 Mar:** In Britain, the National Union of Mineworkers votes to call off the year-long national strike.

• **10 Mar:** President Chernenko of the USSR dies aged 73. Mikhail Gorbachev is named first secretary of the Soviet Communist party on the following day.

• **12 Mar–23 Apr:** A new round of

Ethiopian children receiving aid in a camp.

arms limitation talks takes place between the USSR and USA in Geneva.

• **21 Mar:** In Uitnhage, South Africa, 19 people die when police fire on crowds on the 25th anniversary of Sharpeville.

• **15 Apr:** South Africa announces an end to the ban on mixed race marriages.

• **1 May:** In Poland, 10,000 Solidarity supporters clash with police during a May Day parade.

• **10 May:** In India, Sikh extremists bomb three cities killing 84 people.

• **14 May:** In Sri Lanka, 146 die during Tamil separatist attacks in the holy city of Anuradhapura.

• **10 Jun:** Israel completes withdrawal from Southern Lebanon apart from a 'security zone'.

• **14 Jun:** Shi'ite Muslim gunmen hijack a TWA airliner and demand the release of 700 prisoners held by Israel.

• **2 Jul:** Andrei Gromyko is named president of the USSR. Eduard Shevardnadze becomes foreign minister.

• **10 Jul:** In Auckland harbor, New Zealand, the Greenpeace ship *Rainbow Warrior* is blown up while protesting against French nuclear testing in the area. French agents accept responsibility.

• **27 Jul:** In Uganda, a military coup led by Brig. Okello ousts Milton Obote.

• **15 Aug:** In South Africa, president Botha reaffirms commitment to apartheid and rules out the possibility of parliamentary representation for blacks.

• **17 Aug:** 60 die and 100 are injured in a car bomb explosion in Christian east Beirut. Two days later a car bomb explosion in Muslim Beirut kills 50.

• **13 Sept:** Britain expels 25 Soviet diplomats for alleged spying. The next day USSR expels 25 British diplomats.

• **1 Oct:** Israeli Air Force planes bomb the PLO headquarters in Tunis, killing 60 people, in retaliation for the murder of three Israelis in Cyprus.

• **7 Oct:** Palestinian guerrillas hijack the Italian liner *Achille Lauro* and murder a US hostage.

• **19–21 Nov:** President Reagan and Mikhail Gorbachev meet in Geneva and issue a joint statement condemning nuclear war.

• **2 Dec:** In the Philippines, a court acquits the 26 people accused of the murder of President Benigno Aquino.

CULTURE

• The World Health Organization declares AIDS to be an epidemic.

• Genetic fingerprinting is discovered accidentally by Dr. A. J. Jeffreys in the UK.

• **7 Jul:** West German Boris Becker, aged 17, becomes the youngest winner of the men's singles at Wimbledon.

• **13 Jul:** Rock star Bob Geldof organizes two simultaneous Live Aid concerts (London and Philadelphia) watched on television by over 1.5 billion people worldwide and raising over £50 million for famine victims in Ethiopia.

• **Sept:** The British Antarctic Survey discovers a hole in the ozone layer.

• **13 Nov:** In Columbia, at least 25,000 people die when the Nevado del Ruiz volcano erupts for the first time since 1845.

NUCLEAR CRISIS AT CHERNOBYL

US war planes target Colonel Qadhafi's Libya

POLITICS

• **1 Jan:** Spain and Portugal join the European Economic Community (EEC).

• **9 Jan:** British defense secretary Michael Heseltine resigns after a Cabinet row about the procurement of helicopters in the "Westland affair".

• **7 Feb:** Haitian president-for-life "Baby Doc" Duvalier flees to France after demonstrations against his regime.

• **15 Feb:** President Marcos of the Philippines claims electoral victory despite allegations of vote-rigging.

• **24 Feb:** President Marcos flees the Philippines to the United States; Mrs. Corazon Aquino (widow of Benigno Aquino) is sworn in as president.

• **28 Feb:** Swedish premier Olof Palme is assassinated in Stockholm.

• **2 Mar:** The Australia Bill becomes law, cutting legal ties with Britain.

• **7 Mar:** In South Africa, the state of emergency (imposed 1985) is lifted.

Space shuttle Challenger *explodes in mid-air.*

• **12 Mar:** A referendum confirms that Spain will stay in NATO but not in its command structure and rejects the presence of nuclear weapons in Spain.

• **20 Mar:** Gaullist Jacques Chirac becomes prime minister of France.

• **15 Apr:** US warplanes attack military targets in Tripoli and Benghazi, Libya, following Libyan interference with US military exercises in the Gulf of Sirte.

• **18 Apr:** The South African government rescinds the Pass Laws.

• **26 Apr:** The Soviet nuclear power plant at Chernobyl, Ukraine, explodes releasing dangerous radiation in Europe.

• **8 Jun:** Kurt Waldheim is elected president of Austria, despite allegations of wartime Nazi involvement.

• **12 Jun:** The British government dissolves the Northern Ireland Assembly, set up in 1982.

• **27 Jun:** After New Zealand bans US nuclear-armed warships in its waters, the US declares it cannot be bound by the 1951 ANZUS pact on NZ defense.

• **27 Jun:** The International Court of Justice in The Hague rules that US aid to Contra rebels in Nicaragua is illegal.

• **7 Sept:** Restrictions on civil liberties are imposed in Chile following an assassination attempt on Gen. Pinochet.

• **7 Sept:** Desmond Tutu is enthroned as South Africa's first black archbishop.

• **11–12 Oct:** US president Reagan and Soviet premier Gorbachev hold a summit in Reykjavik, Iceland.

• **20 Oct:** Yitzhak Shamir takes over from Shimon Peres as prime minister of Israel.

• **13 Nov:** US president Reagan admits a secret arms deal with Iran, in the so-called Iran-Contra scandal.

• **25 Nov:** US vice-admiral Poindexter and Col. Oliver North are dismissed from the National Security Council after it is revealed that money from arms sales in Iran funded Contra rebels in Nicaragua.

• **19 Dec:** Soviet dissident Andrei Sakharov and his wife are permitted to return to Moscow after seven years' internal exile.

CULTURE

• Soviet premier Gorbachev institutes a policy of *glasnost* (openness) in the arts and literature, allowing many previously banned works to be published.

• Nicotine chewing gum is developed for smokers wanting to give up.

• The UK newspaper industry is transformed, when Murdoch-owned titles move from Fleet St. to Wapping, and *Today* and the *Independent* are born.

• **24 Jan:** US space probe *Voyager 2* flies past the planet Uranus.

• **28 Jan:** US space shuttle *Challenger* explodes shortly after takeoff killing all seven crew members.

• **8 Apr:** American film star Clint Eastwood is elected mayor of Carmel, California.

• **4 Jul:** In the US, the Statue of Liberty is reopened after refurbishments.

• **22 Nov:** US boxer Mike Tyson becomes the youngest-ever world heavyweight champion, aged 20.

SUPERPOWERS REDUCE ARMS

Ferry disasters in Zeebrugge and the Philippines claim high death tolls

POLITICS

• **20 JAN:** Terry Waite, the Archbishop of Canterbury's special envoy, disappears in Beirut, Lebanon.

• **2 FEB:** In a referendum in the Philippines, 81 percent approve a new US-style constitution.

• **22 FEB:** A force of around 7,000 Syrian troops enters west Beirut in an effort to end fighting between Shia Muslim and Druse forces.

• **26 FEB:** The Tower Commission investigating US arms sales to Iran criticizes senior White House staff.

• **28 FEB:** Soviet premier Gorbachev proposes a separate agreement on the abolition of medium-range nuclear missiles in Europe and drops insistence on the curtailment of US "Star Wars".

• **10 MAR:** Charles Haughey is reelected premier of the Republic of Ireland.

• **19 MAR:** In Czechoslovakia, Gustáv Husák announces far-reaching political and economic reforms.

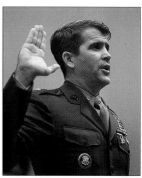

North gives evidence in the Iran-Contra affair.

• **13 APR:** China and Portugal sign an agreement for the return of Macao to Chinese sovereignty in 1999.

• **14 APR:** Gorbachev announces that the USSR is prepared to remove short-range missiles from Eastern Europe.

• **6 MAY:** In the South African general election, the ruling National Party wins an overwhelming victory.

• **17 MAY:** Iraqi Exocet missiles hit the USS *Stark* in the Gulf, killing 37 crew.

• **3 JUN:** In Canada, prime minister Mulroney and leaders of ten provinces sign the Meech Lake Accord recognizing Quebec as a "distinct society".

• **11 JUN:** Margaret Thatcher wins a record third term of office in Britain.

• **20 Jul:** The UN Security Council unanimously adopts a resolution calling on Iran and Iraq to implement ceasefire.

• **7 Aug:** The presidents of Guatemala, El Salvador, Honduras, Nicaragua and Costa Rica sign a peace plan.

• **21 Sept:** US helicopters intercept an Iranian ship caught laying mines in the Persian Gulf.

• **6 Oct:** Fiji becomes a republic after two successive bloodless coups.

• **18 Oct:** US destroyers attack Iranian oil installations in the Persian Gulf in retaliation for Iranian attacks on shipping.

• **19 Oct:** In the US, the Dow Jones Average falls 508 points (23 percent) precipitating massive falls in share values across the world.

• **18 Nov:** In the US, the Congressional report on the Iran-Contra affair blames President Reagan for widespread corruption in the government.

• **7–10 Dec:** At a summit in Washington, D.C., Gorbachev and Reagan sign an accord eliminating intermediate nuclear forces.

CULTURE

• **5 Jan:** Genetic fingerprinting is used for the first time in a criminal investigation (Leicester, UK).

• **24 Jan:** In the UK, 162 police and 33 demonstrators are injured in violent riots outside Rupert Murdoch's News International printing plant at Wapping, London.

• **6 Mar:** Townsend Thoresen cross-Channel roll-on roll-off ferry *Herald of Free Enterprise* capsizes off Zeebrugge, Belgium drowning 187 people.

• **10 Mar:** The Roman Catholic church speaks out against conception by artificial methods.

• **Jun:** The New Zealand All Blacks win the first Rugby Union World Cup beating Wales 49-6.

• **2–3 Jul:** British entrepreneur Richard Branson makes a transatlantic hot-air balloon flight from Sugarloaf mountain, Maine, to Co. Londonderry, Northern Ireland.

• **Aug:** Canadian Ben Johnson sets a new 100m world record at 9.83 secs.

• **Sept:** In Bangladesh, over 20 million are reported homeless after worst floods for 40 years.

• **16 Oct:** In Britain, a freak storm sends winds of 93 mph (149 kph) across the country felling an estimated 15 million trees.

• **21 Dec:** Nearly 3,000 people die in a ferry disaster in the Philippines.

PLO RECOGNIZES ISRAEL

The Iran–Iraq war comes to an end

POLITICS

• **8 FEB:** Mikhail Gorbachev announces that Soviet troops will begin withdrawal from Afghanistan on 15 May.

• **24 FEB:** The South African government announces new curbs on the antiapartheid movement.

• **26 FEB:** Gorbachev makes a television appeal for calm following nationalist unrest in Armenia.

• **29 FEB:** Archbishop Desmond Tutu and 100 clergy are arrested in Cape Town while petitioning parliament.

• **6 MAR:** Three suspected IRA bombers are shot dead in Gibraltar by British security forces.

• **31 MAR:** The US Senate approves support for the Nicaraguan Contras and aid for children caught in the fighting.

• **3 APR:** Ethiopia and Somalia conclude a peace agreement, ending 11 years of border disputes.

• **18 APR:** US forces destroy Iranian oil

Flo-Jo wins the Olympic 100m sprint.

installations in retaliation for Iranian damaging of a US frigate (14 Apr).

• **8 MAY:** François Mitterrand is reelected president of France.

• **2 JUN:** In Australia, the High Court approves the publication of former MI5 officer Peter Wright's book *Spycatcher*, despite UK government opposition.

• **28 JUN–1 JUL:** The National conference of the USSR Communist party resolves to implement *perestroika* (reform of the Soviet system).

• **3 JUL:** The US warship *Vincennes* shoots down an Iranian civil airliner, with the loss of 290 people.

• **6 JUL:** 167 people die in an explosion on the North Sea oil rig *Piper Alpha*.

• **10 Jul:** Ethnic disputes flare up in Burundi between the dominant Tutsi and the Hutus, leaving thousands dead.

• **17 Aug:** Pakistani premier Gen. Zia and the US ambassador to Pakistan are killed when their aircraft explodes.

• **25 Aug:** Peace talks to end the Iran–Iraq war begin in Geneva.

• **28 Aug:** Gen. Jaruzelski of Poland calls for national reconciliation after two weeks of strikes.

• **31 Aug:** In Bangladesh, 25 million people are homeless after flooding.

• **21 Sept:** The Soviet Union declares a state of emergency in Nagorno-Kharabakh, following disturbances between Armenians and Azerbaijanis.

• **30 Sept:** Soviet premier Gorbachev is appointed president while retaining his position as general secretary of the Communist party.

• **8 Nov:** In the US presidential election, Republican George Bush defeats Democrat Michael Dukakis.

• **10 Nov:** The UK resumes diplomatic links with Iran.

• **16 Nov:** Benazir Bhutto is elected prime minister of Pakistan, the first woman to lead a Muslim country.

• **7 Dec:** Gorbachev announces a reduction in Soviet armed forces by 500,000 men.

• **13 Dec:** PLO leader Yassir Arafat renounces terrorism and recognizes the state of Israel in a speech to the UN.

• **21 Dec:** In the UK a Pan Am aircraft is blown up in mid air and crashes over Lockerbie, killing 270 people.

CULTURE

• Novelist Salman Rushdie publishes his controversial novel *Satanic Verses*.

• The Human Genome Project begins to map the entire sequence of genes in human beings.

• Radiocarbon dating shows that the Turin Shroud, believed by some to carry the imprint of Christ's face, in fact dates from the 14th century.

• **27 Jan:** The Reserve Bank of Australia issues a polymer $10 note.

• **18 Jul:** A rock concert is held in Wembley Stadium, London, to mark Nelson Mandela's 70th birthday and to agitate for his release from prison.

• **Sept:** At the Seoul Olympics, Canadian Ben Johnson wins the 100m, but is disqualified for taking steroids.

• **Sept:** US athlete Florence Griffith-Joyner (Flo-Jo) wins the women's 100m; her fashion statements hit the headlines.

THE YEAR OF FALLING BARRIERS

F. W. de Klerk begins social and political reform in South Africa

POLITICS

• **7 Jan:** Hirohito, emperor of Japan since 1926, dies, and is succeeded by his son Akihito.

• **20 Jan:** The Republican George Bush is inaugurated as the 41st president of the United States.

• **14 Feb:** Ayatollah Khomeini, ruler of Iran, issues a *fatwah* or death sentence against the British writer Salman Rushdie for alleged blasphemy in his novel *Satanic Verses*.

• **24 Mar:** The *Exxon Valdez*, a laden oil tanker, runs aground in Prince William Sound, Alaska. An estimated 11 million gallons of oil are spilled.

• **17 Apr:** The trade union Solidarity is legalized in Poland.

• **18 Apr:** Chinese students begin mass pro-democracy protests in Tiananmen Square, Beijing.

• **25 May:** Mikhail Gorbachev is elected president of the USSR by the new Congress of People's Deputies.

The Berlin wall is breached, 10 Nov.

• **3 Jun:** The religious leader Ayatollah Khomeini dies in Iran.

• **3 Jun:** The student protests in Beijing are brutally crushed.

• **4 Jun:** The first partially democratic elections in Poland are held.

• **10 Jul:** A series of nationwide strikes by coalminers starts in the Soviet Union.

• **14 Aug:** South African president P. W. Botha resigns and is succeeded by F. W. de Klerk, who begins to dismantle the apartheid system.

• **23 Aug:** Hundreds of thousands of Latvians, Lithuanians, and Estonians form a human chain to protest against their annexation by the Soviet Union.

• **10 Sept:** Hungary opens its borders with Austria.

• **15 Oct:** Eight prominent African National Congress members are released from prison in South Africa, including Walter Sisulu.

• **17 Oct:** An earthquake in San Francisco kills over 70 people.

• **18 Oct:** The hardline Communist president Erich Honecker of East Germany is ousted and replaced by Egon Krenz.

• **19 Oct:** The Hungarian parliament legalizes opposition parties.

• **23 Oct:** A new Hungarian republic is declared.

• **25 Oct:** The Communist party of Yugoslavia adopts a new policy of political pluralism.

• **26 Oct:** John Major becomes British chancellor of the exchequer.

• **10 Nov:** The Berlin Wall is opened, allowing East Germans free movement to the West.

• **10 Nov:** Todor Zhivkov, president of Bulgaria, resigns.

• **21 Nov:** The British House of Commons is televised for the first time.

• **24 Nov:** The Czech administration resigns following a week of anti-government demonstrations.

• **3 Dec:** The members of the politburo and central committee of East Germany, including prime minister Krenz, resign.

• **10 Dec:** Gustav Husak resigns as president of Czechoslovakia.

• **20 Dec:** US forces begin an assault on targets in Panama to arrest president Noriega.

• **22 Dec:** Nicolae Ceaucescu's government in Romania is overthrown after a battle with security forces. Ceaucescu is executed on 25 Dec.

• **29 Dec:** Dissident Czech writer Vaclav Havel is elected president of Czechoslovakia.

CULTURE

• Meteorologists pronounce 1989 to be the warmest year on record, worldwide.

• Eighty nations agree to limit the use of CFCs to protect the ozone layer.

• **15 Apr:** In a crush at Hillsborough stadium, Sheffield, UK, 96 soccer fans are killed.

• **14 Jul:** A controversial glass pyramid outside the Louvre, Paris, designed by I. M. Pei, is opened.

• **25 Aug:** US spaceprobe *Voyager II* passes the planet Neptune.

BREAK-UP
OF THE SOVIET
UNION

*Saddam Hussein invades Kuwait,
US troops fight back*

POLITICS

• **1 JAN:** Cuba joins the UN Security Council after a 30-year break.

• **3 JAN:** Protesters riot in the Soviet republic of Azerbaijan. Soviet troops are sent to quell the violence.

• **1 FEB:** The Yugoslav government sends troops to quell ethnic unrest in the province of Kosovo.

• **2 FEB:** In South Africa, president de Klerk ends the 30-year ban on the ANC and 33 other opposition groups.

• **11 FEB:** In South Africa, Nelson Mandela is released from prison.

• **25 FEB:** In Nicaragua, a US-backed coalition led by V. B. Chamorro defeats president Ortega's Sandinista government in a general election.

• **26 FEB:** USSR undertakes to withdraw from Czechoslovakia by July 1991.

• **11 MAR:** Augusto Pinochet resigns as president of Chile. Democratically elected Patricio Aylwin succeeds.

Nelson Mandela, free at last, 11 Feb.

• **11 MAR:** Lithuania declares its independence from the USSR.

• **15 MAR:** Gorbachev becomes the first executive president of the USSR.

• **24 MAR:** In Australia, Labor prime minister Bob Hawke wins a fourth term.

• **25 MAR:** The USSR sends tanks to Vilnius, capital of Lithuania, to discourage secession.

• **11 APR:** British customs officers intercept "supergun" parts destined for Iraq.

• **17 APR:** USSR cuts off fuel supplies to Lithuania, imposing economic blockade.

• **4 MAY:** Latvia declares its independence from the USSR.

• **8 MAY:** Estonia declares its independence from the USSR.

- **20 May:** The first free elections since 1937 are held in Romania resulting in victory for the National Salvation Front.

- **28 May:** The National League for Democracy wins the first multiparty elections in Burma for 30 years.

- **12 Jun:** The parliament of the Russian Federation votes to achieve sovereignty from the USSR.

- **20 Jun:** Uzbekistan declares independence from the USSR.

- **23 Jun:** Moldova declares independence from the USSR.

- **1 Jul:** Germany reaches economic and monetary union.

- **16 Jul:** Ukraine declares independence from the USSR.

- **27 Jul:** Belarus declares independence from the USSR.

- **2 Aug:** Iraq invades Kuwait.

- **6 Aug:** The UN Security Council imposes sanctions against Iraq.

- **7 Aug:** President Bush sends troops to Saudi Arabia to prevent Iraqi invasion.

- **23 Aug:** Armenia declares independence from the USSR.

- **3 Oct:** Germany is reunited.

- **24 Oct:** In the Pakistani elections Benazir Bhutto's is defeated by the Islamic Democratic Alliance.

- **7 Nov:** Mary Robinson becomes first woman president of Ireland.

- **22 Nov:** In Britain, Margaret Thatcher resigns and is replaced as prime minister by John Major.

- **2 Dec:** Helmut Kohl becomes chancellor of a united Germany.

- **9 Dec:** Lech Walesa wins the Polish presidential election.

- **9 Dec:** Slobadan Miloseovic is elected president of Serbia.

- **16 Dec:** Fr. Jean-Bertrand Aristide wins the presidential election in Haiti.

CULTURE
- Nintendo video games take off.

- **4 Feb:** New Zealand cricketer Richard Hadlee is the first to take 400 Test wickets.

- **Apr:** Floods swamp vast areas of New South Wales, Queensland, and Victoria.

- **24 Aug:** In Lebanon, Irish hostage Brian Keenan is released after 1,597 days in captivity.

- **15 Oct:** Mikhail Gorbachev wins the Nobel Peace Prize.

- **1 Dec:** French and British workers dig through and meet in the Channel Tunnel.

EUROPEAN COMMUNISM COLLAPSES

US-led forces defeat Saddam Hussein, but do not depose him

Iraqi forces torch an oil well south of Kuwait city.

POLITICS

• **13 JAN:** Soviet troops storm a television station in Vilnius, Lithuania.

• **16 JAN:** Iraq fails to meet the UN deadline for withdrawal from Kuwait; US-led forces launch "Operation Desert Storm" to liberate Kuwait.

• **17 JAN:** Iraq fires Scud missiles against Israel, and against Saudi Arabia two days later.

• **26 JAN:** In Somalia, rebels overrun Mogadishu. President Siyad Barre flees.

• **22–25 FEB:** Iraqis torch hundreds of Kuwaiti oil wells as they retreat.

• **23 FEB:** Military coup in Thailand.

• **26–27 FEB:** Kuwait city is liberated by US troops; Iraqi forces are defeated.

• **28 FEB:** The US suspends operations in Kuwait. Controversially they do not pursue and depose Saddam Hussein.

• **MAR:** Civil war brews in Iraq.

• **17 MAR:** In the USSR, a referendum votes in favor of preserving a federation of equal sovereign republics.

• **9 APR:** Georgia proclaims its independence from the USSR.

• **17 APR:** British, French and US troops enter northern Iraq to establish safe havens for Kurdish refugees.

• **28 MAY:** The Ethiopian People's revolutionary Democratic Front capture Addis Ababa.

• **31 MAY:** A peace agreement ends the civil war in Angola.

• **4 JUN:** The Albanian government resigns after a three-week general strike.

• **3 JUN:** The USSR changes its name to

the Union of Soviet Sovereign (as opposed to Socialist) Republics.

• **17 JUN:** Apartheid is legally ended in South Africa.

• **24 JUN:** An unconditional and unlimited ceasefire is established in Cambodia, ending 12 years of conflict.

• **25 JUN:** Croatia and Slovenia declare independence from Yugoslavia.

• **1 JUL:** A protocol is signed in Prague terminating the Warsaw Pact.

• **31 JUL:** US and USSR sign a Strategic Arms Reduction Treaty (START) reducing long-range nuclear weapon arsenals by one third.

• **18 AUG:** In the USSR, Communist hardliners initiate a coup imprisoning President Gorbachev in his holiday villa.

• **21 AUG:** Latvia declares its independence from the USSR.

• **22 AUG:** Gorbachev returns to Moscow.

• **25 AUG:** Gorbachev resigns as leader of the Soviet Communist party.

• **30 AUG:** Azerbaijan declares its independence from the USSR.

• **6 SEPT:** The Soviet authorities formally grant independence to Latvia, Lithuania and Estonia.

• **30 SEPT:** A military coup in Haiti overthrows President Aristide.

• **8 NOV:** The EC imposes an economic embargo against Yugoslavia in an attempt to halt the civil war .

• **8 DEC:** Russia, Ukraine and Belarus create the Commonwealth of Independent States (CIS).

• **10 DEC:** 12 member states of the EC sign the Maastricht Treaty.

• **19 DEC:** In Australia, Paul Keating replaces Bob Hawke as prime minister and leader of the Australian Labor party.

• **25 DEC:** Gorbachev resigns as president of the (now defunct) USSR.

C U L T U R E

• **JUN:** Leningrad changes its name back to St. Petersburg after referendum.

• **JUL:** China suffers its worst floods since the 1930's.

• **8 AUG:** British citizen John McCarthy, held hostage in Lebanon, is released.

• **5 NOV:** British publishing tycoon Robert Maxwell dies in mysterious circumstances. His business empire, beset by massive debts and financial corruption, collapses.

• **18 NOV:** British citizen Terry Waite, held hostage in Lebanon since January 1987, is released.

YUGOSLAVIA FRAGMENTS

Racial antagonism in the Baltic becomes "ethnic cleansing"

POLITICS

• **1 JAN:** Egyptian Boutros Boutros-Ghali becomes UN secretary-general.

• **2 JAN:** Russia and Ukraine end former Soviet price controls by abolishing state subsidies on goods.

• **6 JAN:** A coup topples the government of Georgian leader Zviad Gamsakhurdia.

• **15 JAN:** The EC recognizes the independence of Croatia and Slovenia.

• **30 JAN:** Russian president Boris Yeltsin meets John Major in London and signs a 15-point declaration on the non-proliferation of nuclear weapons.

• **18 MAR:** South African prime minister F. W. de Klerk is given overwhelming backing in a referendum for his plans to abolish apartheid.

• **22 MAR:** Albanian Communist president Ramiz Aziz is defeated in elections by Democrats.

• **1 APR:** The US pledges $24 billion aid to Russia.

Bill and Hillary Clinton celebrate victory.

• **9 APR:** The EC recognizes Bosnia-Herzegovina.

• **15 APR:** The UN imposes an air traffic embargo on Libya to force it to hand over two suspected terrorists.

• **16 APR:** President Najibullah of Afghanistan is overthrown by Mujaheddin rebels.

• **29 APR–3 MAY:** Los Angeles citizens riot following the acquittal of a white policemen for beating a black motorist.

• **30 MAY:** The UN imposes sanctions on Serbia and Montenegro after fierce attacks on Sarajevo.

• **1 JUN:** At the Earth Summit in Rio de Janeiro, delegates from 178 nations discuss environmental protection.

• **2 Jun:** Denmark votes against ratification of the Maastricht treaty.

• **16 Jun:** Fidel Ramos wins the Philippine presidential election.

• **23 Jun:** Labor party leader, Yitzhak Rabin is elected prime minister of Israel and promises to limit Jewish settlement in the occupied territories.

• **28 Jun:** Relief supplies are airlifted into Bosnia after UN troops take control of Sarajevo airport.

• **29 Jun:** President Boudiaf of Algeria is assassinated by fundamentalists.

• **9 Jul:** Chris Patten is sworn in as the last governor of Hong Kong.

• **13 Aug:** The UN condemns "ethnic cleansing" by the Serbs in Bosnia and votes to use force if necessary to deliver humanitarian aid.

• **16 Sept:** Sterling is devalued and the pound leaves the European Exchange Rate Mechanism.

• **26 Oct:** A Canadian referendum rejects limited autonomy for Quebec.

• **4 Nov:** Democrat Bill Clinton defeats Republican George Bush to become 42nd US president.

• **18 Nov:** Former Pakistan prime minister Benazir Bhutto is teargassed during a demonstration in Islamabad.

• **20 Nov:** NATO forces impose a naval blockade against Serbia in the Adriatic following Serb aggression in Bosnia.

• **6 Dec:** A mosque in Ayodhya, India, is destroyed by a Hindu mob.

• **9 Dec:** US troops arrive in Somalia to oversee international food aid.

• **21 Dec:** Slobodan Milosevic becomes president of the rump state of Yugoslavia.

CULTURE

• **13 Mar:** In Russia, the last edition of *Pravda* is published. It announces suspended publication the next day.

• **12 Apr:** Opening of Euro Disney at Marne-la-Vallée near Paris.

• **13 Apr:** Nelson and Winnie Mandela announce their separation.

• **20 Apr:** Expo '92 opens in Seville, Spain.

• **20 Nov:** Windsor Castle, Britain, is partially destroyed by fire.

• **27 Nov:** Parts of Vienna's Hofburg palace are destroyed by fire.

• **9 Dec:** The Prince and Princess of Wales announce their separation.

• **17 Dec:** Australian prime minister Paul Keating announces that new citizens will no longer swear an oath of allegiance to the Queen.

ATROCITIES
IN BOSNIA

*Eritrea establishes
independence from Ethiopia*

POLITICS

• **1 JAN:** Europe's single market comes into operation.

• **1 JAN:** The Czech Republic and Slovakia become separate states.

• **3 JAN:** Presidents Bush and Yeltsin sign START II committing to a further one third reduction of nuclear missiles.

• **20 JAN:** William Jefferson Clinton is inaugurated as 42nd US president.

• **24 FEB:** Brian Mulroney resigns as Canadian prime minister.

• **24 FEB:** Fishermen in France destroy fish valued at $3.6 million in protest against cheap imports.

• **25 FEB:** The UN votes to create a war crimes tribunal, the first since 1945, to rule on Bosnian atrocities.

• **26 FEB:** A Palestinian extremist bombs the World Trade Center, New York, killing five people.

• **1 MAR:** US begins airdrop of supplies to eastern Bosnia-Herzegovina.

A Sarajevo mother at the grave of her 17-year-old daughter who was killed by snipers.

• **13 MAR:** The Australian Labor party wins its 5th consecutive general election led by Paul Keating.

• **14–17 MAR:** Georgian government forces struggle with rebel forces in Sukhumi, capital of the breakaway province of Abkhazia.

• **20 MAR:** The UN in Bosnia supervises evacuation of civilians from Srebrenica.

• **19 APR:** A 51-day siege of the Branch Davidian headquarters at Waco, Texas, by US federal authorities ends with a fire in which 72 people lose their lives.

• **25 APR:** A referendum in Russia provides a popular mandate for Boris Yeltsin's government.

- **6 May:** The UN declares six "safe areas" in Bosnia: Sarajevo, Tuzla, Zepa, Srebrenica, Bihac and Gorazde.

- **24 May:** Eritrea becomes independent from Ethiopia.

- **27 May:** A bomb explodes outside the Uffizi Gallery, Florence, killing six people.

- **13 Jun:** Kim Campbell becomes Canada's first woman prime minister.

- **26 Jun:** US forces launch a missile attack on Iraqi intelligence headquarters in Baghdad, following reports of a plot to assassinate former president Bush.

- **29 Jul:** In Israel, John Demjanjuk, indicted for war crimes during World War II, is acquitted.

- **13 Sept:** Israeli prime minister Yitzhak Rabin and PLO chairman Yassir Arafat shake hands on the White House lawn to seal an agreement on interim Palestinian self-rule.

- **21 Sept:** Boris Yeltsin suspends the Russian parliament, and Alexandr Rutskoi seizes power.

- **4 Oct:** The rebels led by Rutskoi in the Russian parliament surrender after government forces shell the building.

- **15 Oct:** Nelson Mandela and F. W. de Klerk share the Nobel Prize for Peace.

- **25 Oct:** The Canadian Liberal party, led by Jean Chrétien, sweeps to power in a general election that leaves the Conservatives with only two seats.

- **1 Nov:** The European Community becomes the European Union (EU).

- **14 Dec:** British and Irish prime ministers John Major and Albert Reynolds sign the Downing St. declaration on peace in Northern Ireland.

CULTURE

- US scientists claim to have discovered the gene responsible for homosexuality.

- Release of the films *Jurassic Park* and *Schindler's List*, both directed by Stephen Spielberg.

- **11 Mar:** A doctor is murdered by an anti-abortion activist outside a Florida abortion clinic.

- **24 Jun:** The Republic of Ireland decriminalizes homosexuality.

- **19 Sept:** Australian prime minister Paul Keating announces that Australia will become a republic by the year 2001.

- **23 Sept:** The International Olympic Committee announces that the Games in the year 2000 will be held in Sydney, Australia.

- **Dec:** The Hubble Space Telescope is discovered to have faults in the design of its main mirror and is repaired in orbit.

WHITEWATER SCANDAL BREAKS

Civil war in Rwanda creates two million refugees

POLITICS

• **5 Feb:** A mortar attack on a market place in the Bosnian capital, Sarajevo, kills 68 people and wounds over 200.

• **23 Feb:** Ceasefire between Bosnia and Croatia.

• **25 Feb:** Over 50 Palestinians are killed in a Hebron mosque when an Israeli settler, Baruch Goldstein opens fire with an automatic weapon.

• **24 Mar:** In the US, allegations are made in Congress that President and Mrs. Clinton may have dealt improperly with their investments in the Whitewater Development Corporation in Arkansas.

• **25 Mar:** US troops withdraw from Somalia after 15 months.

• **27 Mar:** Italian general election results in victory for the Freedom Alliance right-wing coalition led by Silvio Berlusconi.

• **31 Mar:** In Bosnia, Serb forces bomb the UN "safe areas" of Gorazde and Srebrenica.

A Los Angeles freeway after January's quake.

• **6 Apr:** The Burundian and Rwandan presidents are assassinated. Violence erupts on a huge scale.

• **8 Apr:** Morihiro Hosokawa resigns as prime minister of Japan after 8 months in office, following accusations of financial misconduct.

• **10 Apr:** US planes under NATO command carry out airstrikes against Serb forces at Goradze.

• **14 Apr:** In Greece, former King Constantine is deprived of his citizenship and his property is nationalized.

• **26–29 Apr:** In South Africa, the African National Congress win the first non-racial general election.

• **4 May:** Israel and the PLO sign an agreement giving Palestine self-rule in the Gaza Strip and Jericho.

• **10 May:** Nelson Mandela is sworn in as president of South Africa.

• **23 Jun:** France sends troops to Rwanda to aid refugees from conflict.

• **29 Jun:** Tomiichi Murayama becomes Japan's first socialist premier since 1947.

• **8 Jul:** North Korean leader Kim Il Sung dies, aged 82.

• **19 Jul:** The Rwandan Patriotic Front claims victory in the civil war; 2 million war refugees desperately need aid.

• **Aug:** Up to 20,000 Cubans flee to the United States after President Castro lifts exit restrictions (reintroduced 9 Sept).

• **31 Aug:** The IRA announces a ceasefire in Northern Ireland.

• **19 Sept:** US troops invade Haiti encountering no resistance.

• **15 Oct:** President Aristide returns to Haiti from exile.

• **21 Oct:** The US and North Korea reach agreement over development of a North Korean nuclear program.

• **25–26 Nov:** An assault on the Chechen capital by Russian-backed forces is defeated by government troops.

• **28 Nov:** A referendum in Norway rejects EU membership.

• **11 Dec:** Russia invades Chechenya.

• **23 Dec:** A US-brokered ceasefire begins in Bosnia-Herzegovina.

CULTURE

• The homosexual age of consent in Britain is lowered to 18.

• **Jan:** Bush fires on the east coast of Australia destroy nearly 2 million acres.

• **Jan:** Southern California is declared a disaster area following an earthquake measuring 6.6 on the Richter scale.

• **12 Mar:** The first women priests in the Church of England are ordained.

• **1 Apr:** Yachtsman Robin Knox-Johnston and the crew of the *ENZA* complete a round-the-world voyage in a record 74 days 22 hr 17 min.

• **8 Apr:** Kurt Cobain, lead singer of the band *Nirvana* is found dead.

• **6 May:** The Channel Tunnel opens.

• **2 Dec:** The Australian government agrees to pay A$13,500,000 to south Australian Aborigines displaced by the nuclear tests of the 50s and 60s.

• **8 Dec:** New Zealand government offers NZ$1,000 million compensation to Maori tribes.

DEATH OF YITZHAK RABIN

World War II veterans celebrate 50 years since peace was declared

POLITICS

• **12 Jan:** Britain announces the end of 25 years of daylight patrols on the streets of Northern Ireland.

• **13 Jan:** In Italy, Lamberto Dini, former treasury minister, is appointed prime minister.

• **19 Jan:** In Chechenya, Russian troops capture the presidential palace in Grozny from rebel forces.

• **17 Jan:** Jacques Delors retires after ten years as president of the EU. Jacques Santer takes over.

• **27 Jan:** In Poland, international leaders and 10,000 survivors commemorate the liberation of the Nazi concentration camp at Auschwitz.

• **12 Feb:** The Bosnian ceasefire (agreed December '94) breaks down; heavy fighting takes place in Bihac.

• **12 Feb:** Civil war in Angola finally ends as UNITA rebels sign peace treaty.

• **20 Mar:** In Japan, a nerve gas attack

Floral tributes to the memory of Yitzhak Rabin.

on a crowded subway train in Tokyo kills ten people and injures thousands.

• **26 Mar:** Seven members of the EU remove border controls.

• **31 Mar:** 20,000 Hutu refugees flee massacres in Burundi.

• **16 Apr:** Canada and the EU reach an agreement on fishing rights in the north west Atlantic.

• **19 Apr:** In Oklahoma City, USA, a terrorist bomb wreaks havoc killing 158 people and injuring hundreds.

• **7 May:** Jacques Chirac is elected president of France.

• **7 May:** In Britain, millions celebrate the fiftieth anniversary of VE day.

• **20 May:** Former Italian prime minister Silvio Berlusconi is to stand trial for corruption.

• **6 Jun:** Shoko Asahara, leader of the Aum Supreme Truth religious cult is charged with the nerve gas attack on the Tokyo subway.

• **11 Jul:** Bosnian Serb forces overrun UN safe areas of Srebrenica, and Zepa.

• **Sept:** NATO bombing forces Serb withdrawal from around Sarajevo.

• **5 Sept:** France begins underground nuclear tests at Mururoa Atoll.

• **18 Sept:** Hong Kong holds its first democratic elections.

• **5 Oct:** The US announces a 60-day ceasefire in Bosnia.

• **16 Oct:** Almost a million blacks march in Washington for the cause of black moral and spiritual renewal.

• **4 Nov:** Israeli prime minister Yitzhak Rabin is shot by a Jewish rightwinger.

• **11 Nov:** Despite widespread condemnation, Nigeria executes writer and campaigner Ken Saro-Wiwa.

• **21 Nov:** At Dayton, Ohio, the US government brokers a ceasefire which divides Bosnia Herzegovina into two sections; one for Muslim Croats and one for Serbs.

CULTURE

• In France, 20,000 year-old cave paintings are found in the Ardèche region.

• In Egypt, US archaeologists find the 67-chamber tomb built for the 50 sons of Ramses II, the largest tomb yet found.

• **17 Jan:** A huge earthquake measuring 7.2 on the Richter scale devastates Kobe in western Japan.

• **27 Feb:** Barings Bank collapses after losses by trader Nick Leeson of more than £800 million.

• **14 May:** New Zealand's yacht *Black Magic* wins the America's Cup.

• **20 Jun:** The oil company Shell UK abandons plans to dump the aged Brent Spar oil platform in the Atlantic after objections from environmentalists.

• **Jul:** Britain has the hottest summer since records began.

• **3 Oct:** After a nine-month trial, US footballer and film star O.J. Simpson is found not guilty of murdering his wife and another man.

• **30 Oct:** Quebec votes against declaring independence from Canada by a narrow margin.

• **24 Nov:** The Republic of Ireland votes by referendum for the legalization of divorce.

MAD COWS AND ENGLISHMEN

Conflict breaks out again between Israelis and Palestinians

POLITICS

• **8 Jan:** Francois Mitterrand, president of France 1981–95, dies aged 79.

• **9 Jan:** In Russia, Chechen rebels seize 3,000 hostages in the town of Kizlyar.

• **20 Jan:** The Fatah faction led by Yassir Arafat wins the majority of seats in elections for the Palestinian Council.

• **24 Jan:** North Korea agrees to allow the International Atomic Energy Authority to inspect nuclear facilities.

• **27 Jan:** In Niger, a military coup puts Col. Ibrahim Barre Mainassara in power.

• **27 Jan:** France conducts a sixth nuclear test in the Pacific despite international protests.

• **29 Jan:** President Chirac of France announces an end to nuclear tests.

• **29 Jan:** In Canada, Lucien Bouchard is sworn in as Quebec premier.

• **1 Feb:** The US donates US$2 million to the UN food assistance program for North Korea following floods in 1995.

The opening ceremony of the Atlanta Olympics.

• **7 Feb:** René Préval becomes president of Haiti, the first peaceful handover of power in 193 years.

• **9 Feb:** In Britain, the IRA calls off its 17-month ceasefire.

• **15 Feb:** In Britain, publication of the Scott Report inquiring into arms sales to Iraq in the late 1980s concludes that the Government misled parliament.

• **23 Feb:** Chinese troops are reported to be massing in Fujian province, the nearest part of the mainland to Taiwan.

• **3 Mar:** In Israel, the third suicide bomb attack in a week, kills 19 people.

• **3 Mar:** In Australia, John Howard becomes prime minister.

• **5 Mar:** A suicide bomb in Tel Aviv kills 12 people; Israel announces that it will take action against the Palestinians.

• **8 Mar:** China begins a series of military exercises off Taiwan.

• **12 Mar:** The arrival of the US aircraft carrier *Independence* brings the number of US vessels off Taiwan to 14.

• **19 Mar:** President Mugabe is returned for a further six years as president of Zimbabwe.

• **20 Mar:** In Britain, the government admits that BSE, "mad cow disease", could be transmitted to humans through eating beef products.

• **11 Apr:** Israeli airstrikes hit a UN base in Lebanon killing 105 civilians.

• **21 Apr:** Chechen rebel leader Dzokhar Dudayev is killed in a Russian rocket attack.

• **22 Jun:** A few months after resigning as Greek prime minister, Andreas Papandreou dies, aged 77.

• **4 Jul:** Boris Yeltsin is re-elected president of Russia despite persistent rumors of his ill-health.

CULTURE
• The World Health Organization warns of a tuberculosis "plague" from a drug-resistant strain of the bacillus.

• **29 Jan:** In Australia, executives of the Elders IXL group and the Bank of New Zealand go on trial accused of the theft.

• **Feb:** In USA, Congress approves a bill making it a criminal offence to place proscribed material on the Internet.

• **21 Feb:** In Australia, the Northern Territory passes legislation allowing terminally ill adults to instruct doctors to end their lives.

• **22 Feb:** In France, president Chirac announces an end to military conscription by the year 2001.

• **13 Mar:** In Dunblane, Scotland, 16 children and their teacher are shot dead in their school by gunman Thomas Hamilton, who then commits suicide.

• **28–29 Apr:** In Port Arthur, Tasmania, a 29-year-old man shoots 32 people dead and wounds 18 others.

• **13 Jun:** Sumitomo corporation in Japan dismiss Yasuo Hamanaka "Mr. five percent" for unauthorized copper trading resulting in enormous losses, deliberately concealed over 10 years.

• **15 Jul:** In Britain, the Prince and Princess of Wales petition for divorce.

• **19 Jul:** The 1996 Olympic Games, celebrating the 100th Olympiad, open in Atlanta, Georgia.

INDEX

PICTURE CREDITS

Abbreviations

AOL   Andromeda Oxford Ltd
HG   Hulton Getty
KC   Kobal Collection
P   Popperfoto
RF   Rex Features

6-8 HG; 10 Melies/KC; 12 HG; 14 A.K.G. Photo; 16 HG; 18 Corbis-Bettmann; 20 HG; 22 The National Motor Museum, Beaulieu; 24 Mary Evans Picture Library; 26 HG; 28 P; 30-32 HG; 34 P; 36 Essenay/KC; 38-42 HG; 44 P; 46 HG; 48 Famous Players/Paramount/KC; 50 Brian Rasic/RF; 52 A.K.G. Photo; 54 KC; 56 Corbis-Bettmann; 58 P; 60-62 HG; 64 P; 66 AOL; 68 Universal/KC; 70 Robert Harding Picture Library; 72 HG; 74 Corbis-Bettmann; 76 RKO/KC; 78-82 P; 84 HG; 86 Walt Disney/KC; 88 Wiener Library; 90 National Archives, Washington; 92 Warner Bros./KC; 94 P; 96 RF; 98 P; 100-102 HG; 104 P; 106 The Futile Press; 108 HG; 110 Los Alamos National Laboratory/Science Photo Library; 112 HG; 114-116 P; 118 A.K.G. Berlin; 120 AOL; 122 P; 124 HG; 126 AOL; 128 P; 130 HG; 132 RF; 134 HG; 136 Corbis-Bettmann/UPI; 138-140 P; 142 HG; 144 RF; 146-150 P; 152 Gökin Sipahioglu/RF; 154 P; 156 Mauru Carraro/RF; 158 RF; 160-162 Sipa Press/RF; 164 Hatami/RF; 166 RF; 168 P; 170 RF; 172 Zihinoglu/Sipa Press/RF; 174 S. Franklin/Sygma; 176 Frilet/Sipa Press/RF; 178 Sisson/Sipa Press/RF; 180 Trippett/Sipa Press/RF; 182 P; 184 Sipa Press/RF; 186 Young/RF; 188-192 P; 194 RF; 196 Chris Harris/RF; 198 Billy Stickland/Allsport

Jacket Picture: Los Alamos National Laboratory/Science Photo Library